CULTURAL WARS IN AMERICAN POLITICS

D1503338

SOCIAL PROBLEMS AND SOCIAL ISSUES

An Aldine de Gruyter Series of Texts and Monographs

SERIES EDITOR

Joel Best

Southern Illinois University at Carbondale

CULTURAL WARS IN AMERICAN POLITICS
Critical Reviews of a Popular Myth

RHYS H. WILLIAMS
Editor

cH

ALDINE DE GRUYTER
New York

About the Editor

Rhys H. Williams is Associate Professor of Sociology at Southern Illinois University at Carbondale. Dr. Williams is coauthor with N. J. Demerath III of *A Bridging of Faiths: Religion and Politics in a New England City* (1992) and is the author of numerous journal articles.

ALDINE DE GRUYTER
A division of Walter de Gruyter, Inc.
200 Saw Mill River Road
Hawthorne, New York 10532

This publication is printed on acid free paper ∞

Library of Congress Cataloging-in-Publication Data
Cultural wars in American politics : critical reviews of a popular
    myth / Rhys H. Williams, editor.
        p. cm. — (Social problems & social issues)
    Includes bibliographical references and index.
    ISBN 0-202-30563-5 (cloth : alk. paper). — ISBN
0-202-30564-3 (pbk. : alk. paper)
        1. United States—Civilization—1970– 2. United States—Politics
and government—1989– 3. Culture conflict—United States.
    4. Politics and culture—United States—History—20th century.
    5. Christianity and politics—Protestant churches. 6. Protestants—
United States—Political activity. I. Williams, Rhys H.
    II. Series
E169.12.C77 1997
973.92—dc21   97-22848
                                                                        CIP

Manufactured in the United States of America

10 9 8 7 6 5 4 3 2 1

For my Family
Katherine, Reese, Louise, Gwyneth, Bronwyn, Jeff,
Mary, Don, Molly, Paul, Sally, John, David and Lauri
always willing to argue politics

Contents

About the Contributors

Bethany Bryson is a doctoral candidate in sociology at Princeton University, Princeton, New Jersey.

Jackson W. Carroll is Ruth W. and A. Morris Williams, Jr. Professor of Religion and Society at the Divinity School of Duke University, Durham, North Carolina.

Nancy J. Davis is professor of sociology and chair of the department of sociology and anthropology at Depauw University, Greencastle, Indiana.

N. J. Demerath III is professor of sociology at the University of Massachusetts, Amherst.

Paul DiMaggio is professor of sociology and chair of the department of sociology at Princeton University, Princeton, New Jersey.

Michael Emerson is assistant professor of sociology at Bethel College, St. Paul, Minnesota.

John H. Evans is a doctoral candidate in sociology at Princeton University, Princeton, New Jersey.

Sally Gallagher is assistant professor of sociology at Oregon State University, Corvallis.

Margaret Seyford Hrezo is assistant professor of political science at Radford University, Radford, Virginia.

Ted G. Jelen is professor and chair of political science at the University of Nevada, Las Vegas, Las Vegas, Nevada.

Paul Kennedy is assistant professor of sociology at Gordon College, Wenham, Massachusetts.

Fred Kniss is associate professor of sociology at Loyola University, Chicago.

Penny Long Marler is associate professor of religion and society at Samford University, Birmingham, Alabama.

Daniel V. A. Olson is associate professor of sociology at Indiana University, South Bend in South Bend, Indiana.

Gerald M. Platt is professor of sociology at the University of Massachusetts, Amherst.

Robert V. Robinson is professor of sociology and director of the Institute of Social Research at Indiana University, Bloomington.

Timothy Shortell is assistant professor of sociology at Brooklyn College, Brooklyn, New York.

David Sikkink is a doctoral candidate in sociology at the University of North Carolina, Chapel Hill.

Christian Smith is assistant professor of sociology at the University of North Carolina, Chapel Hill.

Karen S. Straight is a doctoral candidate in sociology at the University of Massachusetts, Amherst.

Melinda Bollar Wagner is a professor of anthropology and associate chair of the Appalachian Studies Program at Radford University, Radford, Virginia.

Rhys H. Williams is associate professor of sociology at Southern Illinois University, Carbondale.

Yonghe Yang is a statistical analyst with the Gallup Organization in Rockville, Maryland.

Acknowledgments

Over the past couple years a number of manuscripts on the American culture war have arrived on my desk. I received some due to my research interests in politics and religion; I received others as a general courtesy from friends; a few others arrived because I was to be a discussant on a panel session on religion and politics at a scholarly meeting. As the 1996 campaign season heated up "culture wars" themes again appeared in partisan rhetoric and—fairly uncritically—in many media analyses of the campaign. So an edited collection of critical reviews seemed like a natural project. I appreciate the encouragement, support, and feedback I have received for this book from Joel Best, Jay Demerath, John Evans, Paul DiMaggio, Katherine Jahnige, and Fred Kniss. Others whose wisdom contributed to my thinking on this subject, without necessarily knowing it would end up in this book, include Nancy Tatom Ammerman, Steven Brint, Mark Chaves, Gerald Platt, Donald Robinson, Mark Shibley, R. Stephen Warner, Gwyneth Williams, and Robert Wuthnow.

Earlier versions of the introduction and the afterword were presented to the Chicago Area Group for the Study of Religious Communities, directed by Steve Warner, and as a Plenary Address to the Illinois Sociological Association in October 1996, Jack Harkin, President. The comments and questions in both those settings were very helpful.

The manuscript was handled both expertly and cheerfully through its production by Arlene Perazzini. Finally, I greatly appreciate the enthusiasm, wit, and good humor of Richard Koffler of Aldine de Gruyter. He made this project relatively painless, and occasionally fun; I was fortunate to have him as an editor.

Reprint permissions

"Religion, Ideology, and Electoral Politics" by Gerald M. Platt and Rhys H. Williams first appeared in *Society* 25(5, July/August, 1988), 38–45. ©Transaction Publishers. Reprinted with permission.

"Culture Wars? Insights from Ethnographies of Two Protestant Seminaries" by Jackson W. Carroll and Penny Long Marler first appeared in *Sociology of Religion* 56(1, Summer, 1995), 1–20. ©Association for the Sociology of Religion, Inc. Reprinted with permission.

"Have Americans' Social Attitudes Become More Polarized?" by Paul DiMaggio, John Evans, and Bethany Bryson first appeared in *American Journal of Sociology 102*(3, November, 1996), 690–755. © University of Chicago Press. Reprinted and shortened with permission.

1

Introduction

RHYS H. WILLIAMS

Recent headlines trumpet stories of protest, conflict, and even violence: abortion clinics are firebombed in Florida, Georgia, and Oklahoma; Planned Parenthood workers are murdered in Kansas and Massachusetts; a Cincinnati art gallery owner is arrested for exhibiting Robert Mapplethorpe's photographs; a rap group is arrested on obscenity charges; the civil rights—or "special privileges"—of gays and lesbians become electoral issues in Colorado and Oregon; and issues of multiculturalism, freedom of expression, and "political correctness" divide many of the nation's college campuses. To many Americans this does not seem like "politics as usual." These stories and others like them seem to indicate that a new and different type of political conflict has swept the nation.

This new conflict even gets its own soundbite: We are witnessing a "culture war," we are told. The major political cleavage in contemporary American politics is no longer class, race, region, or any of the many social-structural differences that divide the population. Rather, a major realignment of sensibilities and controversial issues means that the body politic is now rent by a cultural conflict in which values, moral codes, and life-styles are the primary objects of contention.

Patrick Buchanan brought the glare of the national spotlight to the phrase "culture war" when he used his address to the 1992 Republican National Convention to declare a "war for the nation's soul." That moment was both the apex and the nadir of a presidential campaign that carried itself as a moral crusade, galvanizing both impassioned constituents and media attention. Oliver North's 1994 Senate campaign in Virginia echoed those themes, with similar outcomes. Their losing efforts led some to discount the notion. However, in 1996 Buchanan's campaign was no less crusadelike, although he often traded issues of sexuality and family structure for issues of economic nativism and class resentment. If anything, however, the war metaphors were more prominent as Buchanan called for "peasants with pitchforks" to "lock and load" and "ride to the sound of the gunfire." Other contenders for the Republican presidential nomination repeated the claim of an encompassing divide over morality and values. The notion was picked up by such other "cultural warriors" as Rush Limbaugh, William Bennett, former secretary of education, and James Dobson, director of the interest group Focus on the Family. And in early 1996 a new general interest periodical on culture and politics was founded and titled, *Culture Wars*.

Not to be outdone rhetorically, much fund-raising literature for liberal political and social causes uses culture wars language with similar tones of alarm. The hallowed principles of journalistic, artistic, and/or academic freedom are threatened, they argue, and only a stout defense of the barricades will prevent a "neo-McCarthy" backlash from overwhelming the social and political progress of the last few decades. The nation is threatened by "moral zealots" who want to dictate all manner of life choices according to their strict neo-Puritan (or, occasionally, neo-Victorian) prejudices.

This is not just the hyperbole of a conflict-obsessed media and partisan direct-mail fund-raisers. Academic, literary, and religious observers have contributed to this portrait. Todd Gitlin (1995) explains "why America is wracked by culture wars." Tom Sine (1995) is "searching for sanity in America's culture wars." Michael Scott Horton (1994) hopes to go "beyond culture wars," while Russell Jacoby (1994) claims that the culture wars "divert education and distract America." Other publications with some version of "culture wars" in their titles include those by Bolton (1992), Cain (1994), Duke and Johnson (1996), Dworkin (1996), Gates (1992), Gerson (1996), Graff (1992), Green, Guth, Smidt, and Kellstedt (1996), Hartman (1991), Nolan (1996), Puckett (1992), Rapping (1994), Shor (1986), and Whitehead (1994). These come from both the academic left and right, and represent both the humanities and social sciences.

The culture war depicted in these volumes is not always the same conflict. For example, Gerson (1996) sees the basic conflict as one between traditionalists, including religious people, and members of the "new class," knowledge workers who are overwhelmingly secular. Dworkin (1996) is concerned with the emergence of what he calls the "imperial self." The sides in the cultural conflict are divided over whether the self is the supreme manifestation of human life, or whether humans should love something beyond the self. Gitlin (1995) is primarily concerned with the Left in America; his thesis is that the "identity politics" of gender and race have fractured the ability of progressive political forces to mobilize large coalitions over broad issues. Green et al. (1996) are mostly concerned with how religious commitments affect voting, and the extent to which evangelical Christians identify with, and participate in, the organized Christian Right.

The most developed and systematic academic version of the culture wars thesis appeared in sociologist James Davison Hunter's 1991 book *Culture Wars: The Struggle to Define America*. The book became a widely selling and widely cited work, and is often thought to be the source of Buchanan's phrase. *Culture Wars* offered an encompassing critique of the conflicts in contemporary politics and culture. Hunter divided America [or Americans; whether he intended his insights to apply to average citizens is a matter of some debate—see Davis and Robinson (1996), Hunter (1996a)] into two opposing camps, the "orthodox" and the "progressives," based on a single dimension, the locus of moral and social authority. This division is intractable, in Hunter's view, and has an internal logic that leads inevitably to escalating conflict (1991:42, 49, 52, 58, 64, 290–91). While *Culture Wars* did contain many qualifying statements about the extent and depth of the "war," its tone of urgency (the book opens with "Stories from the Front," which are examples of cultural conflict labeled "Dispatches") and its tendency to sweeping analyses painted a gloomy portrait. In subsequent interviews Hunter expanded upon the seriousness of the cultural conflict he described, upped the rhetorical ante with the title of his next book (*Before the Shooting Begins*, 1994), and has responded directly to some of his academic critics (1996a, 1996b).

The essays collected in this volume add more measured analyses to what I view as this overheated rhetoric. The chapters gathered here engage several versions of the culture wars thesis on their own terms, assess their accuracy, and examine their theoretical logic. As the essays show, whether the level of analysis is individual attitudes, subcultural values, political party dynamics, or culturewide ideological currents, Hunter's all-encompassing bipolar ideological axis is overly simplistic and masks as much variance as it illuminates. Further, careful examination of the actual cultural divides in the American body politic reveals why politicians such as Pat Buchanan are more successful in generating news copy than in winning elections.

Nonetheless, if articulated broadly enough, there is something in the culture wars thesis. Certainly the rhetoric resonates with sizable portions of the electorate, and because it does it can be a successful mobilizing metaphor for certain kinds of politicians and issue activists. Also, several of the most contentious and passionate issues in current politics revolve around what can be called "cultural" issues. The culture wars thesis does have the great benefit of calling attention to the extent to which contemporary politics is more than just a matter of dividing the economic pie. Too often academic observers proceed from the assumption that politics is just the surface manifestation of economic interests; people who vote against their interests must be in some way deficient—either they do not perceive their interests "correctly" or they suffer from "false consciousness."

Quite to the contrary of this materialist, interest-based assumption, the symbolic aspects of our collective life are great sources of both conflict and solidarity. People do act in the public arena based on assumptions about what the "good society" is, what we must do to achieve it, and what constitutes a "moral" life. Hunter noted correctly that public culture can have a powerful shaping effect on the ideological practices of interest groups and the opinions of individuals. Sometimes the worldview assumptions about the public moral order are indeed incompatible with rival assumptions; and when moral worldviews align with social structural differences, political conflict can easily turn from civil politics to cultural war. India, Ulster, the Balkans, Sudan, and the Middle East all serve as potent reminders of just how volatile a mixture religion and politics can be. In sum, a broad reading of culture wars has much to recommend it, and those who study religion and politics must issue a quick assent.

Indeed, a broad interpretation of the idea of "cultural wars" has great relevance to American politics. This relevance springs from three sources: First, there is religion's continuing vitality in American life, both as a source of meaning and as a salient social division. Religion's political efficacy is well documented, both historically (e.g., Noll 1990; Thomas 1989; Williams and Alexander 1994) and currently (e.g., Demerath and Williams 1992; Smith 1996; Williams and Demerath 1991; Williams 1996).

Interacting with religion's potency has been the fluidity of class divisions in American society. Class matters greatly in politics—few would deny that. But American culture has shown great ambivalence in its dealings with class as a social identity (e.g., Burke 1995). Class is often individualized, or made a matter of life-style as much as economics, or occasionally denied altogether. While there has been and continues to be class resentment in American culture, it has not transformed itself into a sustained socialist movement (e.g., Laslett and Lipset 1974). Class position reflects well on a person's worth, but only as an achieved status. For example, politicians often feel obligated to play down their backgrounds of class privilege—as George Bush did in both 1988 and 1992—by accusing opponents who call for redistributive reforms of trying to stir up "class antagonisms." Whereas religion has, at times, been a good source of collective identity for American political action, class has just as often not been.

Finally, the United States currently has several large "cultural production" industries; that is, industries whose main products are, in essence, symbols. The entertainment industries are one example; news media and higher education are two others. The institutions that comprise these industries are in the business of producing and disseminating symbols, are populated by "knowledge class" professionals to whom culture is extremely important (e.g., Brint 1994), and in some way or other touch the lives of many people not directly connected to them. Thus it is perhaps not surprising to find that the culture wars rhetoric has particularly resonated within these circles. Culture, is after all, what these institutions are about; further, the entertainment, news, and academic industries are often given to hyperbole in assessing either their own importance or their difficulties and "crises." Many of the culture wars titles mentioned above focus specifically on either the arts or higher education. And many of the conservative political activists who have popularized the culture wars phrase have been particularly successful at attacking the "cultural elite" that supposedly governs the fine arts and university worlds—worlds from which many Americans do in fact feel estranged. Indeed, one might argue that American populism's primary target shifted from the 1890s' economic plutocrats to the 1980s' cultural arbiters. For these three reasons—the vitality of religion, the ambivalence about class, the prominence of the culture industries—it is precisely around "culture" that some of America's most visible political contests cohere.

These important points about cultural politics make it all the more important that the culture wars thesis be assessed without the hyperbole and partisan rancor that have accompanied the spread of the term in popular political analysis. There is cultural conflict in American life, but is it war? Distinctly different worldviews and moral visions undergird many of our political differences, but are those the only source of conflict? Is there, as Hunter's version of the thesis maintains, only one really crucial cultural divide in contemporary culture: whether one has an orthodox or a progressive vision of moral authority? Is cultural conflict so thorough, and so intractable, that our institutions have lost their ability to moderate it? And, perhaps most important, is the cultural divide that Hunter claims organizes the conflict between political elites now spreading to the general public?

These are some of the questions that motivate the authors appearing in this collection. The chapters, taken as a whole, assess Hunter's version of the culture wars thesis, examine other sources of political tension and conflict, explain how that conflict is often moderated, and offer other ways of understanding the current ideological landscape. After a brief review of the narrow version of the culture wars thesis—that contained in Hunter's book—this introduction concludes with a review of each of the book's sections.

HUNTER'S CULTURE WARS THESIS

In *The Restructuring of American Religion* (1988), Robert Wuthnow argued that since World War II changes in American culture and institutions—in particular the rise of mass access to higher education, and the divisive politics of the civil rights struggle and the Vietnam War—had produced a new cleavage in American religion: the older divisions of Protestant, Catholic, and Jew have been cross-cut by a liberal-conservative divide running through all three groups. Where religious and denominational identity, largely articulated in terms of doctrine, theology, and religious practices, had been the focus of conflict, now issues of ideology and culture cross-cut identity divisions. As a result, conservative Protestants, for example, now have more in common with conservative Catholics and Jews than they do with liberal Protestants. In a subsequent book Wuthnow (1989) focused again on what he called the "struggle for America's soul," but his subtitle divided the combatants into three camps: evangelicals, liberals, and secularists.

A less noted restructuring also implied by Wuthnow's book is the "public-private" dichotomy in American religion, most forcefully articulated by Martin Marty (1970). Marty had distinguished public from private denominations by their attitudes and strategy toward the church and society. Public groups articulated a plan of social reconstruction through institutional change, and they entered the public arena through political and social activism. In the 1950s and 1960s these were the liberal, mainline denominations. Private groups understood change as occurring through a "hearts and minds" strategy of individual conversion, generally eschewing public politics. Evangelical Protestant denominations represented this orientation. The rise of the Christian Right in the late 1970s, among other changes, have led scholars to question this distinction (e.g., Jacobsen and Trollinger, forthcoming). For example, one can find both themes even within small, religiously homogeneous groups firmly within one side or the other of the liberal-conservative divide (Williams and Blackburn 1996).

James Hunter's *Culture Wars* expanded the scope of Wuthnow's claims even as it narrowed the source of, and explanation for, the conflict. Hunter located the liberal-conservative cleavage (which he termed orthodox vs. progressive) in the differing sources of authority each side uses, and further claimed that the division between the sides has expanded beyond religion into secular politics, becoming in that process the most important structuring cleavage in contemporary society. For Hunter, orthodox people locate authority in a transcendent source outside society and human construction, while progressives draw upon human reason, science, and contemporary culture as their authority references. Because these differences are at the level of the "worldview," they do more than just shape our moral, social, and political ideas; they also mold our very perceptions of reality (cf. Berger 1967; Evans 1996), our sense of how the world "should" be *and* how it in fact "is." One can easily see why these differences are not amenable to compromise; indeed, Hunter maintains that even recognizing the potential authenticity of rival worldviews can be a threat to the coherence of one's own (1991:52, 58, 131). The result is an inevitable heightening of cultural and political conflict.

In pursuing this argument, Hunter—and his critics—use the term "culture" in two ways. First, culture is defined as the beliefs, values, ideas, and moral commitments that people share; these have become the *objects* over which the two sides struggle. Given American society's religiosity, and the centrality of sexuality, family, and gender to many religiomoral traditions, issues such as abortion, gay rights, public prayer, and pornography have thus taken center stage. Second, culture is the *means* with which contemporary politics is pursued. Media strategies, soundbites, photo opportunities, and symbolic displays of life-style legitimation (e.g., politicians campaign in Texas wearing cowboy hats and in Iowa wearing overalls; gay activists wear pink triangles sewn on their clothing; bumper stickers that say Vote have the "t" shaped as a cross) are the tools with which this war is pursued. In this sense of the term, culture is the storehouse or repertoire of symbols that people wield in their attempts to shape their world.

This dual meaning is significant for assessing the extent to which the culture war is a reality. If culture is primarily beliefs and values, the differences between orthodox and progressive persons should show up in surveys and interviews. As people articulate what is important to them, two sides should emerge that demonstrate different understandings of moral authority, opposing opinions on particular social issues, and incompatible visions of how society "ought" to be organized.

However, if culture is used primarily to articulate the means through which war is waged, other ways of examining current conflicts are also required. One must examine the "public culture" of politics: the rhetoric through which appeals are made, the symbols used to dramatize issues and mobilize partisans, and the logical structures of conflicting claims and the impact that structure has on conflict. This requires more of an "ideological" analysis, with the attendant recognition that public culture often gains its own momentum. This can produce a situation in which people feel locked into positions they do not fully support, and the public conflict feeds on itself.

In recognition of this dual meaning in the term "culture," this book is divided into different sections in order to investigate the culture war thesis in several ways. The sources of data include general public opinion surveys, voting studies, in-depth interviews, case studies of particular institutions, analysis of campaign rhetoric, and comparisons with other nations. Some authors examine culture as the object of contention, others treat it as the tools for conflict. Most of the authors here criticize at least some aspects of Hunter's narrow version of the culture wars thesis; at the same time almost all push for broader understandings of cultural conflict in political life.

THE BOOK SECTIONS

The book is divided into three sections. The first section contains chapters that use public opinion data to examine the extent to which the general

American public, and a sample of institutional elites, is divided on cultural issues. There is little support in these chapters for a culture wars argument that has but one dimension. Also, there is only sporadic evidence for a polarizing tendency in public opinion, an important point, as much of Hunter's argument is hinged on the realignment of political opinions, based in moral worldviews, that runs across traditional structural cleavages of race, class, and religion.

Demerath and Yang use General Social Survey (GSS) data from the National Opinion Research Center to examine attitude clustering first in the general population, then among religious groups. They find a variety of cross-cutting cleavages rather than a single, bipolar ideological divide. Similarly, Davis and Robinson do something of a two-stage analysis. First, they study survey data of the general population and find attitude diffusion rather than unidimensional clustering. Then they move beyond the bipolar question to seek the extent to which the "religiously orthodox," a group likely to be seen as mobilized cultural warriors (e.g., Green et al. 1996), form a homogeneous attitudinal bloc. Even within that population there is a lack of homogeneity on political and social issues. To the extent that conservative religiosity does produce attitude-clusters they focus on family and gender issues.

DiMaggio, Evans, and Bryson examine the relative polarization of public opinion over time, and find a polarizing clustering only on specific issues—significantly, issues that have experienced some of the most fervent cultural politics in the last two decades. Thus, the conflict that has occurred over those issues does seem to be amenable to explanation via public attitudes. But just as significantly, there is not the general realignment toward polarized opinion blocs upon which so many versions of the culture wars thesis rely. Their overall conclusion does not support the idea that Americans' social attitudes have recently polarized. Finally, Shortell uses a data set composed of "elites" from a variety of institutional sectors to search for the different attitudinal dimensions of ideology and for the effects of religion on political conservatism generally. Since many conservative activists have proclaimed the importance of traditional religion to maintaining America's moral center, and Hunter's argument relies heavily on the idea that elites lead public discourse, this is an important place to search for the culture wars cleavage. Instead, Shortell contends that ideology is a multidimensional concept, varying by both content and structure, and various ideological divisions do not align identically among different subsamples. While he does find a consistently significant ideological divide on issues of personal morality, it is influenced by both religious affiliation and religious commitment. Thus, among this sample of elites, there is neither a thorough cultural realignment nor a bipolar ideological division.

In sum, while there is evidence for the importance of cultural issues as political divisions, and some significant "clustering" among particular issue-types, the most important conclusion to be drawn from the chapters in this section is that the war rhetoric is vastly overheated—the culture war simply cannot find very many reliable soldiers.

The second section shifts the level of analysis to investigate the existence of culture wars within a variety of institutions. While Shortell's study of elite attitudes does not show the clearly polarized ideological blocs Hunter's book implies, it may well be the case that the culture war exists within institutions such as political parties, mainstream religious organizations, or the seminaries that train religious leaders. These are institutions that have culture production as a major aspect of their purpose; further, they are settings more likely to be dominated by activists and partisans—groups often too small to be noticeable in random samples of the entire population. Again, however, the results are mixed. While there are certainly cultural cleavages that lend themselves to vibrant political contests, the unidimensional cultural war is again missing-in-action.

Carroll and Marler report on their ethnographic work within Protestant religious seminaries, and report some moderate support for a culture wars argument. However, their analysis makes clear that it is more faithful to the way this "war" is experienced by those in it if we understand the cultural conflict to be as much a matter of cultural "style" as it is an issue of polarized opinions. That is, it is not simply differences in cognitive attitudes and beliefs that separate people. Aspects of personal and group life-styles act as cues, forming identity and marking group boundaries. Seminarians are learning who they are religiously at least in part by learning who they are not—but it is not merely a matter of beliefs and attitudes; stylistic boundaries such as speech patterns and dress are as important as cognitive commitments to particular doctrinal issues.

Jelen examines a central institution of American politics, the alignment of loyalties to the major political parties and the resulting partisan identification. He finds moderate support for an argument that charts a political realignment and polarization among Protestants. It is more significant among Evangelicals than it is among so-called mainline Protestants (an argument consistent with Green et al. 1996), but it still fits imperfectly along the poles that are aligned with Democrat-Republican partisanship. Political parties, as organizations, have more cross-cutting divisions than a single ideological divide.

Similar conclusions emerge from Hrezo and Wagner's case study of the Virginia Senate campaign of Oliver North. They expand their analysis of a particular case by considering the Christian Right's general dilemma with the classical tension between "realism" and "idealism" in political theory. Realism understands politics as compromise; one learns to live in the world and fashion the world in ways that are acceptable even if not perfect. Idealism understands the world as an extension of the moral order in the universe. As a result the idealist must transform politics into a purer moral exercise rather than settle for corrupting compromises. The success in the Virginia political primary of the idealist perspective—and its movement-style politics pursued by Christian Right activists—led to failure in the general election, where realist compromises were required. Again, one can see a cultural divide within a single political institution, the Virginia Republican party, but it is again marked largely by cultural style rather than issue-positions per se. And importantly, the culture wars ship crashed on the rocks of the compromises necessary to win general elections. The tensions between movement politics and institutional politics is a subject taken up in the Afterword.

Finally, Smith and his colleagues use in-depth interviews with a large sample of American Protestants to demonstrate almost no culture wars talk at the grass-roots level. There are plenty of divisions between people, and much disagreement over social and cultural issues, but there is no single organizing axis of conflict. Indeed, many of Smith's respondents find themselves supporting *both* sides of the authority dimension that Hunter describes as the crucial boundary. This is an important point. On many issues that are presented as either/or choices by activists, or rendered as such by media reports, many people actually hold opinions consistent with "both" sides.

In other words, actual public opinion is more of a both/and than either/or (see a similar argument in Williams and Demerath 1991). It is not that the "average" person's opinions are necessarily muddled or inconsistent, as some analysts charge (e.g., Converse 1964); nor is it that "moderate" public opinion is but a statistical artifact that is "contentless" (Hunter 1996a:247) and without "coherence or teleology as a system of moral public reasoning" (Hunter 1996b:247). Rather, it is that many people do not reason by applying absolutist moral principles on a case-by-case deductive basis. Instead, they hold and understand the usefulness of two potentially contradictory positions, using them situationally in varying relevant contexts. It may well be that the standard instrument for ascertaining opinions, the survey questionnaire, is too often unable to detect such nuances. If so, that in itself does not bode well for any narrow thesis of bipolar cultural conflict.

The third section of the book criticizes the culture wars thesis by offering several competing conceptualizations of the American political landscape. Hunter (1996a) has warned that analysts should not make either of two mistakes: they must not reduce "culture" to nothing but aggregated individual opinions; and they must not be fooled by the moderate character of so many individual opinions into thinking that American politics still has a "strong center." The chapters in this section do neither. First, several of them examine the very kinds of "public culture" that Hunter argues is crucial to understanding societal conflict and social change. And second, the authors here rarely feel compelled to choose between the dualism of a "strong center" or a bipolar "war" argument. Instead, they again show American political contests to have multiple dimensions that cut across the body politic in various ways, and that inspire various levels of conflict.

Demerath and Straight use examples from Demerath's ethnographic data from several countries around the world to examine the differences between U.S. cultural politics and the literal wars in other countries. They offer five analytic distinctions, based in religiopolitical relations, that suggest why it is unlikely for the United States to develop large-scale cultural violence over state power. This chapter is an important caveat to taking America's war imagery too seriously, and offers a comparative angle on the institutional processes in the United States that often defuse conflict.

Platt and Williams articulate the post–New Deal ideological divide as "individualist" versus "collectivist." In these terms, both major political parties are coalitions that lean opposite ways on different issue types. Rhetoric from the 1984 and 1988 presidential campaigns illuminate this division, while consideration of the historical development of the post–New Deal parties cautions against thinking of this divide as a necessary principle of American politics. Dan Olson offers a similar ideological landscape by separating sexuality-morality issues from economic justice issues when studying public opinion. He finds that the two issue types produce four different opinion publics. His conclusion offers an interesting rationale as to why the logic and practices of institutional politics actually mitigate against the polarized conflict that the culture wars thesis proposes. As a result, the war rhetoric is appropriately downgraded in Olson's title to cultural "tensions."

Fred Kniss separates the fundamental ideological axes of American politics yet again, this time into two different dimensions relating to the "moral order" that is embodied in every worldview. Rather than making his axes the *content* of the ideological principles involved, Kniss labels them according to their functional orientation—they represent the locus of "moral authority" and the locus of the "moral project" for social change. He demonstrates the extent to which the two axes he articulates capture the situations of many marginal social groups, such as the Quakers or Mennonites, better than content-based bipolar distinctions. Kniss's data on intra-Mennonite conflict show the ways in which larger ideological divisions have confounding impacts on peripheral groups, and how those groups can in turn affect the larger political culture.

Finally, the Afterword sums up the general critical assessment of the narrow version of the culture wars thesis and provides a rationale for understanding why a broader vision of cultural politics is useful. Some differences in the social processes that distinguish movement-style politics from routinized, institutional politics reveal why it is easy to be misled by culture war rhetoric, and why the disjunctures between political culture and political institutions continue to foster such conflict.

In toto, data from other countries, public opinion surveys, in-depth interviews, campaign rhetoric, institutional ethnographies, and the experiences of minority religious groups show the extent to which the cultural dimensions of American politics are crucially important. But these cultural manifestations take a variety of forms, with a variety of consequences. There is not a "culture war" in the United States—and asserting it only serves to mask the many important ways in which culture in fact shapes our collective political life.

Thus the title of this collection. The culture war is an American "myth" in two senses of the word. First, following the everyday use of myth as something that is not literally true, the culture war is a myth. It does not actually exist either in the streets or in the many indicators used here to assess whether there are cultural cleavages that could be mobilized into warlike conflict. But myth also has a more anthropological meaning—as *mythos*. In this sense, while the culture wars may not be literally true the resonance of the idea expresses a truth about American politics. That truth understands the important role that culture plays in our political history and the ways in which symbols and stories help form who we are and who we are against. Political conflict, just like political solidarity, is expressed symbolically, and that must be analyzed correctly and understood in order to grasp the past, the present, or the future of American life.

REFERENCES

Berger, Peter L. 1967. *The Sacred Canopy*. New York: Anchor/Doubleday.

Bolton, Richard, ed. 1992. *Culture Wars: Documents from the Recent Controversies in the Arts*. New York: New Press–Norton.

Brint, Steven G. 1994. *In an Age of Experts: the Changing Role of Professionals in Politics and Public Life*. Princeton, NJ: Princeton University Press.

Burke, Martin J. 1995. *The Conundrum of Class: Public Discourse on the Social Order in America*. Chicago: University of Chicago Press.

Cain, William E., ed. 1994. *Teaching the Conflicts: Gerald Graff, Curricula Reform, and the Culture Wars*. New York: Garland.

Converse, Philip E. 1964. "The Nature of Belief Systems in Mass Publics." Pp. 206–61 in *Ideology and Discontent*, edited by David Apter. New York: Free Press.

Davis, Nancy, J., and Robert V. Robinson. 1996. "Rejoinder to Hunter: Religious Orthodoxy—An Army without Foot Soldiers?" *Journal for the Scientific Study of Religion* 35:249–51.

Demerath N. J. III, and Rhys H. Williams. 1992. *A Bridging of Faiths: Religion and Politics in a New England City*. Princeton, NJ: Princeton University Press.

Duke, James T., and Barry L. Johnson. 1996. "The Culture War in Congress." *Research in the Social Scientific Study of Religion* 7:43–73.

Dworkin, Ronald W. 1996. *The Rise of the Imperial Self: America's Culture Wars in Augustinian Perspective*. Lanham, MD: Rowman and Littlefield.

Evans, John H. 1996. "'Culture Wars' or Status Group Ideology as the Basis of U.S. Moral Politics." *International Journal of Sociology and Social Policy* 16(1/2):15–34.

Gates, Henry Louis. 1992. *Loose Canons: Notes on the Culture Wars*. New York: Oxford University Press.

Gerson, Mark. 1996. *The Neoconservative Vision: From the Cold War to the Culture Wars*. Lanham, MD: Madison.

Gitlin, Todd. 1995. *The Twilight of Common Dreams: Why America Is Wracked by Culture Wars*. New York: Metropolitan.

Graff, Gerald. 1992. *Beyond the Culture Wars: How Teaching the Conflicts Can Revitalize American Education*. New York: Norton.

Green, John C., James L. Guth, Corwin E. Smidt, and Lyman A. Kellstedt. 1996. *Religion and the Culture Wars: Dispatches from the Front*. Lanham, MD: Rowman and Littlefield.

Hartman, Geoffrey H. 1991. *Minor Prophesies: The Literary Essay in the Culture Wars*. Cambridge, MA: Harvard University Press.

Horton, Michael Scott. 1994. *Beyond Culture Wars: Is America a Mission Field or Battlefield?* Chicago: Moody.

Hunter, James Davison. 1991. *Culture Wars: The Struggle to Define America*. New York: Basic Books.

———. 1994. *Before the Shooting Begins: Searching for Democracy in America's Culture War*. New York: Free Press.

———. 1996a. "Response to Davis and Robinson: Remembering Durkheim." *Journal for the Scientific Study of Religion* 35(3):246–48.

———. 1996b. "Reflections on the Culture War Hypothesis." Pp. 243–56 in *The American Culture Wars: Current Contests and Future Prospects,* edited by James L. Nolan. Charlottesville: University Press of Virginia.

Jacobsen, Doug, and William Vance Trollinger, Jr. Forthcoming. *Re-Forming the Center: American Protestantism 1960 to the Present*. Grand Rapids, MI: Eerdmans.

Jacoby, Russell. 1994. *Dogmatic Wisdom: How the Culture Wars Divert Education and Distract America*. New York: Doubleday.

Laslett, John H. M., and Seymour Martin Lipset, eds. 1974. *Failure of a Dream? Essays in the History of American Socialism*. Garden City, NY: Anchor/Doubleday.

Marty, Martin E. 1970. *Righteous Empire: The Protestant Experience in America*. New York: Dial.

Nolan, James L., Jr., ed. 1996. *The American Culture Wars: Current Contests and Future Prospects*. Charlottesville: University Press of Virginia.

Noll, Mark A., ed. 1990. *Religion and American Politics*. New York: Oxford University Press.

Puckett, Walter. 1992. *Bringing the Church Off the Slippery Slope: Recovery from Culture Wars.* Columbus, GA: Brentwood Christian Press.

Rapping, Elayne. 1994. *Mediations: Forays into the Culture and Gender Wars.* Boston: South End.

Shor, Ira. 1986. *Culture Wars: School and Society in the Conservative Restoration, 1969–1984.* Boston: Routledge and Kegan Paul.

Sine, Tom. 1995. *Searching for Sanity in America's Culture Wars.* Grand Rapids, MI: Eerdmans.

Smith, Christian, ed. 1996. *Disruptive Religion: The Force of Faith in Social Movements.* New York: Routledge.

Thomas, George M. 1989. *Revivalism and Cultural Change.* Chicago: University of Chicago Press.

Whitehead, Fred, ed. 1994. *Culture Wars: Opposing Viewpoints.* San Diego: Greenhaven.

Williams, Rhys H. 1996. "Religion as Political Resource: Culture or Ideology?" *Journal for the Scientific Study of Religion* 35(December):368–78.

Williams, Rhys H., and Susan M. Alexander. 1994. "Religious Rhetoric in American Populism: Civil Religion as Movement Ideology." *Journal for the Scientific Study of Religion* 33(March):1–15.

Williams, Rhys H., and Jeffrey Neal Blackburn. 1996. "Many Are Called but Few Obey: Ideology and Activism in Operation Rescue." Pp. 167–85 in *Disruptive Religion: The Force of Faith in Social Movements,* edited by Christian Smith. New York: Routledge.

Williams, Rhys H., and N. J. Demerath III. 1991. "Religion and Political Process in an American City." *American Sociological Review* 56:417–31.

Wuthnow, Robert 1988. *The Restructuring of American Religion: Society and Faith Since World War II.* Princeton, NJ: Princeton University Press.

———. 1989. *The Struggle for America's Soul: Evangelicals, Liberals, and Secularism.* Grand Rapids, MI: Eerdmans.

I

THE VIEW FROM PUBLIC OPINION DATA

2

What American Culture War?
A View from the Trenches as Opposed to the Command Posts and the Press Corps

N. J. DEMERATH III and YONGHE YANG

Few descriptions of American society have made a quicker transition from jargon to cliché than the phrase "culture war." Since sociologist James Hunter first deployed it in 1991 in the title of his popular book, the label and its connotations have found their way into newspeak, political soundbites, and kitchen seminars the country over. It now seems almost universally assumed that the war is already upon us with mounting casualties. By 1994 and the appearance of Hunter's second book on the topic, its title seemed ironically and somewhat quaintly tempered in asking what might be done *Before the Shooting Begins.*

But, of course, wars come in different forms. These include the manipulative contests between officers in search of medals, the self-fulfilling prophesies of moral provocateurs, and the exaggerated fantasies of entrepreneurial reporters confusing fact with fiction for lack of a firsthand view. There is no question that all of the above are implicated to some degree in the current contest. Certainly there are sufficient extremists on both the left and the right to begin the action. Whether true-believers or movement professionals, they have a clear interest in ginning up the confrontation. Nor do they lack complicit coverage on the part of analysts anxious to sell books, newspapers, and airtime.

At one level, the mere acceptance of the phrase "culture war" is ipso facto evidence of its reality—especially in the hyperspace of a putative postmodernism. However, at another level it is worth checking on the fundamentals. Quite apart from those proudly leading the march to battle (and those reporting on them) it is worth asking who is following. Regardless of the skirmishes occurring among movement devotees, it is hardly idle to ask the mood of the citizen foot soldiers at large. At least that is the conviction behind the research reported here.

Following a brief review of the recent literature advancing the thesis of increasing American polarization, we shall subject the thesis to extensive testing with the help of pooled data from the National Opinion Research Center's General Social Surveys for the years 1977, 1985, and 1993. Since much of the thesis concerns polarization within rather than between formerly homogeneous institutions, we shall give special attention to several key religious denominations across the ideological spectrum.

POLARIZATION REVIEWED

Cassandras of division and polarization are hardly new among American pundits. Politicians have often used the theme as part of a classic "divide and conquer" strategy. Survey researchers from Karl Marx forward have noted bipolar conflicts in the ranks. Recently, however, several sociologists have given the theme particular prominence by describing a cultural conflict that threatens the very fabric of American society itself.

In 1988, Robert Wuthnow noted a growing and ineluctable conservative-liberal rift in American religion that goes beyond religious issues per se and threatens to spill into the political arena. Previous conflicts between religious liberals and religious conservatives were somewhat muted because they were allocated into distinct denominational camps that had relatively little to do with each other, but this conflict "cuts across denominational lines" (Wuthnow 1988:219).

According to Wuthnow, the tensions between religious liberals and religious conservatives originated in the theological split between modernists and fundamentalists earlier in this century. By the mid-1970s, however, disputes flared over a series of social and moral controversies concerning abortion on demand, pornography, homosexuality, women's rights, and school prayer. As these disputes moved aggressively to the center of the political stage during the 1980s, they have increasingly led to bitter partisan politics—again not just between parties but sometimes within and beyond them. The result has been a polarization of public opinion "that may have sweeping ramifications for the future of American religion" (ibid., 315).

In Wuthnow's presentation, the American public is almost evenly divided between these two conflicting camps. He reported that 43 percent of those surveyed identified themselves as religious liberals (19 percent as very liberal); 41 percent identified themselves as religious conservatives (18 percent as very conservative); and only 16 percent found it impossible to identify with one or the other of these labels. He then observed that similar patterns of differentiation existed within denominational boundaries. For example, half of Southern Baptists are liberals and half are conservatives; among Methodists, the ratio is 1.15 to 1; and among Catholics the ratio is 1.38 to 1.

However, the result was not just apparent within the religious community; it also divided America's vaunted "civil religious" tradition. Breaking apart one of America's most politically sacred mantras, Wuthnow described an emerging conservative civil religion dedicated to "one nation under God," and a distinct liberal civil religion pursuing "liberty and justice for all." And, of course, the presence of two civil religions belies the function of the one unifying umbrella so important to Emile Durkheim ([1912] 1915) and Robert Bellah (1967). When two or more civil religions collide, the results are very uncivil indeed.

Wuthnow stopped short of an extreme characterization of a culture engulfed in flames or embroiled in war. However, a more recent proponent of the polarization thesis was less constrained. James Hunter's book *Culture Wars* (1991) portrays polarization on a much larger canvas that goes far beyond religion itself. Hunter reports an increasingly volatile ideological polarization between the culturally "orthodox" and the culturally "progressive" in American society. He views contemporary public discourse on social and moral issues as a war between two competing moral visions that have encompassed all Americans, religious and nonreligious alike. The cultural divide between the orthodox and the progressive is so prevalent that it cuts across religious and other distinctions that have long divided Americans, turning them into irrelevant anachronisms.

Like Wuthnow, Hunter says that the major lines of division on the religious scene are no longer born out of theological and doctrinal disagreements—as between Protestants and Catholics or Christians and Jews or between Protestant denominations. Rather, there are more fundamental disagreements over the sources and substance of moral truth. For example, the progressives within Protestantism, Catholicism, and Judaism express similar ideological concerns, as do the culturally orthodox within each of these traditions. Hunter's battlegrounds are almost identical to those recognized by Wuthnow: government spending, women's rights, sexual morality, social policy, political ideology, civil liberty, and so on.

Richard Neuhaus (1992) also refers to "what is happening" as "cultural warfare." He insists that the cultural warfare is not restricted to the quarrels within the "high culture" of editors, book writers, dance directors, and other cultural elites. It is more fundamental and comprehensive as a war between different ideas about who we are and who we ought to be. Although Neuhaus does not use the word *polarization,* his analysis depicts the nation as tending toward two widely conflicting groups who have fundamentally opposed understandings of social reality and moral authority.

Meanwhile, others have added fuel to the fire. Of course, there are any number of analyses in the long tradition of American "value conflicts," and Guth, Smidt, Kellstedt, and Green (1993) and Goggin (1993) are among those who chronicle and catalog the divisions surrounding abortion in particular. However, the theme of a widespread, deep-seated, and desperate conflict is apparent in just the subtitles of three recent works. Thus, British author Os Guinness (1993) has made a special point of America's "Time of Reckoning"; William Bennett (1992) signals alarm over "The Fight for Our Culture and Our Children"; Todd Gitlin (1995) asks "Why America Is Wracked by Culture Wars." In fact, DiMaggio, Evans, and Bryson (1996) have recently charted the rapid rise of "culture war" references in the media at two-month intervals for the period 1990–1995.

But in all of this, there is a paucity of compelling evidence of empirical polarization, especially at the individual level. Wuthnow's assertion that the public is evenly divided into two opposing moral camps is based on respondent self-labeling rather than on scientific evaluations of individual social and moral positions. This is potentially misleading not only because self-placement is subjective, but also because it is virtually guaranteed to generate polarization when the respondents are asked to identify with one of two opposing ideological positions.

Hunter's observations are based primarily on qualitative evidence, such as opposing views in public discourse, passionate rhetoric of religious leaders, case studies of social activists, and the growth of cross-denominational ideological alliances. This says more about polarized movements and organizations than polarization among the citizenry as individuals. As Hunter himself acknowledges, polarization is more apparent at the institutional or organizational level due to the public rhetoric of cultural elites, the activism of special purpose groups, and particularly media attention and dramatization. But how is the general public related to this hypothetical polarization? Are there distinct ideological clusters among ordinary Americans on the basis of their ideological orientations? Has there been a gravitation to extreme positions as opposed to a meeting at the moderate middle? And how is this related to the organizations within one important institutional sector, namely, religious denominations? These are the questions that frame the analysis to follow.

DATA AND METHODS

The data are from the annual General Social Survey (GSS) of the National Opinion Research Center at the University of Chicago. Specifically, we pool seven GSS subfiles for the years 1977, 1985, 1988, 1989, 1990, 1991, and 1993. These surveys include all the important variables necessary to operationalize the ideological disputes at the heart of the culture wars hypothesis. They also escape the problem of other surveys in which one or more crucial variables are missing, making cluster results incomparable across surveys.

However, quite apart from missing variables, our analyses have a fairly high proportion of missing values. This is partly due to our use of scales built from multiple variables, where a single missing response disqualifies the respondent from the aggregate. A more fundamental source is the GSS variable rotating design. Since its inception, the GSS has employed a three-year-cycle rotation design under which most of its items appear on two of every three surveys. Hence, some of the important variables for our analyses are missing in some surveys. For example, in 1984, 1986, and 1987, the factor scales cannot be constructed in the same way due to missing values on some variables. Consequently, these three surveys have to be excluded from the analyses. Since 1988, GSS has changed its rotation design to an across subsamples split-ballot design. For our purposes, the new design guarantees the availability of all the variables we need to construct the seven scales in all the five surveys after 1988. The disadvantage of the new design is that it generates more missing values within each survey because rotating items are now asked of only two-thirds of the respondents in each survey. Therefore, all the rotating variables contain at least one-third missing values by design. Based on the reduced sample size, the actual rate of missing data is less than 50 percent.

Our analyses pivot around seven constructed scales concerning abortion, civil liberty, women's rights, racial justice, sexual morality, political ideology, and religious intensity. The first five are the results of factor analyses, while the last two are based on the GSS single-item variables POLVIEWS and RELITEN (cf. Yang 1996 for methodological details). All variables are coded such that smaller values represent more liberal views and larger values indicate more conservative inclinations. Together, these scales embody virtually all of the important issues that constitute the major battlefields in the putative war. However, we did exclude a measure of economic liberalism because it generates too many missing values in the data and, even when included, does not alter the overall patterns.

The basic statistical technique is that of cluster analysis (cf. Yang 1996). Each respondent in the surveys is considered a separate object to be evaluated on the seven criterion variables. Geometrically, each object can be conceptualized as a point in the seven-dimensional space. Cluster analysis is applied to these objects so that those close together in this space are grouped into the same cluster. As to the number of clusters, the literature strongly suggests two polarized clusters: hence a two-cluster solution would be most appropriate. However, both Wuthnow and Hunter admit the possibility of a middle ground, and the postcluster canonical discriminant analysis needs at least three clusters to calculate two canonical variables for visual display. Therefore, we will request a three-cluster solution. It is important to note that this would not conceal a truly bifurcated data structure with only two polar groups.

IN SEARCH OF POLARIZATION

Many clustering methods have been developed in different fields of research, and most of them are believed to be biased toward finding clusters of particular size, shape, and dispersion. To reduce such biases, we applied different clustering methods to the same GSS data, including Average Linkage and Ward's Minimum Variance, which simulation studies find perform best in recovering known cluster structures in artificial data sets (SAS 1990). Very similar clustering patterns emerge from these cluster analyses. We choose the clustering patterns derived from the K-means method for interpretation. Also, to avoid too laborious repetition, we will only present and examine the clusters derived from the 1977, 1985, and 1993 surveys. The 1977 survey is the earliest survey in which all the variables are available to construct the seven scales, and 1993 is the latest. The 1985 survey is selected not only because it lies in the middle of the time span, but also it involves the fewest missing values.

As requested, each cluster analysis produced three clusters. The spatial distributive patterns and ideological characteristics of these clusters are summarized in the three figures and three tables that follow. Figures 1 through 3 show the scatterplots of the clusters as presented in a two-dimensional canonical discriminant function space. Statistically, the canonical discriminant functions are the best discriminators among the clusters. They are used here to reveal how the clusters are different from each other and in what respects. By examining these plots we can see if the polarization hypothesis is plausible.

There are two remarkable features in the three scatterplots. First, they depict nearly identical clustering patterns in the three years except that the 1993 sample is much smaller due to missing observations. In all three instances, the clusters are primarily differentiated on the first canonical function, although cluster two is also slightly different from the other two clusters on the second canonical function. In cluster analysis terminology, we may say that the cluster solutions have a high degree of replicability across data sets. If a cluster solution is repeatedly discovered across different samples from the same general population, it is plausible to conclude that this solution has some generality.

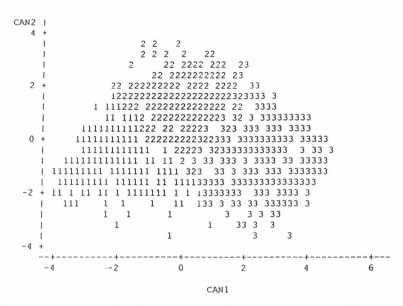

Figure 1. Canonical plot of cluster membership, 1977. Note: 506 obs had missing values. 583 obs hidden.

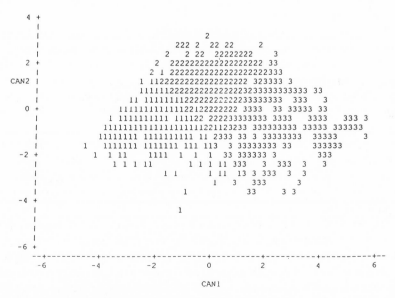

Figure 2. Canonical plot of cluster membership, 1985. Note: 453 obs had missing values. 640 obs hidden.

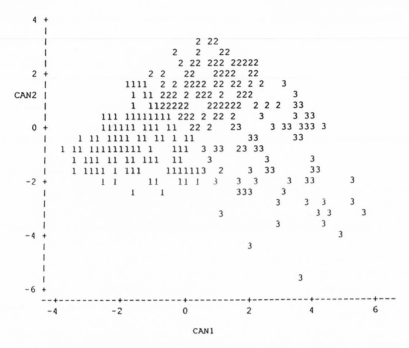

Figure 3. Canonical plot of cluster membership, 1993. Note: 1238 obs had missing values. 132 obs hidden.

The second notable feature in these plots is the lack of spatial differentiation between these clusters. There are no obvious boundaries, and the clusters are not clearly separated from one another by blank or low-density space. In fact, the spatial distribution of these points is even denser and the boundaries even fuzzier than the plots could reveal because hundreds of objects are still hidden due to coinciding values. The canonical variables apparently do not discriminate very well among the three clusters. Obviously, these plots present little evidence of clear-cut ideological differentiation among the respondents in any of these years, let alone ideological polarization. Based on these plots, we cannot even determine if these are "real" clusters in the data or if there is an arbitrary partition of a continuous cloud of points.

Cluster analysis is especially helpful in uncovering underlying structures in the data that are not readily apparent by visual inspection or by appeal to other authorities, but while the clustering strategy is often described as structure-seeking, its operation can also seem structure-imposing. A clustering procedure will always sort objects into different groups and generate a classification even if no particular structure exists in the data (cf. Everitt 1980). This intrinsic ambiguity presents no problem when clusters in the

Table 1. Canonical Structure and Cluster Means, 1977 (*N* = 1024; ANOVA *P* > *F*, .0001)

	First Canonical Correlation	Second Canonical Correlation	Liberal Cluster Mean (*N* = 358)	Moderate Cluster (*N* = 359)	Conservative Cluster (*N* = 307)
Abortion	.4516	.6758	−.8530	.2500	.5880
Civil liberty	.8171	.0017	−.8482	−.0816	.9526
Sexual morality	.6819	.5029	−.9693	.4067	.5658
Women's rights	.7098	−.0214	−.7152	−.0857	.8681
Racial justice	.8122	−.4557	−.5614	−.5061	1.1897
Political ideology	.2662	.2316	−.3718	.1646	.2060
Religious intensity	.3989	.3682	−.6057	.2778	.3234

data are sufficiently well-separated so that they can be easily identified through visual inspection [cf. Yang (1996) on America's "new denomina-tionalism"]. However, when the clusters are poorly separated, it is up to the researcher to decide if the clusters produced by the clustering procedure are "real" rather than artifactual (Bonner 1964). Such a decision has to be based on the interpretability of the cluster solution, and on an examination of the differences between these clusters. We will first examine the discriminant functions to obtain more information on the general characteristics of these clusters. The most important statistics resulting from the postcluster canoni-cal discriminant analyses are summarized in Tables 1 to 3.

The first two columns of these tables report the canonical structures, represented by correlation coefficients between each canonical function and the seven original scales. The first canonical variable is more discrimi-nating than the second because it has the highest multiple correlation with the clusters. These correlations are .855, .870, and .863 in 1977, 1985, and 1993, respectively (not shown on tables). Notice that in Tables 1 to 3 the first canonical variable has high positive correlations with all the criterion vari-ables. Therefore, the first canonical variable can be substantively interpreted as a scale measuring general conservatism. Respondents who score higher on the first canonical function are more conservative, and those who score lower are more liberal, as measured on the seven scales. This means that in all three plots, cluster 1 is more liberal than cluster 2, which in turn is more liberal than cluster 3.

The second canonical variable is also statistically significant, that is, the three clusters are significantly different on the second canonical discrimi-nant functions as well. The second canonical variables have extremely consistent cross-variable correlation patterns: they have high positive cor-relations with antiabortion attitudes, high religiosity, and strict sexual moral-ity, but high negative correlations with the racial justice scale. Their

Table 2. Canonical Structure and Cluster Means, 1985 (*N* = 1081; ANOVA *P* > *F*, .0001)

	First Canonical Correlation	Second Canonical Correlation	Liberal Cluster Mean (*N* = 375)	Moderate Cluster (*N* = 394)	Conservative Cluster (*N* = 312)
Abortion	.6429	.4975	−.8339	.3372	.5915
Civil liberty	.7166	−.0830	−.6806	−.0633	.9571
Sexual morality	.6858	.4477	−.9020	.4035	.6455
Women's rights	.7237	−.0915	−.6489	−.0563	.9555
Racial justice	.7508	−.5251	−.4496	−.4535	1.2371
Political ideology	.3028	.3303	−.4579	.2986	.2145
Religious intensity	.3455	.3897	−.5708	.3212	.2407

correlations with other scales are too low to be of practical significance. The second canonical variables have less straightforward interpretations due to their incoherent correlations with the original scales. The only indisputable conclusion is that they do not embody any strong and coherent ideology since they are positively associated with some conservative views and negatively associated with others. This means that individuals in cluster 2 are not systematically different from the other two clusters on the second discriminant function. As we will argue momentarily, this lack of a strong and coherent ideology is characteristic of moderate Americans who occupy the vast middle ground in the cultural conflict.

The next three columns in the three tables report the standardized cluster means on each of the seven scales. These numbers are again in standard deviation units, which show the cluster mean on a particular scale relative to the overall mean of the scale in the sample. For instance, in the 1977

Table 3. Canonical Structure and Cluster Means, 1993 (*N* = 368; ANOVA *P* > *F*, .0001)

	First Canonical Correlation	Second Canonical Correlation	Liberal Cluster Mean (*N* = 179)	Moderate Cluster (*N* = 126)	Conservative Cluster (*N* = 63)
Abortion	.5781	.5695	−.7546	.8407	.4217
Civil liberty	.6902	−.0895	−.5618	−.0385	1.2979
Sexual morality	.7036	.3631	−.7464	.6200	.7186
Women's rights	.7241	−.2640	−.4969	−.0598	1.4324
Racial justice	.6861	−.6023	−.3284	−.3256	1.6969
Political ideology	.3300	.2938	−.4597	.4049	.3896
Religious intensity	.4616	.3760	−.5747	.6903	.0724

sample, the mean of cluster 1 on the sexual morality scale is more than one standard deviation below the overall mean. Again, these tables exhibit almost identical patterns: on average, individuals in cluster 1 express liberal views on all issues, those in cluster 3 display conservative tendencies on all aspects, and those in cluster 2 feature no coherent ideologies. For all tables, the significance level of analysis of variance using cluster membership as the independent variable and the seven scales as dependent variables is .0001. This demonstrates that the clusters are significantly different on all these criterion variables in all three years.

The discriminant analyses indicate that the three clusters displayed in the scatterplots are significantly different on all the scales, especially on the first canonical discriminant functions. These three clusters roughly represent three relatively distinct ideological orientations among the sampled individuals. Since very similar clustering patterns emerged from all these samples, we can be reasonably confident that the clustering procedures accurately reflected the underlying structure of the data and, by analogy, of the general population. Based on the interpretations of the canonical functions, we label the clusters according to their location on the first canonical function. From the left to the right along the horizontal axis, the three clusters can be identified as liberal, moderate, and conservative, respectively.

CLUSTER VALIDATION

The tentative tripartition of the sample into three ideological clusters is intuitively appealing. However, as we have noticed, there are no manifest boundaries between these clusters, and this ambiguity suggests the possibility of an arbitrary partition of a relatively homogeneous population. To establish the validity of these clusters, we examine cross-cluster variations on some external variables. One of the most efficient validation procedures involves variables that are theoretically relevant to the intended classification but not used to generate the cluster solution.

Table 4 contains the basic information. Unfortunately, almost all the relevant external variables are categorical, and this makes significance tests difficult. In the following discussion, we will illustrate each cluster's basic demographic characteristics and how members of each cluster responded to some relevant GSS questions. Thus, beginning with demographic characteristics, there are more younger people among liberals than among moderates and conservatives. For example, in 1977, about 55 percent of those classified as liberals were between 18 and 35 years of age, as compared to only 15 percent among conservatives.

Table 4. Cross-Cluster Variations on External Variables

External Variables	1977			1985			1993		
	Lib.	Mod.	Con.	Lib.	Mod.	Con.	Lib.	Mod.	Con.
Age 18–35 (%)	54.5	40.4	15.0	47.3	37.8	14.5	39.3	31.9	17.5
Male (%)	50.6	40.2	45.2	47.3	43.9	42.9	44.8	40.4	40.8
Black (%)	10.3	12.6	11.9	9.3	13.3	12.5	9.5	13.2	11.6
From South (%)	21.6	33.3	44.8	29.2	31.0	47.5	24.7	35.7	43.8
Average years of schooling* (%)	13.1	11.9	10.0	13.7	12.5	10.7	13.8	12.9	11.6
Attend church service nearly every week or more often (%)	12.5	51.3	41.8	13.1	50.5	49.1	15.2	58.8	43.9
Support prayer in school (%)	46.6	69.3	77.0	37.4	60.6	72.5	43.5	68.8	78.8
Fundamentalists (%)	18.0	31.8	41.1	20.0	36.8	47.2	24.7	42.9	44.9
Think we are spending too little on improving the conditions of blacks (%)	27.6	28.5	19.1	39.8	31.2	18.2	1.8	32.4	28.7
Support tougher laws against divorce (%)	25.6	55.9	63.4	33.4	59.2	71.2	35.3	54.0	65.7
Favor legalization of marijuana (%)	m	m	m	m	m	m	33.1	17.3	7.0
Favor ERA (%)	79.9	65.6	51.6	m	m	m	m	m	m
Oppose gun control (%)	25.3	28.5	25.7	25.7	27.1	26.9	15.1	18.1	20.7
Voted in the last presidential election (%)	63.4	68.0	61.2	67.6	72.7	65.9	70.6	69.9	64.3
Voted Democratic candidate in the last presidential election (%)	55.8	53.5	51.1	47.8	33.8	29.9	50.2	33.2	35.3

*, significant at the .0001 level; m, data missing.

As discovered in many other studies, liberals also tend to be better educated. In both 1977 and 1985, the liberals on average have three more years of schooling than the conservatives. However, it is worth noting that a subsequent analysis (not shown here) shows that there is no positive relationship between higher educational levels and greater polarization of the sort that might be expected according to Hunter's more refined thesis of a greater cultural war among "elites." The thesis may well apply to movement leaders, political rhetoricians, and moral entrepreneurs. However, it does not describe societal elites in the broader sense of those standing in the higher reaches of the status and class distribution. If anything, this is a stronghold of moderation.

Regional differences also contribute to ideological diversity, as noted by other researchers (e.g., Stump 1984a, 1984b). Conservatives are more likely to be residing in the South, that is, the southern region in Zelinsky's (1961) classification of religious regions. In all three samples, about 45 percent of the conservatives are from the South, compared with about one-third of the moderates and only one-quarter of the liberals. Liberals are slightly more likely to be male than moderates and conservatives, although the practical significance of this difference may be trivial. Finally, African Americans are less likely to be found in the liberal clusters.

The rest of the variables shown on the left side of Table 4 are relevant because they incorporate some of the most important issues in the current public debate. Before we examine cross-cluster variations as a validation procedure, it is important to understand that there is no bias involved in the selection of these variables. They are chosen not because they confirm or refute any preexisting presumptions, but rather for two other reasons: First, they are frequently used to measure ideological orientations in the literature, so their validity has been widely accepted if not painstakingly established. Second, they are available in all three data sets and have not been used in generating the cluster solutions.

Clearly liberals differ dramatically from members of the other two clusters in their frequency of church attendance. Only 13 percent of them attended church services nearly every week or more often in the 1977 sample, 13 percent in 1985, and 15 percent in 1993. Although the comparisons between the moderates and the conservatives are not so striking, moderates are clearly more likely to be regular churchgoers than conservatives. In 1977 and 1993, the difference is about 10–15 percentage points.

The U.S. Supreme Court has ruled that no state or local government may require prayer or Bible readings in public schools. However, the controversy over the issue of school prayer continues—as does prayer itself in perhaps as many as one-quarter to one-third of public schools across the country. Less than half of the liberals support school prayers, as compared to more than 60 percent among the moderates and around three-quarters among the conservatives. Meanwhile, the conservatives in the three samples are about twice as likely as the liberals to belong to fundamentalist churches.

On social policy issues, the liberals are more likely to believe that we are spending too little on improving the conditions of Blacks although the differentiation is not so clear in some respects. For example, in 1977 the liberals and moderates are virtually indistinguishable on this measure, and in 1993 there is only a 4-percentage-point difference between the moderates and conservatives. The liberals generally do not support tougher laws against divorce. They are much less likely to state that divorce in this country should be more difficult to obtain than it is now. In 1993, about one-third of the liberals favor the legalization of marijuana, as compared to 17 percent among the moderates and only 7 percent among the conservatives. Concerning an Equal Rights Amendment for women, there is a 14-percentage-point difference between both liberals and moderates, and moderates and conservatives. However, the three clusters show little variation in their attitudes toward gun control. The overwhelming majority of the samples support gun control by roughly a three-to-one margin. In terms of political participation, as measured by voter turnout rate in presidential elections, no consistent pattern can be observed. Members of the three clusters are equally likely to vote, although the moderates may have a slightly higher proportion. Among those who voted, the liberals are most likely and the conservatives are least likely to vote for Democratic candidates. Nonetheless, the distinction is minimal in 1977 and, in all three instances, the differences between the moderates and the conservatives are negligible.

In summary, these data yield several overall patterns. First, there are significant variations across the clusters on most of the variables presented in Table 4. The liberals are generally younger, better educated, less religious, from non-South regions, and express more liberal views on most social issues including school prayer, government spending, divorce laws, drug legalization, and women's rights. The conservatives are found on the other end of the ideological spectrum and the moderates occupy the middle ground. This pattern of differentiation on external variables illustrates that the clustering procedures effectively sorted the respondents into three groups based on their overall ideological orientations. Thus, we can be confident that on average the three clusters are different not only on variables used in the cluster analyses but also on variables not involved in developing the cluster solutions.

Second, on some variables, such as gun control and political participation, the three clusters are not very different from one another. On other variables, substantial variations can be observed only between the liberals and the conservatives and not between all pairwise comparisons. For example, the moderates and the conservatives are almost equally likely to vote for Democratic presidential candidates. Based on different but conceptually

Table 5. Changing Proportion (%) of Liberals, Moderates, and Conservatives—1977, 1985, 1993

	1977	1985	1993
Liberals	35	35	49
Moderates	35	37	34
Conservatives	30	28	17
N	(1024)	(1081)	(368)

related variables from the same sample, Table 4 reveals a pattern similar to Figures 1 through 3: the three clusters are relatively distinct in their ideological profile but the boundaries are not always clear. This has obvious and important implications for the culture war and polarization theses.

Finally, another pattern with implications concerns the changing proportions of liberals, moderates, and conservatives in the pooled samples for 1977, 1985, and 1993. Since the proponents of a polarized culture war all argue that this is a phenomenon on the increase, there should be a sharp decrease of moderates with corresponding growth among liberals and especially conservatives, who are after all most likely to "begin the shooting." According to Table 5, the reality is markedly different. Recalling that the issues involved are standardized, the proportion of conservatives has actually declined over the fifteen-year period from 30 percent to 17 percent; the moderates have remained remarkably stable, and the liberals have experienced the single large growth spurt from 35 percent in 1985 to 49 percent in 1993. These figures hardly suggest whole armies itching for battle.

INTRA-ORGANIZATIONAL STRUGGLES: THE CASE OF DENOMINATIONS

To this point, we have made little mention of religion. Although both Wuthnow and Hunter suggest that it is a propelling polarizing force, it is not at all clear that it is a cause or a consequence, even where polarization occurs. Of course, there is very little doubt that there are modal disagreements between religious denominations on the moral matters at issue here. Indeed, it is empirically demonstrable that these matters are now more important than either conventional religious differences or distinctions in socioeconomic variables in producing a "new denominationalism" in America (Yang 1996). The question here, however, concerns the differences *within* denominations. If Wuthnow and Hunter are correct, polarized battles should be rending the old tents and leaving many exposed to a new kind of cultural storm.

It is neither realistic nor necessary to study all denominations in the GSS samples. Most of them are simply too small for separate examination, and a reasonable alternative is to select several major denominations so that all types of denominations are represented. Of course, focusing on larger denominations increases the possibilities of finding intradenominational polarization. Nonetheless, we shall look specifically at the American Baptist Association, Southern Baptist Convention, United Methodist Church, Lutheran Church–Missouri Synod, Presbyterian Church in the United States, the Episcopal Church, Jews, the Mormon Church, and evangelical and fundamentalist churches. Even with these relatively larger denominations, it is still necessary to pool several annual surveys to ensure a sufficient sample size. The composite sample comprises 9047 respondents from the 1985, 1988, 1989, 1990, 1991, and 1993 surveys. These six surveys were selected because they are more up-to-date and they include all the criterion variables measuring ideological variations.

Space precludes providing the separate scatterplots for the cluster analyses performed for each of the nine denominations, using the same criterion variables as above [see Yang (1996) for the full presentation]. In each case, plots were distributed within a two-dimensional canonical space. Substantive interpretations of the two-axis CAN1 and CAN2 are provided in Table 7 (see pp. 34–5), which reports the total canonical structures represented by the correlation coefficients between the canonical variables and each of the seven scales for each of the denominations involved.

Suffice it to say that there are indeed well-separated ideological clusters within most of these denominations. For example, the respondents from the Presbyterian Church in the United States are clearly divided in their attitudes toward the seven issues, as are the United Methodists and the Evangelicals and Fundamentalists (a finding to which we return below). From Table 7 we can see that there are clear differences within these groups, especially on issues of abortion, civil liberty, women's rights, and racial justice. The opposing signs for the first and second clusters (C1 and C2) show that views between the clusters along this range of issues are virtually non-overlapping. All of the other denominational groupings show a clear distinction on at least some of the internal variable issues, particularly on issues of women's rights and racial justice. Based on these issues, attitudes of individuals in cluster 1 may be identified as distinctly more liberal than the attitudes of individuals that appear in cluster 2. In cases where the signs are not opposing there are still some significant differences in coefficient magnitude, indicating a consistent ideological difference between the two clusters. Notice that the differences in political ideology and religious intensity are also often acutely marked (the scales themselves prevent negative values).

However, these data are deceptive. Closer examination reveals that these apparent polarizations represent fundamentally different underlying struc-

Table 6. Cluster Means (Centroids) on Canonical Discriminant Functions

	Southern Baptist Convention		United Methodist Church		Lutheran Church-Missouri Synod		Evangelicals and Fundamentalists	
	CAN1	CAN2	CAN1	CAN2	CAN1	CAN2	CAN1	CAN2
Cluster 1	-.477	.062	-.425	.015	-.672	.165	-2.248	-.302
Cluster 2	2.403	-.007	3.226	.056	3.404	-.141	2.778	-.357
Cluster 3	-.543	-3.308	.795	-4.524	-1.591	-3.435	.193	4.411

Table 7.   Cluster Means on Internal Variables

Denominations Clusters	American Baptist Association		Southern Baptist Convention		United Methodist Church		Lutheran Church Missouri Synod	
	C1	C2	C1	C2	C1	C2	C1	C2
Abortion	.130	.522	.016	.695	−.275	.530	.031	.114
Civil Liberty	.343	1.417	.061	1.439	−.179	.901	−.343	1.270
Women's Rights	−.026	1.339	−.090	1.185	−.239	1.211	−.123	.951
Racial Justice	−.275	2.026	−.048	1.670	−.120	1.662	−.173	1.559
Sexual Morality	9.619	11.60	9.774	10.909	9.169	11.185	9.196	11.273
Political Ideology	3.98	45.000	4.323	4.023	3.961	5.111	4.333	5.091
Religious Intensity	2.079	2.600	1.788	2.159	1.681	2.222	1.902	2.091

tures than the polarization hypothesis assumes. Thus, while there are commonly two well-separated clusters of respondents in these denominations, this does not necessarily imply a contest of ideological extremes. In fact, the vast majority of those in the liberal cluster are more likely to be ideological moderates than liberals. To see this, we need to examine the cluster means on the canonical variables presented in Table 6 (see p. 33) for the four denominations that exhibit at least a modicum of separation on the first canonical variables. The canonical coefficients are standardized so that the canonical variables (CAN1 and CAN2) have means equal to zero and pooled within-cluster variances equal to one. This means that all the scores in Table 6 are in standard deviation units. In this theoretical context, zero is the neutral point on the ideological spectrum represented by the particular canonical variable.

For each of these denominations, let us concentrate on the first canonical variable and the first two clusters. Table 6 shows that, for all four denominations, cluster 1 has negative means on the first canonical variable and cluster 2 has positive means. The corresponding figures (Figures 1 to 3) have accurately reflected this pattern: cluster 1 is located to the left of cluster 2. As Table 6 shows, cluster 2 is much farther to the right of the midpoint than cluster 1 is to the left. This means that cluster 1 is only slightly liberal, and it can be more appropriately characterized as ideological moderate than liberal. The apparent separation between cluster 1 and cluster 2 along the first discriminant function is more likely to be an ideological differentiation between the moderates and the conservatives, rather than an ideological polarization between the liberals and the conservatives as the polarization hypothesis suggests.

However, there is further evidence against the intradenominational polar-

Table 7.   (cont.)

Presbyterian Church in the U.S.		Episcopal Church		Jewish		Mormons		Evangelical and Fundamentalists	
C1	C2	C1	C2	C1	C2	C1	C2	C1	C2
−.717	.796	−.481	.824	−1.125	.606	.501	−.299	−.443	.836
−.824	1.131	−.498	−.182	−.696	.011	−.311	.810	−.541	.994
−.433	.328	−.320	.567	−.596	.622	.251	1.142	−.228	.498
−.380	.594	−.240	1.696	−.379	−.484	−.268	1.270	−.448	.119
7.571	10.600	8.508	9.500	6.222	10.667	10.759	10.00	9.267	11.250
3.571	2.400	4.200	4.250	3.148	4.000	4.519	5.000	3.800	4.417
1.905	1.400	1.785	2.000	1.833	2.333	2.241	1.000	1.667	3.000

ization hypothesis. Polarization implies (and its proponents claim) an approximately even division between the liberal and the conservative clusters. However, a prominent feature of the clustering patterns is the disproportionate cross-cluster frequency distributions. In most denominations the overwhelming majority of the respondents are classified into cluster 1, which means that the vast majority of the sample have been identified as ideological moderates or maybe weak liberals and only a tiny minority have been recognized as conservatives. In most denominations, it is the small minority of conservatives who express distinct, intense, unwavering, and consistent values and beliefs. Conservatives are more upset about the state of America, are more anxious to affect social policy, and are more extreme in their views.

Finally, it is ironic that our only compelling evidence of intradenominational polarization is found among Evangelicals and Fundamentalists. These two camps are generally portrayed as conservative or orthodox monoliths, but each seems to host groups of roughly equal size that are equally separated from the middle of the ideological scale embodied by CAN1 in Table 6. This seems to be an ideal structure of ideological polarization, since CAN1 can indeed be interpreted as a scale of ideological conservatism. And while the evidence might also be ideal for those seeking confirmation of intradenominational polarization, it may be cold water for those portraying a larger culture war provoked and sustained by a united and resolute right flank. Of course, Nancy Ammerman's qualitative treatment of *Baptist Battles* (1990) provides abundant letter and verse for the disputes at issue on this end of the spectrum. The fact that our data do not confirm a widespread split among her Southern Baptist troops suggests again that the warfare may be confined to the generals.

CONCLUSION

The polarization thesis envisions a polarized American public immersed in deep ideological debate and culture war. In cluster analysis terminology, it stipulates a public divided into two separate clusters defined by orthogonal ideological convictions. In testing this hypothesis, we performed cluster analyses on several national samples, using different clustering methods. None of these analyses provides any hint of ideological dichotomy in the data. All produce three poorly separated clusters, which we have labeled liberal, moderate, and conservative along an ideological continuum. While there is an appearance of intradenominational polarization, this turns out to be more apparent than real under closer inspection. Indeed, the only cases that justify the warfare label are the Evangelicals and Fundamentalists—two groups that are generally depicted as waging the war rather than consumed by it.

The polarization argument is off-base in several important respects. First, it fails to emphasize the force and forces of moderation, though in fairness it should be noted that both Wuthnow and Hunter acknowledge this possibility. Second, it oversimplifies American ideological diversity and vastly exaggerates the cultural divide among us. Third, in focusing only on the two extremes, it rests its case on the testimony of the few who call to arms rather than the many who fail to respond. Fourth, polarization and cultural warfare depend upon rival ideologies that go beyond single issues and are consistent and coherent across several issues taken together. Fifth, qualitative evidence (like its quantitative counterpart) has both virtues and liabilities; one must be wary of arguments that rest solely on the passionate rhetoric and confrontational activities of opposing "special purpose groups"—for example, pro-life and pro-choice social movement organizations. The antagonisms between movement "elites" are not necessarily reflected among either rank and file members or the great unmobilized mass—as the elites themselves know full well.

Meanwhile, the notion of a culture war has been positively provocative as well as negatively misleading. This chapter is hardly alone in picking up the gauntlet. Jackson Carroll and Penny Marler (1995) find only scant support for the culture war model in their recent ethnographies of two Protestant seminaries—one liberal and one conservative. William McKinney (1995) is also skeptical, based on his reading of American denominational communities. Michele Dillon (1995) has recently argued that the larger debate over abortion constitutes more "normal discourse" than "culture war." Paul DiMaggio, John Evans, and Bethany Bryson (1996) have recently taken an instructively different route through a different set of GSS data but emerge with very compatible conclusions. Demerath (1995) places the matter in a more comparative context by arguing that America's cultural skirmishes really amount to democracy at work and reveal important differences of both cause and consequence when compared to the bloody battles raging in countries such as Northern Ireland, Guatemala, Israel, and India. Clearly the issues are important; just as clearly, they deserve the attention of more scholarship rather than further stereotyping.

REFERENCES

Ammerman, Nancy Tatom. 1990. *Baptist Battles.* New Brunswick, NJ: Rutgers University Press.

Bellah, Robert N. 1967. "Civil Religion in America." *Daedalus 96*:1–21.

Bennett, William J. 1992. *The De-Valuing of America.* New York: Summitt.

Bonner, R. E. 1964. "On Some Clustering Techniques." *I.B.M. Journal of Research and Development 8*:22–32.

Carroll, Jackson W., and Penny Long Marler. 1995. "Culture Wars? Insights from Ethnographies of Two Protestant Seminaries." *Sociology of Religion 56*:1–20.

Demerath, N. J. III. 1995. "Lamb among the Lions: America's 'Culture Wars' in Cross-Cultural Perspective." Paper presented at "Two Parties?" Conference at Messiah College, Pennsylvania.

Dillon, Michele. 1995. "The American Abortion Debate." *Virginia Review of Sociology 2*:115–32.

DiMaggio, Paul, John Evans, and Bethany Bryson. 1996. "Have Americans' Social Attitudes Become More Polarized?" *American Journal of Sociology 102* (November):690–755.

Durkheim, Emile. [1912] 1915. *The Elementary Forms of the Religious Life.* New York: Free Press.

Everitt, B. 1980. *Cluster Analysis.* New York: Halstead.

Gitlin, Todd. 1995. *The Twilight of Common Dreams: Why America Is Wracked by Culture Wars.* New York: Metropolitan.

Goggin, Malcolm L., ed. 1993. *Understanding the New Politics of Abortion.* Los Angeles: Sage.

Guinness, Os. 1993. *The American Hour.* New York: Free Press.

Guth, James L., Corwin E. Smidt, Lyman A. Kellstedt, and John C. Green. 1993. "The Sources of Anti-Abortion Attitudes." In *Understanding the New Politics of Abortion,* edited by M. Goggin. Los Angeles: Sage.

Hunter, James Davison. 1991. *Culture Wars: The Struggle to Define America.* New York: Basic Books.

———. 1994. *Before the Shooting Begins: Searching for Democracy in America's Culture War.* New York: Free Press.

McKinney, William. 1995. "Can Religious Communities Survive America's Culture War?" Manuscript, Hartford Seminary, Hartford, Connecticut.

Neuhaus, Richard John. 1992. "Can Atheists Be Good Citizens?" Pp. 295–308 in

Being Christian Today: An American Conversation, edited by R. J. Neuhaus and G. Weigel. Washington, DC: Ethics and Public Policy Center.

SAS Institute, Inc. 1990. *SAS Stat User's Guide,* Version 6, 4th ed. Cary, NC: Author.

Stump, Roger W. 1984a. "Regional Differences in Religious Affiliation in the United States." *Sociological Analysis 45*(4):283–99.

———. 1984b. "Regional Migration and Religious Commitment in the United States." *Journal for the Scientific Study of Religion 23*(3):292–303.

Wuthnow, Robert. 1988. *The Restructuring of American Religion: Society and Faith Since World War II.* Princeton, NJ: Princeton University Press.

Yang, Yonghe. 1996. "The Structure and Dynamics of Ideological Pluralism in American Religion." Ph.D. dissertation, Department of Sociology, University of Massachusetts, Amherst.

Zelinsky, Wilbur. 1961. "An Approach to the Religious Geography of the United States." *Annals of the Association of American Geographers 51*(June):139–93.

3

A War for America's Soul?
The American Religious Landscape

NANCY J. DAVIS and ROBERT V. ROBINSON

> There is a religious war going on in this country. It is a culture war as critical to
> the kind of nation we shall be as the Cold War itself, for this war is for the soul
> of America.
> —Pat Buchanan at the 1992 Republican National Convention

Metaphors of "culture war" abound in recent scholarship on religion, in
mass media coverage of religion and politics, and in the speeches of politicians appealing to religious blocs. Religious traditionalists are portrayed as a
monolithic, politically conservative phalanx marching lockstep into battle
against the forces of religious modernism or secularism. In this chapter we
ask whether the rumors of culture war are exaggerated. We investigate
whether religious divisions exist among Americans in their views on a range
of issues, including schooling, sexuality, reproductive rights, gendered divisions of labor, racial equity, social welfare, and economic justice. We also
focus in some detail on whether those at one end of the religious spectrum—
the religiously orthodox—constitute the united, politically conservative
front that the widely used label "Religious Right" implies.

In his influential book *Culture Wars* (1991), James Davison Hunter argues
that traditional religious antagonisms between Protestants and Catholics and
between Christians and Jews have been superseded by an intractable conflict between the religiously orthodox and moral progressives. The *orthodox*
are those who believe that God is the ultimate moral arbiter of right and
wrong, that the word of God as recorded in sacred texts is inerrant and
timeless, and that God takes an active role in people's everyday lives. *Progressives,* who include religious modernists as well as agnostics and atheists,
believe that humans are the ultimate judge of right and wrong, that morality

39

is an evolving, open quest that must be judged in its historical and cultural context, and that humans are responsible for their own fates (ibid., 44–45). For Hunter, as well as for Robert Wuthnow (1988), who makes a similar distinction between religious conservatives and religious liberals, Americans with traditional religious beliefs take more conservative stances than religious modernists or secularists on a wide range of issues—abortion, sex outside marriage, prayer in public schools, the division of labor between women and men, equality between racial groups, and economic redistribution (Hunter 1991:97, 109–116; Wuthnow, 1988:114, 219–23, 248).

We agree with Hunter and Wuthnow that religious traditionalists are more conservative than modernists on issues of sexuality, reproductive rights, family, and gendered divisions of labor, but disagree that they are more conservative on issues of racial and economic equality.[1] Many studies have found that religious conservatism is associated with social conservatism (e.g., Woodrum 1988a, 1988b; Olson and Carroll 1992). Yet other studies have found that religious conservatism is either uncorrelated with economic justice attitudes (e.g., Hart 1992:221; Olson and Carroll 1992) or is correlated with *liberal* attitudes on questions of economic justice (e.g., Johnson, Tamney, and Halebsky 1986; Tamney, Burton, and Johnson 1989; Jelen 1990:124). We argue that the religiously orthodox have a "status" interest (Gusfield [1963] 1986) in defending their way of life against secular encroachment that leads them to relatively conservative positions on family and gender issues, but they also have an economic interest, due to their socioeconomic and racial composition, in government efforts to equalize differences between rich and poor and between Whites and people of color.

GENDER AND FAMILY-RELATED ISSUES

In a classic book, *Symbolic Crusade,* Joseph Gusfield ([1963] 1986) characterized the late nineteenth- and early-twentieth-century movement to prohibit the sale and use of alcohol as an attempt by small-town, middle-class, native-born Protestants to defend their declining status and influence against the increasing influx of urban, working-class, foreign-born Catholics and Jews. In the "status politics" of the fight over temperance, abstinence and alcohol became symbolic in a struggle over whose ways of life, values, and tastes would be recognized by law. Much the same analysis can be made of the efforts of traditional religionists today to defend what they see as a disappearing way of life in the face of encroaching secularism. The orthodox, who have a conception of timeless and absolute morality that does not shift with changes in the secular world, are more apt to see themselves as facing a hostile secular world than are moral progressives, who accommodate to that world. For the orthodox, the family is seen as a bulwark against secular encroachment, as one of the few remaining domains where particularistic religious expression is allowed, and as the paramount way to ensure that children will internalize their parents' moral understandings (Ammerman 1987; Davidman 1991; Bendroth 1993:98). We argue that, for most of the orthodox, public schools are seen as undermining and relativizing religious beliefs that parents are teaching their children at home; in their view, schools should support and strengthen religious conviction by presenting a Judeo-Christian worldview and allowing time for prayer. In the eyes of the orthodox, the institution of marriage is being undermined by permissive attitudes toward "casual sex," pornography, homosexuality, and sex outside marriage.

Scripture, which is open to multiple interpretations on many issues, is no less so with respect to gender relations (contrast "Wives, submit yourselves unto your own husbands, as unto the Lord" [Ephesians 5:22–23] with "There is neither Jew nor Greek, there is neither bond nor free, there is neither male nor female; for ye are all one in Christ Jesus" [Galatians 3:28]). Yet for most traditionalist Christians, domestic roles for women, as the primary guardians of their children's religious upbringing, take on elevated importance in the face of a hostile and expanding secular world. Orthodox Judaism, like traditional Christianity, stresses the importance of family, women's primary duty as wife and mother, and the limitation of sexuality to marriage (Danzger 1989:104–5, 153; Davidman 1991:160, 162). Orthodox-sponsored organizations, such as Jews for Life and Agudath Israel, have mobilized against abortion, women's work outside the home, pornography, and gay rights (Hunter 1991:94–95, 100).

Thus, the status interest of the religiously orthodox as a group attempting to defend a timeless moral code in the face of secular change leads them to conservative positions on gender and family-related issues. Along with Wuthnow (1988:168, 201–3), Hunter (1991:49, 122), and others (e.g., Klatch 1992; Woodrum 1988a, 1988b), we expect the orthodox to be less supportive than moral progressives of women taking on positions that compete with those of wife and mother; more opposed to liberalized abortion laws and birth control, which make motherhood voluntary (Luker 1984); and more opposed to sex education, pornography, homosexuality, and sex outside marriage, which are seen as separating sexuality from marriage and the rearing of children. We also expect more favorable attitudes toward school prayer among the religiously orthodox than among moral progressives.

RACIAL AND ECONOMIC ISSUES

Issues of racial and economic equality are among the most contested in the contemporary political arena, as can be seen in recent debates over affirmative action; immigration; the minimum wage; tax cuts for the middle-class, well-to-do, and corporations; regulations on the movement of jobs overseas; welfare reform; government jobs provision; Medicare and Social Security; and national health care. While the religiously orthodox are widely assumed to be more conservative than theological progressives on racial and economic issues, we suggest that the orthodox may be no more conservative than moral progressives on these issues and may even be more liberal. Because our data do not allow us to address the question of attitudes toward gender inequality (aside from the more narrow concern of women's and men's involvement in the family, workplace, and government), we limit our arguments here to attitudes toward racial and economic inequality.

Since sacred texts are ambiguous on questions of racial and economic justice, the biblical literalism of the religiously orthodox does not inevitably lead them to opposition to racial and economic equality. Biblical texts have been used to justify both equality and inequality and have helped spawn and sustain popular social movements with very different goals. Historically, orthodox Christianity has been associated with slavery and abolition, with segregation and civil rights, and with economic populism and conservatism. Max Weber ([1922] 1964:46–59), in his discussion of the indeterminacy of religion as a political force, argued that the same religious tradition and sacred texts may support either "priestly" or "prophetic" traditions. Williams and Alexander note that priestly orientations "support, legitimate, and reinforce the status quo in its power arrangements," while prophetic orientations "challenge extant political arrangements" (1994:4). Based solely on the lack of a clear direction that a strict biblical reading gives the religiously orthodox, we would expect no relationship between religious orthodoxy and racial or economic conservatism. However, as Hunter (1991:63–64) acknowledges and as we will show, the religiously orthodox draw disproportionately on the less advantaged segments of society—the working class and poor, the less educated, and racial and ethnic minorities. To the extent that the disadvantaged among the orthodox have an economic and racial interest in government policy that would benefit them (Robinson and Bell 1978; Davis and Robinson 1991), we would expect the orthodox, *as a group,* to be more liberal on economic and racial issues than progressives, *as a group.* In other words, if the orthodox are comprised disproportionately of the disadvantaged, then the economic and racial interests of disadvantaged individuals among the orthodox should make the orthodox, on average, more favorable toward policy that promotes equality between classes and races than moral progressives, who tend to draw from the more privileged of society. Our expectation then is that in the zero-order (that is, without controls for race and socioeconomic position), the religiously orthodox should be more liberal on economic and racial issues than moral progressives. However, since, as we noted above, the effect of biblical literalism on racial and economic issues is unclear, we expect no effect of religion on such issues when the racial and socioeconomic composition of the religiously orthodox and progressives is taken into account.

Based on these arguments, we hypothesize:

H_1: *The religiously orthodox are more conservative than moral progressives on family-related and gender issues.*

H_2: *Without controls for race and socioeconomic variables, the religiously orthodox are more liberal than moral progressives on issues of race and class inequality. With controls, the orthodox are no different from moral progressives on issues of race and class inequality.*

ARE THE SIDES POLITICALLY MONOLITHIC?

Both Wuthnow and Hunter noted that public opinion is complex and that the religious division between religious traditionalists and modernists only "tends to" align with political divisions. Nonetheless, there is a strong suggestion in their work that each of the sides is comprised of like-minded people. Wuthnow (1988:133, 239, 256) depicted the antagonists in the religious divide as "almost separate religious communities" that have spawned civil religions that "frequently appear to be at fundamental odds with one another" and interpreted public opinion surveys as indicating "political uniformity" within each side. Hunter, as the title of his book conveys, used language that depicts even greater polarization and hostility between the two sides, each of which "operates within its own constellation of values, interests and assumptions" and is "worlds apart" from the other (1991:128). That for Hunter (ibid., 42, 49) the struggles over social, political, and economic issues share a common root in "fundamentally different" moral cosmologies also points to a degree of commonality of opinion within each side. Finally, neither Wuthnow nor Hunter devotes much attention to whether either group is divided in its political stance along the lines of race, class, or gender. Yet, however much Wuthnow and Hunter imply political uniformity within the two sides of the religious divide, the imagery of monolithic camps or voting blocs has been drawn far more sharply by media pundits, politicians, and leaders of parachurch organizations such as the Moral Majority and the Christian Coalition.

We have several reasons for believing that neither the religiously orthodox nor moral progressives are monolithic. We focus our arguments and
analyses specifically on the religiously orthodox because they have had
greater success of late than theological progressives in mounting a political
movement and a national presidential campaign, which suggests that they
may have a more developed and consistent ideology than moral progressives (but see Warner 1988). The widespread use of the label "Religious
Right" to refer to the orthodox and the absence of a corresponding label for
the other side of the religious spectrum also points to the perception of
greater ideological consistency on the conservative end of the religious
spectrum.

First, our argument above concerning the ambiguity of sacred texts, regardless of the issue, suggests that a literal interpretation of these will not
direct the orthodox in a clear ideological direction. If the religiously orthodox are pulled in a conservative direction on gender and family-related
issues based on their status interests but in a liberal direction on racial and
economic issues based on the economic interests of the disadvantaged
among them, then this should break down ideological consistency across
issues. The priestly and prophetic traditions within the same religion suggest
that the orthodox may not be consistently conservative across a range of
issues.

Second, although the religiously orthodox draw disproportionately on the
disadvantaged, they are, of course, comprised of both advantaged and disadvantaged members. Thus the religiously orthodox may be divided along
the lines of race, class, and gender on many specific issues. For the religiously orthodox to advance a united conservative front requires that the
self-interest of groups who would be hurt by conservative positions or policy
be superseded by religious authority, which is unlikely given the ambiguous
message of Scripture. We expect that women are less accepting than men of
the idea that women should work in the home and men in the workplace,
that Blacks take more liberal stances than Whites on issues of racial equality,
and that working-class and poor people are more favorable than middle-
class and affluent people toward government efforts to reduce the gap
between rich and poor. These divisions may impede consensus or commonality of viewpoints among the orthodox.

Third, as Converse (1964) argued, elites may hold more consistent ideological positions across a range of issues than does the public generally. In
other words, there may be considerably less adherence to a "party line"
among rank and file adherents of moral orthodoxy than among the leadership. The national leaders of orthodox groups often present broad political
agendas as *gestalts* encompassing a wide range of issues [e.g., the Moral
Majority's "Agenda for the 1980s" and, more recently, the Christian Coalition's "Contract with the American Family" (Pohli 1983:532; Jelen

1990:118)]. Perhaps it is because so many analyses of religious traditional-ists focus on the speeches or writings of elites who head parareligious orga-nizations that the impression is formed of the orthodox as monolithically and consistently conservative in their politics. In the process the rich, multi-faceted kaleidoscope of political views in these communities goes unrecog-nized. Surveys of ordinary Americans (e.g., Jelen 1991; Tamney et al. 1989; Hart 1992) and ethnographies of Protestant Fundamentalist, Catholic Pen-tecostal, and Orthodox (and Hasidic) Jewish congregations (e.g., McGuire 1982; Pohli 1983; Ammerman 1987; Neitz 1987; Stacey and Gerard 1990; Davidman 1991) have found considerable diversity, complexity, egalitari-anism, or incorporation of secular ideologies in the attitudes of religious traditionalists.

Thus, we hypothesize:

H$_3$: *The religiously orthodox are not uniformly conservative on gender, racial, and economic issues.*

H$_4$: *The religiously orthodox exhibit little consensus on specific issues.*

H$_5$: *The religiously orthodox are divided by sex, race, and class in their atti-tudes. Specifically, women take more liberal positions than men on questions of gender relations; people of color take more liberal positions than Whites on racial issues; and working-class and poor people take more liberal positions than middle-class and affluent people on economic issues.*

THE RELIGION MODULE OF THE
GENERAL SOCIAL SURVEY

In testing these hypotheses, we analyze data from the National Opinion Research Center's General Social Survey (GSS) for 1991. This is a national sample of the noninstitutionalized population of the United States, eighteen years of age or older. The 1991 GSS had 1517 respondents, of which 1359 or 89.6 percent also completed a questionnaire for the International Social Survey Programme (ISSP) module on religion; 158 individuals did not com-plete the ISSP questionnaire. Our sample consists of the respondents to the ISSP module.

MEASURES

We measure religious orthodoxy versus progressivism by a three-item index. Respondents were asked:

(a)   Which one of these statements comes closest to describing your
      feelings about the Bible?
      1.   The Bible is an ancient book of fables, legends, history and
           moral teachings recorded by man.
      3.   The Bible is the inspired word of God but not everything
           should be taken literally, word for word.
      5.   The Bible is the actual word of God and it is to be taken
           literally, word for word.
(b)   How much do you agree or disagree with the following? The course
      of our lives is decided by God.
      1.   Strongly disagree.
      2.   Disagree.
      3.   Neither agree nor disagree.
      4.   Agree.
      5.   Strongly Agree.
(c)   How much do you agree or disagree with the following? Right and
      wrong should be based on God's laws.
      1.   Strongly disagree.
      2.   Disagree.
      3.   Neither agree nor disagree.
      4.   Agree.
      5.   Strongly Agree.

The three items are summed to form an index that ranges from 3 to 15.
(The first item is scored from 1 to 5 so that it will carry the same weight
as the other two items). High scores indicate religious orthodoxy or
traditionalism.[2]

The attitudinal variables that we analyze are described briefly below. All
of these are coded so that the high pole represents the conservative position.
Information on many of the dependent variables was collected from randomly selected subsamples of two-thirds or one-half of the GSS respondents.
Because these subsamples do not perfectly overlap from item to item, it is
not possible to form indexes of similar questions on family, gender, racial,
and economic issues.

THE AMERICAN RELIGIOUS LANDSCAPE

The rhetoric of culture war in the mass media suggests a religious topography resembling two peaks separated by a chasm. Academics writing about
this religious division have disagreed in their mapping of the religious ter-

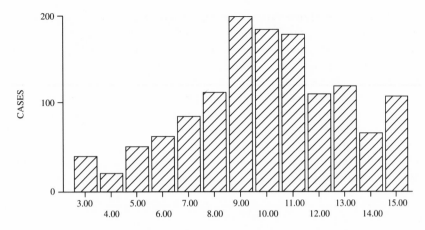

Figure 1. Distribution of religious orthodoxy/progressivism.

rain. Using a self-assessed measure of religious conservatism,[3] Wuthnow (1988:133) finds that the religious spectrum has large conservative and liberal wings, each containing over two-fifths of Americans, and a small middle ground of less than one-fifth of the population. Consistent with this imagery, Wuthnow (ibid., 21) refers to the "chasm" or "ravine" dividing the two sides. Hunter (1991:159) expects that approximately 20 percent of Americans hold strongly to the orthodox vision (see also Greeley 1989:19) and 20 percent to the progressive view, leaving roughly 60 percent in the middle.

Figure 1 shows that the distribution of religious orthodoxy fits Hunter's topography more than Wuthnow's. The distribution is approximately normal with a mean of score of 9.97 and a standard deviation of 2.98. Nearly two-thirds (64.8 percent) of Americans occupy a middle ground between the extremes of orthodoxy and progressivism, falling within one standard deviation of the mean (as compared with 68.3 percent in the normal distribution). The cases tend to skew toward the conservative end of the religious spectrum; 21.9 percent of Americans are at the orthodox pole of the distribution (more than one standard deviation from the mean), while 13.3 percent are at the progressive pole.

The sizable middle ground between the extremes of the religious spectrum has received little attention from scholars or the mass media. Hunter (1994:86, 106), in a study of American attitudes toward abortion, notes that the common characterization of the middle as "muddled" may misrepresent the views of this group. Muddled individuals should hold moral cosmologies that are internally contradictory, for example, the belief that God decides the course of people's lives but that God's laws should not determine right and wrong. We operationalized muddled individuals as those who, on the three items in the orthodoxy scale, had at least one extreme score (1 or 5) counterbalanced by at least one extreme or moderately extreme score (1, 2, 4, or 5) in the opposite direction. Using this definition, we find that only 10.8 percent of the 881 people in the middle are muddled, leaving 89.2 percent who take consistently moderate positions. Of course, even some of the individuals classified as muddled may have moral cosmologies that are well-considered and nuanced but not in accord with generally held notions of orthodoxy and progressivism. That most Americans in the middle hold consistently moderate positions between the extremes of orthodoxy and progressivism further suggests that orthodoxy/progressivism is better conceived as a continuum ranging from consistently orthodox people through moderates to consistently progressive people rather than as polarized religious "camps."

WHO ARE THE RELIGIOUSLY ORTHODOX?

Our hypothesis (H_2) that the religiously orthodox are more liberal than moral progressives on racial and economic issues is based on the assumption that the orthodox draw disproportionately on the poor and working class, the less educated, and racial and ethnic minorities. A regression analysis of the social determinants of religious orthodoxy that we reported in an earlier paper (Davis and Robinson 1996c) confirms this. The orthodox are significantly more likely than progressives to have low incomes (standardized coefficient = −.074), to have less prestigious occupations (−.064), to be less educated (−.144), and to be African Americans (.173), Latinos (.078), or American Indians (.100) than to be Whites.

ARE THE RELIGIOUSLY ORTHODOX MORE CONSERVATIVE THAN MORAL PROGRESSIVES ON FAMILY-RELATED AND GENDER ISSUES?

We expected the religiously orthodox to be more conservative than moral progressives on issues relating to the family and gendered divisions of labor. In Table 1, we show standardized regression coefficients for the effect of religious orthodoxy/progressivism on these issues, controlling for social characteristics of respondents (their sex, race, occupational prestige, income, business ownership, education, age, rural or southern residence, denomination, and religious attendance).[4] Positive coefficients in the table

Table 1. Standardized Regression Coefficients for Religious Orthodoxy/
Progressivism in Models Explaining Attitudes toward Family-Related
Issues and Gendered Divisions of Labor

Issue	Standardized Regression Coefficient for Orthodoxy/Progressivism
Family-Related Issues	
Favors prayer in public schools	.271*
Opposes sex education in public schools	.122*
Rejects birth control for teens	.115*
Opposes abortion on demand	.128*
Views premarital sex as wrong	.220*
Views extramarital sex as wrong	.191*
Views homosexuality as wrong	.224*
Supports antipornography law	.156*
Gendered Divisions of Labor	
Family suffers when woman is employed	.126*
Husbands as breadwinners, wives as homemakers	.187*
Women should run homes, not country	.051
Women not suited for politics	.103*
Would not vote for a woman presidential candidate	.080

Note: Models with controls for sex, race/ethnicity, occupational prestige, income,
business ownership, education, age, rural and southern residence, denomination,
and religious service attendance.
* $p < .05$.

mean that the orthodox are more politically conservative than moral progressives on a given issue, while negative coefficients indicate that the orthodox take a more politically liberal stance than progressives on an issue.

Consistent with our expectations, the orthodox are significantly more
likely than progressives to oppose the Supreme Court ruling forbidding a
mandatory Bible prayer in public schools, to oppose sex education in public
schools, to oppose making birth control available to teens, to oppose legal
abortion on demand, to believe that sexual relations before marriage, outside marriage, and between adults of the same sex are always wrong, and to
favor making pornography illegal.

Attitudes toward women's involvement in the home, workplace, and
politics are also conditioned by religious belief. The orthodox are significantly more likely to agree that family life suffers when a woman has a full-
time job, to believe that the husband should work and the wife should look
after the home and family, and to maintain that most men are better suited
emotionally for politics than are most women. Only on two of the questions
on gendered divisions of labor—the belief that women should take care of
running their homes and leave running the country to men and unwilling-

ness to vote for a qualified woman for President—do the orthodox *not* differ significantly from progressives.

ARE THE RELIGIOUSLY ORTHODOX MORE LIBERAL THAN MORAL PROGRESSIVES ON RACIAL AND ECONOMIC ISSUES?

Our hypothesis (H_2) that, *in the zero order,* the religiously orthodox are more liberal than moral progressives on issues of racial and economic equality is based on the assumption, just confirmed, that the orthodox are disproportionately comprised of racially and economically disadvantaged groups who have an interest in racial and economic equality. We also expected under H_2 that, *controlling for race and socioeconomic position,* the religiously orthodox are no different from moral progressives on these questions because religious texts are ambiguous or contradictory on such issues. Table 2 presents the zero-order correlations and standardized regression coefficients (i.e., with controls for social characteristics) of religious orthodoxy/progressivism with attitudes toward racial and economic inequality.

Looking first at attitudes toward racial inequality, we find mixed results on our hypothesis H_2. Contrary to our expectation, there is no tendency for religious orthodoxy to be associated with liberal racial attitudes in the zero-order, and orthodoxy is positively correlated with attitudes toward racial inequality in two cases: unwillingness to support a qualified black candidate for President (.099, $p < .02$) and support for laws against racial intermarriage (.177, $p < .001$). Nonetheless, the second part of H_2, which states that, controlling for racial and socioeconomic characteristics, the religiously orthodox do not differ from progressives in their attitudes toward racial justice, is confirmed by the consistently nonsignificant standardized regression coefficients. In separate regression analyses of non-Latino Whites (available on request) we found that, as with the entire sample, orthodox cosmology has no net effect on any of the racial attitudes. Thus, the racial composition of the orthodox has little to do with their attitudes on racial inequality. Additional analyses of the effect of social characteristics on racial attitudes (available on request) suggest that what makes the orthodox more conservative as a group on the questions of a black presidential candidate and laws against miscegenation is their tendency to draw upon less affluent, less educated, and older Americans. Nonetheless, with proper controls for social characteristics, orthodoxy, as we expected, has no net effect on any of the five racial attitudes.

Table 2. Standardized Regression Coefficients for Religious Orthodoxy/Progressivism
in Models Explaining Attitudes toward Racial and Economic Inequality

	Effects of Orthodoxy/Progressivism	
Issue	Zero-Order Correlation	Standardized Coefficient
Racial Inequality		
Government spending on Blacks is too high	.032	.055
Opposes government special treatment for Blacks	−.016	.003
Would not vote for black presidential candidate	.099*	.043
Opposes school busing	−.034	−.043
Favors law against racial intermarriage	.177*	.067
Economic Inequality		
Government should not reduce income gap	−.066*	−.017
Government should not provide jobs for all	−.143*	−.088*
Government should not pay for medical care	.024	.004
Government should not help the poor	−.080*	−.035
Government welfare spending is too high	.032	.077
Government spending on Social Security is too high	−.078*	−.069*
Profits should go to shareholders over workers	−.160*	−.130*
Has little confidence in organized labor	−.083*	−.094*

NOTE: Standardized coefficients are for models with controls for sex, race/ethnicity, occupational prestige, income, business ownership, education, age, rural and southern residence, denomination, and religious service attendance.
* $p < .05$.

Turning to attitudes toward economic inequality, we see that the negative zero-order correlations indicate, consistent with H_2 and contrary to widespread understandings of religious orthodoxy (e.g., Wuthnow 1988; Hunter 1991; Klatch 1992), that the religiously orthodox are *more* likely than moral progressives to support government efforts to reduce the income gap between the rich and poor (−.066; $p < .01$), support government provision of jobs for all who want one (−.143, $p < .001$), believe that government should improve the standard of living of the poor (−.080, $p < .01$), that too little is being spent by government on Social Security (−.078, $p < .002$), and that companies should give more of their profits to workers and less to shareholders (−.160, $p < .001$), and have confidence in organized labor (−.083, $p < .01$). That the standardized coefficients, with social characteristics controlled, tend to be smaller than the zero-order correlations suggests that part of the reason for the relative economic liberalism of the religiously orthodox is their tendency to draw on less advantaged groups. Nonetheless, even with controls, the standardized coefficients show that the orthodox are more liberal on government jobs provision, spending on Social Security, giving profits to workers over shareholders, and trust in organized labor,

suggesting that they may interpret sacred texts as supporting economic justice for the poor.

ARE THE RELIGIOUSLY ORTHODOX
MONOLITHIC?

Our findings above that the orthodox are pulled in two different directions on family/gender issues as opposed to economic issues suggest that
they are not monolithically conservative as they have been widely portrayed. Their conservatism on family and gender issues is counterbalanced
by economic liberalism. In order to get a better sense of the political sensibilities of the orthodox, we conduct several analyses separately for this
group. To ensure that we analyze only those respondents who conform most
closely to the beliefs underlying religious orthodoxy, we include in our
sample of religious conservatives only those who were further than one
standard deviation (2.979) from the mean (9.967) on the orthodoxy/
progressivism scale, that is, those who scored 13 or higher. This yields a
sample of 297 respondents or 21.9 percent of the original sample.[5]

We begin with a test of hypothesis H_3 that the religiously orthodox are not
uniformly conservative across a range of issues. In contrast to our analyses
above of whether the orthodox, as compared to progressives, are *relatively*
conservative, in these analyses we look at their *absolute* conservatism—
whether the bulk of the religiously orthodox take conservative positions on
specific issues. In Table 3, we show the percentage of the religiously orthodox who take the conservative stance, when responses to questions are
collapsed into three categories: liberal, moderate (including "don't know"),
and conservative.[6] Not surprisingly, the bulk of orthodox religionists take
conservative positions on school prayer, abortion, premarital and extramarital sex, homosexuality, and pornography.[7] Yet, surprisingly, three-quarters of
the orthodox favor sex education in public schools;[8] they are evenly split on
whether the birth control pill should (47 percent) or should not (49 percent)
be made available to teenagers without their parents' consent; and nearly
one-quarter (24 percent) feel that abortion should be available for any reason. Consistent with H_3, on only one of the thirteen remaining gender, race,
and class attitudes—school busing—does a majority of the religiously orthodox take the conservative position. Although Wuthnow (1988:114) and
Hunter (1991:110–15) expect religious conservatives to take antistatist positions, generally only a minority of this group opposes government efforts to
help African Americans or the poor.

Under hypothesis H_4, we expected the orthodox to show considerable

Table 3.   Percentages of the Religiously Orthodox Taking Conservative Stances on
Attitudes toward Family-Related Issues, Gendered Divisions of Labor, and Racial
and Economic Inequality

Issue	Conservative (%)	Standard Deviation	N
Family-Related Issues			
Favors prayer in public schools	80.5	.749	195
Opposes sex education in public schools	20.8	.817	197
Opposes birth control for teens	49.3	.987	197
Opposes abortion on demand	73.9	.858	199
Views premarital sex as wrong	61.0	.924	297
Views extramarital sex as wrong	91.9	.454	297
Views homosexuality as wrong	90.2	.458	297
Supports antipornography law	56.1	.576	198
Gendered Divisions of Labor			
Family suffers when women is employed	47.8	.895	297
Husbands as breadwinners, wives as homemakers	48.9	.887	297
Women should run homes, not country	29.9	.908	197
Women not suited for politics	35.0	.942	197
Would not vote for woman presidential candidate	14.2	.715	197
Racial Inequality			
Government spending on blacks is too high	17.5	.706	154
Opposes government special treatment for blacks	39.4	.794	198
Would not vote for black presidential candidate	14.2	.709	197
Opposes school busing	58.9	.953	197
Favors law against racial intermarriage	26.1	.879	199
Economic Inequality			
Government should not reduce income gap	40.4	.935	297
Government should not provide jobs for all	38.4	.946	297
Government should not pay for medical care	15.2	.740	198
Government should not help the poor	17.7	.740	198
Government spending on welfare is too high	37.7	.765	154
Government spending on Social Security is too high	3.0	.556	297
Profits should go to shareholders over workers	9.8	.618	297
Has little confidence in organized labor	27.3	.882	198

NOTE: Weak and strong responses (e.g., strongly agree and somewhat agree) were combined to
compute the percentages who are conservative or liberal. Middle responses and "don't know"
were combined to form the moderate category.

dissensus on specific issues. The standard deviation is generally used as a
summary indicator of the degree of consensus or dissensus in a distribution.
For three-category items, the standard deviation has a lower limit of 0.0
(unanimity) and approaches an upper limit of 1.0 (maximum dissensus) as
the sample size increases.[9] The standard deviations of the items in Table 3
suggest considerable dissensus among orthodox religionists. Moderate stan-

dard deviations (.4 to .6) are found on some questions—sex outside marriage, homosexuality, pornography, and spending on Social Security—but there is nearly as much dissensus as possible (> .9) on many issues, including women's role in the home and in politics, whether birth control should be made available to teenagers, whether premarital sex is wrong, whether school children should be bused to achieve racial integration, and whether government should reduce the gap between rich and poor and provide jobs to those who want them. The standard deviations, which are skewed toward the high end of the possible range, that is, toward dissensus, do not indicate the political uniformity that the widespread use of such terms as "factions," "camps," or "blocs" implies.

We hypothesized under H_5 that the self-interest of genders, races, and classes leads some religiously orthodox people to take liberal positions while others take conservative stances. Table 4 summarizes a set of regression analyses in which each of the twenty-six attitudes considered in Table 3 is regressed on gender, race, socioeconomic variables, and other social characteristics. We report in Table 4 the list of those variables that relate significantly to each attitude. As expected, women among the religiously orthodox are more likely than men to disagree that the family suffers when a women take a full-time job, that husbands should work and wives look after the home, and that women should run their homes and leave running the country to men. Women are also more likely than men to support government efforts to improve the living standards of Blacks and reduce the income gap between rich and poor and to believe that the government is spending too little on welfare. Women may support redistributive and welfare programs more because their wages are lower than men's and because welfare programs are targeted to help single mothers and their children.

Consistent with H_5, African Americans are more likely than Whites to support government efforts to reduce racial and economic inequality. Similarly, socioeconomic position significantly affects attitudes toward economic inequality. People with low incomes are more likely than those with high incomes to support government efforts to provide jobs for all and help the poor and to favor increased welfare spending. Less-educated people are also more likely than the well-educated to support government efforts to reduce the income gap and to aid the poor. Workers are more likely than business owners to feel that government spending on Social Security is not high enough.

While we expected divisions along lines of race, gender, and class to be limited to those attitudes where groups have obvious self-interests in their outcomes, we also find divisions along these lines on some sexuality issues. Women generally take more conservative positions than men on issues of abortion, sex outside marriage, and pornography, perhaps because sex is seen as a resource by women and, as such, they have more of an interest

Table 4. Significant Effects of Social Characteristics in Regressions Explaining Attitudes toward Family-Related Issues, Gendered Divisions of Labor, and Racial and Economic Inequality among the Religiously Orthodox

Issue	Significant Standardized Regression Coefficients	R^2	N
Favors school prayer	Latino (−.397)	.184	195
Opposes sex education	Asian (.159), Income (.223), Age (.209)	.177	197
Rejects birth control for teens	Income (.214)	.167	197
Opposes abortion on demand	Female (.180), African American (−.343)	.210	199
Views premarital sex as wrong	Female (.165), Age (.153)	.232	297
Views extramarital sex as wrong	Female (.212), African American (−.225)	.138	297
Views homosexuality as wrong	[no significant effects]	.081	297
Supports antipornography law	Female (.150), African American (−.212), Latino (.160), Age (.153)	.291	198
Family suffers if woman is employed	Female (−.180), Education (−.248)	.159	297
Husbands as breadwinners; wives as homemakers	Female (−.293), Education (−.242), Age (.204)	.213	297
Women should run homes, not country	Female (−.203), Education (−.269), Age (.249)	.222	197
Women not suited for politics	American Indian (.190), Education (−.228)	.178	197
Would not vote for woman President	American Indian (.250)	.156	197
Gov't spending on Blacks is too high	African American (−.446)	.282	154
Opposes government special treatment for Blacks	Female (−.134), African American (−.506), Latino (−.150)	.364	198
Would not vote for Black President	African American (−.221)	.144	197
Opposes school busing	African American (−.207), Income (.201), Age (.194)	.191	197
Favors law against racial intermarriage	African American (−.268), Latino (−.151), Education (−.278)	.316	199
Government should not reduce income gap	Female (−.154), African American (−.149), Education (.117)	.179	297
Government should not provide jobs for all	African American (−.291), Education (.140), Income (.114)	.202	297
Government should not pay for medical care	African American (−.199)	.126	198
Government should not help the poor	African American (−.253), Education (.174), Income (.129)	.231	198
Government welfare spending is too high	Female (−.222), African American (−.241), Income (.288)	.287	154
Government spending on Social Security is too high	Asian (.186), Owner (.105)	.163	297
Profits should go to shareholders over workers	African American (−.127), Asian (−.113)	.154	297
Has little confidence in organized labor	[no significant effects]	.069	198

NOTE: Models with controls for rural and southern residence, denomination, and religious service attendance. Reference category is non-Latino White males who do not own a business. All coefficients shown are significant at $p < .05$.

than men in restricting sex to marriage and increasing the cost of nonmarital sex by limiting abortion. African Americans are more liberal than Whites on abortion and sex outside marriage, and less opposed than Whites to pornography. People with low incomes are more favorable than those with high incomes to sex education in public schools and to making birth control available to teens, perhaps because pregnancy among teenagers is higher among the poor.

CONCLUSION AND DISCUSSION

Through an analysis of a national survey of Americans, we tested several hypotheses regarding the existence of a "culture war" in the United States. While it has become commonplace to portray America as split into warring moral camps, we find that most Americans fall in the middle ground between the poles of religious orthodoxy and moral progressivism. The religious landscape is better conceived as a continuum ranging from orthodoxy through a large middle ground to progressivism, rather than as two opposing camps.

We confirmed our hypothesis that the religiously orthodox are more conservative than moral progressives on family-related issues and gendered divisions of labor, reflecting, in our view, their status interest in defending both the patriarchal family and women's role as socializer of the next generation of believers as the last bulwarks against increasing secularism. Our hypothesis that the tendency for the orthodox to draw disproportionately on disadvantaged groups makes them more favorable than progressives toward racial equality received mixed support. On three out of five racial issues, the orthodox do not differ, in the zero-order, from progressives. On two of the racial issues, the composition of the orthodox (lower income and education and older age) makes them more conservative than progressives. Nonetheless, with proper controls for social background variables, the orthodox are no less favorable toward racial equality than are progressives.

Our hypothesis that the composition of the orthodox helps make them more favorable than progressives toward economic equality was confirmed. In the zero-order, the orthodox are considerably more liberal than progressives on many economic issues. Even with controls for social characteristics, the relative economic liberalism of the orthodox holds up, contrary to widely accepted understandings of orthodoxy (e.g., Ammerman 1987:208; Flake 1984:117–29; Wuthnow 1988; Hunter 1991; Klatch 1992).

The orthodox are thus pulled in two directions. In their support of economic redistribution, the religiously orthodox may draw on economic self-interest and a prophetic interpretation of the Bible that calls for efforts to promote economic justice, much as did Populists and Catholic labor activists in the late nineteenth century, Appalachian coal miners in the 1920s and 1930s, and the Southern Tenant Farmers Union in the 1930s (Williams and Alexander 1994; Billings 1990; Johnson et al. 1986). At the same time, however, the conservatism of the religiously orthodox on gender and family-related issues is priestly in its effort to uphold the status interest of the orthodox in an existing patriarchal and heterosexual family structure, where labor is divided along gender lines and motherhood is women's raison d'être.

Our further analyses of the religiously orthodox, the group most often seen as having the potential to mobilize large numbers of people in a united conservative front, suggest that any statements about the political inclinations of this group must be made with caution. On only a limited number of family-related issues does a majority of the orthodox take a conservative stance. On other family issues (teaching sex education in public schools and making birth control available to teens) and on nearly all issues related to gendered divisions of labor, race, and economic inequality, less than half of the orthodox are conservative. Moreover, disagreement is more common than consensus in the opinions of the religiously orthodox, and the orthodox are sharply divided on many political issues along lines of race, class, or gender (see also Warner 1988:298).

Thus, even religiously orthodox Americans, the group that the mass media, political and religious leaders, and some academics would expect to be ideologically consistent and politically conservative, are moderate or even liberal on many issues, show little political uniformity on specific concerns, and are divided along lines of race, class, and gender. In view of the political indirection, disunity, and division that we find among the religiously orthodox, we must ask whether the culture war they are said to be engaged in with theological progressives exists mainly in the minds of media pundits, leaders of political movements, and academics. Our study of the religiously orthodox also leads us to question the widespread use of the political label "Religious Right" as synonymous with religious orthodoxy, traditionalism, Evangelicalism, or Fundamentalism. Many media analysts would have applied these labels to all the members of our sample who are religiously orthodox, painting them with a broad brush as monolithically conservative on a host of family, gender, racial, and economic issues. Yet, as we have shown, this label fits only a minority of traditional religionists. While the mass media, the leadership of parareligious organizations such as the Christian Coalition and some scholars would send the religiously orthodox forth to battle with the forces of religious modernity and secularism, the orthodox themselves appear to be marching to different orders.[10]

NOTES

1. In his 1988 book, *The Restructuring of American Religion,* Wuthnow (1988:218–23) argues on theoretical grounds and cited survey evidence that religious conservatives are conservative on economic issues. More recently, in *God and Mammon in America,* Wuthnow (1994) finds little correspondence between church attendance and economic attitudes and rarely discusses the conservative/liberal division in religion that was the focus of his earlier book.

2. Factor analysis of these items yielded a single factor with an eigenvalue of 1.84. Cronbach's alpha, a measure of reliability, is .68 for the three items.

3. Wuthnow (1988:343n) uses a measure of self-assessed religious conservatism/liberalism. Respondents were asked: "Where would you place yourself on this scale in terms of your RELIGIOUS views?" Respondents were then handed a card with a 6-point scale ranging from conservative (1) to liberal (6). "Religious conservatives" are respondents who selected 1 or 2 and "religious liberals" are those who selected 5 or 6.

4. Independent variables are coded as follows: *Age* is measured in years. Race/ethnicity is a dummy variable series consisting of *African American, Asian, Latino,* and *American Indian,* with non-Latino White as the reference category. Sex is a dummy variable labeled *Female,* with male as the reference category. *Education* is measured in years of schooling. *Income* refers to family income before taxes in twenty-one categories, with midpoints representing each category. *Occupational prestige* is a scale developed for NORC (see Siegel 1971). Individuals without an occupation are coded to the mean for employed persons, so that in regression analyses this variable indicates effects among employed persons only. *Ownership* is a dummy variable indicating whether the respondent or spouse owned a business versus worked for someone else (reference category). *Rural* is a 10-category ordinal variable ranging from large central city (over 250,000 people) to open country. *South* is a dummy variable indicating residence in the South versus all other regions of the country (reference category). *Religious service attendance* ranges from 0 (never attends) to 8 (attends more than once a week). Denomination is a dummy variable series consisting of *Methodist, Lutheran, Presbyterian, Episcopalian, Other Protestant, Catholic, Jewish,* and *none/other,* with *Baptist* as the reference category.

5. We conducted all analyses on four other subsamples of respondents: (1) those who scored 12 and above on the scale, (2) those who scored 14 and above, (3) those who were Protestant and identified themselves as "fundamentalists," and (4) those who were Protestant or Catholic and reported a "born-again" experience, with similar results to those reported in the text (details available on request from the authors).

6. Further details on these analyses of the religiously orthodox and our response to a comment by Hunter (1996) are reported in Davis and Robinson (1996a, 1996b).

7. What constitutes the "liberal" stance on pornography is not clear since some liberals oppose pornography on grounds that it is degrading or injurious to women, while other liberals support the right to circulate pornography on free speech grounds.

8.   It may be that the orthodox favor sex education in public schools but believe this should teach abstinence rather than effective birth control.

9.   The upper limit is approximate because the equation used in computing the standard deviation depends on the number of cases minus one ($N - 1$). The actual upper limit for 200 cases is 1.003; for 300 cases, it is 1.002; and for 1,000,000 cases, it is 1.000.

10.   Parareligious organizations of the religiously orthodox, such as the Christian Coalition, have had an impact on American politics. Yet even if we accept the claim of this organization to have 1.7 million members (Gallman 1995), this is only 4.3 percent of the roughly 39 million American adults that our analyses suggest are religiously orthodox.

REFERENCES

Ammerman, Nancy. 1987. *Bible Believers: Fundamentalists in the Modern World.* New Brunswick, NJ: Rutgers University Press.

Bendroth, Margaret. 1993. *Fundamentalism and Gender: 1875 to the Present.* New Haven, CT: Yale University Press.

Billings, Dwight B. 1990. "Religion as Opposition: A Gramscian Analysis." *American Journal of Sociology* 96:1–31.

Converse, Philip E. 1964. "The Nature of Belief Systems in Mass Publics." Pp. 206–61 in *Ideology and Discontent,* edited by David E. Apter. New York: Free Press.

Danzger, M. Herbert. 1989. *Returning to Tradition: The Contemporary Revival of Orthodox Judaism.* New Haven, CT: Yale University Press.

Davidman, Lynn. 1991. *Tradition in a Rootless World: Women Turn to Orthodox Judaism.* Berkeley: University of California Press.

Davis, Nancy J., and Robert V. Robinson. 1991. "Men's and Women's Consciousness of Gender Inequality: Austria, West Germany, Great Britain, and the United States." *American Sociological Review* 56:72–84.

———. 1996a. "Religious Orthodoxy in American Society: The Myth of a Monolithic Camp." *Journal for the Scientific Study of Religion* 35:229–45.

———. 1996b. "Rejoinder to Hunter: Religious Orthodoxy—An Army without Foot Soldiers?" *Journal for the Scientific Study of Religion* 35:249–51.

———. 1996c. "Are the Rumors of War Exaggerated? Religious Orthodoxy and Moral Progressivism in America." *American Journal of Sociology* 102:756–87.

Flake, Carol. 1984. *Redemptorama: Culture, Politics, and the New Evangelicalism.* New York: Penguin.

Gallman, Vanessa. 1995. "Christian Coalition Struggling to Balance Political, Spiritual Aspects of Their Mission." *Knight-Ridder Washington Bureau,* September 10.

Greeley, Andrew M. 1989. *Religious Change in America.* Cambridge, MA: Harvard University Press.

Gusfield, Joseph R. [1963] 1986. *Symbolic Crusade: Status Politics and the American Temperance Movement,* 2nd ed. Urbana: University of Illinois Press.

Hart, Stephen. 1992. *What Does the Lord Require?: How American Christians Think about Economic Justice.* New York: Oxford University Press.

Hunter, James Davison. 1991. *Culture Wars: The Struggle to Define America.* New York: Basic Books.

———. 1994. *Before the Shooting Begins: Searching for Democracy in America's Culture War.* New York: Free Press.

———. 1996. "Response to Davis and Robinson: Remembering Durkheim." *Journal for the Scientific Study of Religion 35*:246–48.

Jelen, Ted G. 1990. "Religious Belief and Attitude Constraint." *Journal for the Scientific Study of Religion 29*:118–25.

———. 1991. *The Political Mobilization of Religious Beliefs.* New York: Praeger.

Johnson, Stephen D., Joseph B. Tamney, and Sandy Halebsky. 1986. "Christianity, Social Traditionalism and Economic Conservatism." *Sociological Focus 19*:299–314.

Klatch, Rebecca. 1992. "Complexities of Conservatism: How Conservatives Understand the World." Pp. 361–75 in *America at Century's End,* edited by Alan Wolfe. Berkeley: University of California Press.

Luker, Kristin. 1984. *Abortion and the Politics of Motherhood.* Berkeley: University of California Press.

McGuire, Meredith B. 1982. *Pentecostal Catholics: Power, Charisma, and Order in a Religious Movement.* Philadelphia: Temple University Press.

Neitz, Mary Jo. 1987. *Charisma and Community: A Study of Religious Commitment within the Charismatic Renewal.* New Brunswick, NJ: Transaction.

Olson, Daniel V. A., and Jackson W. Carroll. 1992. "Religiously Based Politics: Religious Elites and the Public." *Social Forces 70*:765–86.

Pohli, Carol Virginia. 1983. "Church Closets and Back Doors: A Feminist View of Moral Majority Women." *Feminist Studies 9*:529–58.

Robinson, Robert V., and Wendell Bell. 1978. "Equality, Success and Social Justice in England and the United States." *American Sociological Review 43*:125–43.

Siegel, Paul S. 1971. *Prestige in the American Occupational Structure.* Ph.D. dissertation, University of Chicago.

Stacey, Judith, and Susan Elizabeth Gerard. 1990. "We Are Not Doormats: The Influence of Feminism on Contemporary Evangelicals in the United States." Pp. 98–117 in *Uncertain Terms: Negotiating Gender in American Culture,* edited by Faye Ginsburg and Anna Tsing. Boston: Beacon.

Tamney, Joseph B., Ronald Burton, and Stephen D. Johnson. 1989. "Fundamentalism and Economic Restructuring." Pp. 67–82 in *Religion and Political Behavior in the United States,* edited by Ted G. Jelen. New York: Praeger.

Warner, R. Stephen. 1988. *New Wine in Old Wineskins: Evangelicals and Liberals in a Small-Town Church.* Berkeley: University of California Press.

Weber, Max. [1922] 1964. *The Sociology of Religion,* translated by Ephraim Fischoff. Boston: Beacon.

Williams, Rhys H., and Susan M. Alexander. 1994. "Religious Rhetoric in American Populism: Civil Religion as Movement Ideology." *Journal for the Scientific Study of Religion 33*:1–15.

Woodrum, Eric. 1988a. "Moral Conservatism and the 1984 Presidential Election." *Journal for the Scientific Study of Religion* 27:192–210.

———. 1988b. "Determinants of Moral Attitudes." *Journal for the Scientific Study of Religion* 27:553–73.

Wuthnow, Robert. 1988. *The Restructuring of American Religion: Society and Faith Since World War II.* Princeton, NJ: Princeton University Press.

———. 1994. *God and Mammon in America.* New York: Free Press.

4

4

Have Americans' Social Attitudes Become More Polarized?

PAUL DIMAGGIO, JOHN EVANS, and BETHANY BRYSON

Polarization, fragmentation, and division have become familiar themes in American political discourse. A leading newsweekly entitles a special issue "Divided We Stand" (*U.S. News and World Report,* July 10, 1991). The editor of the *Columbia Journalism Review*'s special "culture wars" issue asserts flatly, "There is increasing polarization in American society" (Berry 1993). Some social scientists share these perceptions, writing of "deep and abiding cultural fragmentation" (Hunter 1994:vii), "the cultural chasm that has opened up in American society since the sixties" (Guinness 1993:167), the trend "toward ideological polarization in domestic and social concerns" (Wyszomirski 1994:37), or "the sharpening cultural polarization of U.S. society after the mid-1970s" (Ellison and Musick 1993:379). These views are echoed by much of the general public: in June 1995, 86 percent agreed that "there was a time when people in this country felt they had more in common and shared more values than Americans do today."[1]

Yet despite widespread claims and perceptions, little systematic research bears on ideological polarization per se. The impressive body of recent scholarship on aggregate opinion change (Page and Shapiro 1982, 1992; Chafetz and Ebaugh 1983; Smith 1990b; Davis 1992; Hochschild 1995; but see Yang and Demerath 1996) has focused on central tendencies, addressing polarization only in the important but limited sense of differences between particular social groups.

Opinion polarization is interesting because of its potential causal relationship to such phenomena as political conflict and social volatility. But too often the presence of polarization is inferred from the political conflict or volatility it is presumed to cause. Noting increased partisanship in Congress in summer 1995, retired Senator Warren Rudman (R-N.H.) worried: "We may be seeing in Congress a microcosm of what's happening out in the country . . . .What we are seeing is a polarization out there in the country, and what is happening in Congress is a reflection of that."[2]

To assume, as Senator Rudman did, that the political surface reflects a deeper collective condition is natural, reasonable—and potentially misleading. We shall ask if Senator Rudman, and the many others who believe the American public has become more polarized, are right. To do so, we analyze twenty years of data from the General Social Survey (GSS) and National Election Study (NES) to see if Americans' opinions on domestic social issues have indeed become more polarized in recent decades and to identify the extent, nature, and locus of such polarization as may have occurred. . . .

WHAT IS POLARIZATION?

Given polarization's prominence in contemporary political discourse, the literature provides strikingly little guidance in defining it.[3] Perhaps the best place to begin is with what polarization is *not*. Polarization is not noisy incivility in political exchange: although the two things may (or may not) be associated empirically, polarization refers to the extent of disagreement, not to the ways in which disagreement is expressed. Nor is polarization reducible to the balance of responses between agreement and disagreement with survey items (except in the limiting case of two-point scales). It is in the extremity of and distance between responses, not in their substantive content, that polarization inheres.[4]

Polarization is both a state and a process. Polarization as a state refers to the extent to which opinions on an issue are opposed in relation to some theoretical maximum. Polarization as a process refers to the increase in such opposition over time. We focus here on polarization in the latter sense.

To analyze change in the degree of polarization, we must be able to measure it. In order to measure it, we must be able to define it. And to define polarization, we must be clear about why we are interested in it. Our premise is that, other things being equal, attitude polarization militates against social and political stability by reducing the probability of group formation at the center of the opinion distribution and by increasing the likelihood of the formation of groups with distinctive, irreconcilable policy preferences.

Given that premise, we need a theory of, or at least some intuitions about, opinion aggregation as a foundation for measurement. We have four such intuitions. (They are testable in principle, but it is beyond the scope of this article to do so.)

Two of these intuitions refer to properties of single distributions:

1.   Other things being equal, the more dispersed opinion becomes, the more difficult it will be for the political system to establish and maintain centrist political consensus (the *dispersion principle*).
2.   Other things being equal, the greater the extent to which opinions move toward separate modes (and the more separate those modes become), the more likely it is that social conflict will ensue (the *bimodality principle*; see Esteban and Ray 1994).

Two other intuitions refer to relationships *among* distributions:

3.   Other things being equal, the more closely associated different social attitudes become (both within and across opinion domains), the greater the likelihood of implacable conflict (the *constraint principle*; see Converse 1964).
4.   Other things being equal, the greater the extent to which social attitudes become correlated with salient individual characteristics or identities, the more likely it is that they will become the foci of social conflict (the *consolidation principle*; see Blau 1977).

Thus polarization is multidimensional in character. Each of our four principles suggests a distinct dimension, and a distinct measure, of polarization. . . .

Studies of intergroup agreement and disagreement typically use one of two measures; the difference in means or the proportion of each group responding in a certain manner (e.g., agreeing somewhat or agreeing very much with a given position). Although either measure is adequate for many purposes, each suppresses some information relevant to understanding intergroup differences. Focusing on the mean reveals nothing about the shape of the distribution. Focusing on the proportion at one end of the scale withholds information about the pattern of response in the rest of the scale.

We have argued that within-population polarization is a function of both *dispersion* and *bimodality*. Similarly, we contend that *between-population* polarization depends on both the spread between sample means and the peakedness of opinion within each sample. The intuition behind this assertion is that political conflict between groups is a function of both between-group polarization, which increases the likelihood of conflict, and within-group polarization, which reduces it (by making it difficult for advocates of any position to claim to speak for the group as a whole). Therefore, we regard two groups as polarized in a manner likely to lead to intergroup conflict only to the extent that (a) between-group differences are substantial *and* (b) within-group polarization is minimal.

To capture both facets of polarization we must use two measures. We inspect difference of means over time to see if between-group differences have become greater or smaller. But we add to this an analysis of change over time in kurtosis for each group. In some cases, taking account of change in within-group kurtosis leads to different conclusions than would examining changing means alone.

Each of our four principles, and the measure that derives from it, taps a distinct dimension of opinion polarization. Polarization can be said without qualification to increase only when opinion distributions become more (1) dispersed, (2) flat or bimodal, (3) closely associated, and (4) closely linked to salient social identities. Increases on different dimensions indicate polarization of different kinds, with potentially different consequences. Polarization can be said *not* to occur only absent increases in dispersion, bimodality, and consolidation (interitem constraint being a necessary but insufficient condition).

DATA, MEASURES, AND ANALYTIC STRATEGY

To map change over time in Americans' attitudes requires high-quality national sample surveys that ask the same questions on a regular basis and also collect data on a wide range of background variables. We rely on the two leading sources of such items, the General Social Survey (GSS) and the National Election Study (NES).

The NES is a personal-interview sample survey conducted by the University of Michigan Center for Political Studies in presidential and midterm election years. The GSS is a regularly administered, personal-interview sample survey of U.S. households conducted by the National Opinion Research Center (NORC) at the University of Chicago (Davis and Smith 1991, 1992).

Because we are interested in attitude constraint, as well as in the spread and bimodality of particular attitudes, we identify several issue domains upon which to focus. Most assertions that opinion polarization has increased refer to social or cultural issues. Few observers discern growing polarization of opinion on economic or foreign policy. Therefore, we use data on opinions about social issues (e.g., abortion, race, gender roles, sexuality, and crime) over which polarization is most likely to be observed.

The NES fields longer surveys with more opinion items in presidential election years. (Before 1972, the NES was a much smaller survey, with few attitude questions.) When we could, we used items repeated in off-year surveys. Other items were asked only in presidential election years from 1972 to 1992. We used relevant GSS items for each year they were asked from 1974 through 1994. Items from both surveys were rescaled as required to assign conservative answers higher scores. Cases coded "don't know" and "not applicable" were treated as missing. . . .

Variables

NES. . . . Several items report respondents' self-locations on 97-point "feeling thermometers" that gauge the "warmth" of respondents' feelings toward particular groups. We analyzed attitudes toward Blacks, poor people, liberals, and conservatives. (Although liberals and conservatives are not social issues, we included these items as measures of polarization in affective responses to alternative political identities.[5]

Three other NES attitude items were used. A seven-point item on attitudes toward government assistance for minorities (with "7" marking the most negative) ranged from "government should help minority groups" to "minority groups should help themselves."[6] A seven-point scale tapped views on gender equality (1 = women and men should have an equal role; 7 = a women's place is in the home). A four-point abortion scale ranged from support for an unlimited right to abortion (1 = never be forbidden) to the view that abortions should never be permitted (with the value "4").[7]

In addition to the opinion items we used several NES measures to identify subsamples. A six-point education scale was used to identify respondents with college degrees or with no formal education beyond the final year of high school. Age, gender, and region were recorded in the usual manner. Political philosophy was tapped with a seven-point self-identification scale ranging from extremely to slightly liberal (1–3) to extremely to slightly conservative (5–7). Voting is by self-report for this year's presidential election. Party identification and race are by self-report. Political activism is a six-point scale (ACTIVE) based on questions on voting, efforts to influence the votes of others, attending candidate rallies, displaying candidate buttons or stickers, donating money to a political party or (1980 and thereafter) candidate, or volunteering for a party or candidate. "Activists" are those who scored "3" or higher.

GSS. The GSS posed two challenges. First, the GSS adopted a split ballot design between 1988 and 1993; therefore, most questions of interest were asked of only some respondents in those years. Thus we could not scale some attractive items together because they appeared on different ballots.[8] Second, many relevant GSS items were dichotomous and thus ill-suited to recording changes in polarization, except for between-group differences. . . . Six simple attitude scales were constructed that combined tapping attitudes on related issues.[9] First, views of abortion are tapped by an additive scale of seven items, each specifying a condition under which "it should be possible for a pregnant woman to obtain a legal abortion." Second, a racism scale is based on answers to 8 questions tapping attitudes toward African Americans (or, for African-American respondents, white Americans). The questions asked about acceptance of varying degrees of racial integration in schools, willingness to vote for African-American (White) presidential candidates, attitudes toward busing, toward residential segregation, and toward antimiscegenation laws and segregated social clubs, and attributions of responsibility for African Americans' economic disadvantage. A third scale sums responses to three items about women's participation in the public sphere. A fourth is based on four items, with responses ranging from "strongly agree" to "strongly disagree" on a four-point scale, about women's family role. Fifth, a sexuality scale is based on three items eliciting attitudes toward premarital sex, extramarital sex, and homosexuality, with four-point scales ranging from "always wrong" to "not wrong at all." And, finally, a crime-and-justice scale combines responses to questions about capital punishment, gun control, and courts' treatment of criminals. The all-domain constraint and between-group difference analyses also employed dichotomous items on school prayer, sex education, and divorce law. All items were rescaled as needed to assign conservative views higher values.

We used a question about educational attainment to identify college graduates and those with high school–level education or less. Age, gender, and region were measured in the usual manner. "Voters" are respondents who report voting in the most recent presidential election. Race was coded by the interviewer except for cases in which interviewers were in doubt. Questions on liberal/conservative self-identification and party affiliation are similar to those in the NES. We classified as religious conservatives Roman Catholics and evangelical Protestants who attended church nearly every week or more. Religious liberals include mainstream Protestants and Jews and respondents without religious affiliation. [Our classifications of evangelical Protestants and mainstream Protestants and Jews follow Smith (1990a)].

Strategy of Exposition

Because we calculated several measures of polarization using data on 13 scales representing several dozen items over more than 20 years for full samples and several subsamples, we face a striking data-reduction challenge. We rely on graphic means to reduce the welter of statistics to a form that the reader can grasp.

We begin by asking if polarization has increased among all Americans

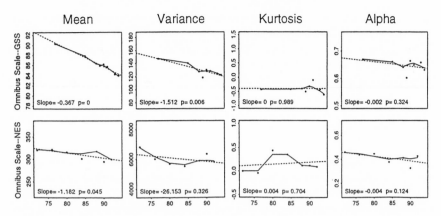

Figure 1. Within-population polarization, full sample; GSS 1974–1994 and NES 1972–1994 omnibus scales; *x*-axis = year.

with respect to the full range of social attitudes in both surveys. We illustrate results for each opinion variable with four graphs (see Figure 1). The horizontal axis of each represents time and ranges from 1972 to 1994 for all graphs for ease of comparison. The results of plotting means across time ("Mean") replicate and extend in time findings reported in other studies (e.g., Page and Shapiro 1992). We include them for the assistance they offer in interpreting more central results.

The crucial findings appear in the second, third, and fourth graphs in each row. The second reports variance (dispersion, *y*-axis) over time (*x*-axis). The third reports kurtosis (peakedness/bimodality) over time. The fourth (for multi-item scales only) reports change over time in Chronbach's alpha (constraint). Each graph includes point observations, a linear regression line of the *y*-axis against year, and a smoothed loess (locally weighted regression) line depicting change in slope. Slope and *P*-values from linear regressions appear as text on each graph. (Because *y*-axis metrics are unstandardized, slopes cannot be compared across items, but they can be compared across groups within items.) We then use the same procedure to report results for specific issue domains: racial attitudes, attitudes about women's roles, crime, abortion and sexual behavior, and feelings toward the poor, liberals, and conservatives. (All analyses entail comparison among items or scales with constant ranges over time. One cannot compare variance, kurtosis, or alpha across items of differing range.)

We next explore change over time in variance, kurtosis, and alpha on the same scales and items for several subgroups—college graduates, voters, the politically active, and people under 30—to see if polarization has occurred more within "attentive publics" (Arnold 1990) and the young than within the population at large. These analyses are reported in the manner described above. In order to conserve space, particular results are presented only when (a) they differ from those for the sample as a whole and (b) at least one measure of polarization exhibits a significant time trend. . . .

Finally we ask if specific pairs of groups have become more polarized in relation to one another over time (the consolidation principle). Comparisons are between groups based on age (younger than 35 years old vs. older than 45 years old); gender (women vs. men); race (African Americans vs. Whites); educational level (college graduates vs. people with no formal education beyond high school); faith tradition (religious conservatives vs. religious liberals); ideology (conservative vs. liberal); region (South vs. other); and party affiliation (Republican vs. Democrat).[10] For each comparison we present two sets of lines in a single panel, the horizontal axis of which represents time. The thicker set of lines within each panel plots the means for each group over time. The slope of a regression of the absolute intergroup difference against time, and the time coefficient's P-value are reported at the top of the panel to test for trends. The left y-axis indicates the mean values. A second, thinner pair of lines depicts change over time in kurtosis for each group, as well as (at the bottom of the panel) the slope (and P-value) of kurtosis plotted against time for each group. The right y-axis reports kurtosis values. We attend to trends that are significant at $P \leq .10$, a generous rule of thumb chosen because each series has few observations (6–15) and to ensure that we do not underestimate the degree to which polarization has occurred.

RESULTS

We begin with the full samples, first analyzing scales based on many social attitudes and then looking at specific issue domains. We next search for polarization within particular subsamples and conclude with an analysis of polarization between groups.

Within-Group Polarization in the Population as a Whole

To test the proposition that contemporary U.S. opinion is characterized by increasing interdomain constraint and polarization (Hunter 1991; Bennett 1992; Guinness 1993), we begin by analyzing omnibus scales, which are a combination of all opinion scales and items described. . . .[11] Whether social conservatism is a homogeneous ideological entity is of course an empirical matter. Existing studies suggest that constraint is greater among social attitudes than between them and opinions on economic or foreign policy, but report that some social attitudes (e.g., toward crime and toward gender) have moved in different directions during the years in question (Smith 1990b; Davis 1992; Page and Shapiro 1992). So these analyses test only the most strongly framed assertions of growing polarization across a unidimensional divide.

Have public attitudes on a wide range of social issues scaled together become more polarized? Apparently not (see Figure 1). A significant decline in variance on the GSS omnibus scale indicates less polarization, while NES scale variance was stable. Kurtosis (bimodality) did not change, although NES data show a partial depolarizing trend reversed in the mid-1980s. Ideological constraint is unchanged on both scales.

The omnibus scales are blunt measures. They effectively demonstrate the absence of polarization on a wide sociocultural front—an important corrective to the rhetoric of "culture war" and the dire warnings of many political commentators. But perhaps polarization *has* occurred with respect to a *subset* of social and cultural issues.

The reader may find it helpful to inspect a three-dimensional graphic presentation of a scale that illustrates a polarization pattern. . . . Figure 2

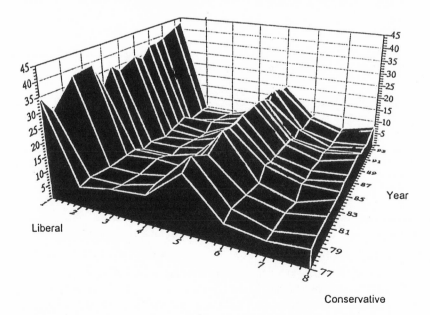

Figure 2.   Distributions by year, attitudes toward abortion, full sample; GSS 1977–1994.

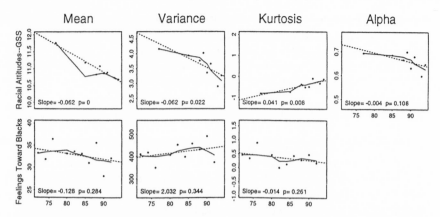

Figure 3. Within-population polarization, full sample; GSS 1977–1994 and NES 1972–1994; feelings toward Blacks and racial attitudes; x-axis = year.

illustrates change over time in the GSS abortion scale. Americans were sharply divided on abortion at the series' onset in 1977, with separate modes at the far left and center points of the scale. Opinion polarized further after 1977, with variance increasing throughout the period (from 5.19 to 5.96 in 1994) and bimodality starting at −1.08, peaking at −1.32 in 1984, and remaining stable thereafter. We turn now to results for specific issue domains (see Figures 3–7).

Race and Poverty. The GSS racial-attitudes scale demonstrates a trend toward *less* polarized (and more liberal) racial attitudes, with variance down and kurtosis up (Figure 3). But, consistent with past research (Jackman and Muha 1984; Schuman, Steeh, and Bobo 1985), broad endorsement of racial integration does not imply support for policies that help minorities or sympathy for poor people. Although variance in response to the NES aid-to-minorities question declined through the early 1980s, it increased after that (Figure 4). Kurtosis behaves similarly, rising (less polarization) until the mid-1980s, then declining. Feelings toward poor people polarized by *both* measures over this period (Figure 4). Thus, despite emerging consensus favoring racial integration, views of the poor, and, after 1984, of government assistance for minorities became more polarized.

Gender. Public attitudes on gender issues have become both more liberal and *less* polarized over time (not shown). Variance in all three gender-attitude measures (two GSS scales and an NES item) declined significantly from the mid-1970s to the mid-1990s. For both measures tapping acceptance of women's occupancy of public roles, bimodality also declined, as did ideological constraint for the GSS public-roles scale.

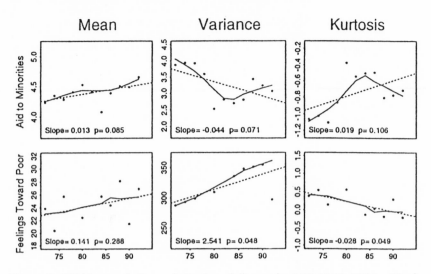

Figure 4. Within-population polarization, full sample, NES 1972–1994, attitudes toward aid to minorities and feelings toward poor people; *x*-axis = year.

Crime and Justice. Crime is perceived as a "wedge" issue in political campaigns. But public attitudes on crime and justice have become *less* polarized since the 1970s, with linear decline in variance and alpha and linear rise in kurtosis (not shown).

Attitudes toward Liberals and Conservatives. Even if Americans' views on substantive issues have not polarized sharply, perhaps they have become more divided in their affective reaction to political labels, as tapped by the NES feeling thermometers. Apparently not. Only a decline in kurtosis for feelings toward conservatives demonstrates polarization, and the positive *k* value indicates that substantial agreement remains (not shown).

Abortion and Sexuality. No issue represents contemporary social conflict as vividly as does abortion, the struggle over that has become symbolic of the so-called culture wars (Hunter 1994). This reputation is deserved. Of all the measures we analyzed, only the GSS abortion scale evinces polarization in all three senses: increased dispersion, bimodality (though this peaked in the mid-1980s), and (within-domain) ideological constraint (Figure 5; see also Hout 1995). By contrast, we find no polarization of attitudes on sexual morality, and a small but significant decline in constraint.

Conclusion. We find little support for the widely held belief that Americans have become sharply polarized on a wide range of social and cultural

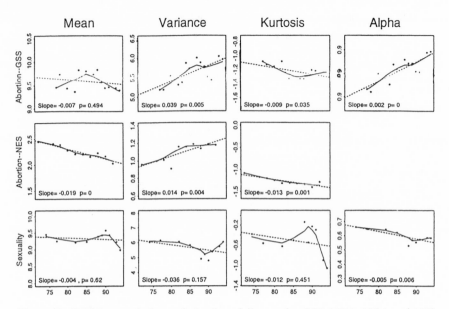

Figure 5. Within-population polarization, full sample, GSS 1974–1994 and NES 1972–1994, abortion and sexuality; x-axis = year.

opinions in the past two decades. Instead we find a variety of trends on specific issues. Americans have become more united in their views on women's role in the public sphere, in their acceptance of racial integration, and in their opinions on matters related to crime and justice. These trends represent movement toward consensus on liberal views on racial integration and gender and on tougher positions on crime. By contrast, Americans have become more divided in their attitudes toward abortion and, less dramatically, in their feelings toward the poor. The fact that division on these latter issues has increased without large directional change in central tendencies confirms the importance of inspecting change in distributions as well as in means.[12]

Within-Group Polarization in Subgroups

Focusing upon the public as a whole may obscure trends toward polarization within particular subgroups. We look at several such groups below: voters, the politically active, college graduates, and the young. A finding of polarizing trends among these groups would be consequential because the first three play a disproportionately important political role, and changes among the young may presage longer-term shifts. (Figures 6 and 7 depict

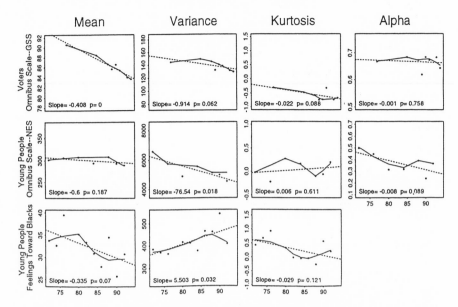

Figure 6. Within-population polarization, voters and young people, GSS 1974–1994 and NES 1972–1994, omnibus scales and feelings toward Blacks; x-axis = year.

results for only those variables where the subgroup evinced significant polarization by at least one criterion *and* where the general population did not.) . . .

Participants in the Political System. The politically active are known to be unrepresentative of the general population in numerous ways (Verba, Schlozman, and Brady 1995) and it is possible that, as attentive observers of political debates, their views have also become more polarized. We focus here upon voters in the most recent election (GSS and NES) and on people who had scores of three or more on the NES activism scale. If political volatility reflects opinion polarization, such polarization should appear first among the most politically engaged.

Voters differed from the public at large in only two respects (Figure 6). First, as for the general public, voters' GSS omnibus scales became less dispersed; but, unlike the public as a whole, they became modestly flatter. This result demonstrates the utility of viewing polarization multidimensionally: variance in opinion declined at the same time that voters migrated slightly away from the center of a narrowing range. Second, constraint on crime and justice issues remained unchanged among voters, although it declined for the general public (not shown).

Only the NES included measures of political activism, restricting analyses to NES opinion items (Figure 7). Activists experienced less polarization than

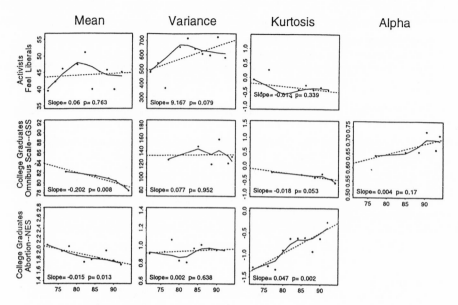

Figure 7. Within-population polarization, activists and college graduates, GSS 1974–1994 and NES 1972–1994, feelings toward liberals, omnibus scale and attitudes toward abortion; x-axis = year.

the general public in their attitudes toward poor people (no significant change, although signs of greater bimodality appear toward the series' end; not shown). Only in their feelings toward liberals (which increased in variance during the conservative mobilization of the late 1970s and early 1980s) did activists display more polarization than the general public.

College Graduates. Many public-opinion scholars believe that because well-educated people attend to news media and value logical consistency among beliefs more highly, they exhibit greater ideological constraint in response to opinion surveys (Converse 1964). It follows that college graduates may participate in political trends such as polarization more actively than less attentive publics. Although this view is controversial (Judd and Milburn 1980; Kiecolt 1988) and the views of well-educated persons grew more similar to those of other Americans by the early 1970s (Nie, Verba, and Petrocik 1976), we look at college graduates separately to ensure giving polarization a fair test.

Because they are politically attentive, college graduates should be especially subject to polarization. One might also expect to find greater dispersion of opinion among college graduates because, due to the rapid expansion of higher education, that group became composed of persons from increasingly diverse backgrounds through the 1970s and 1980s.

Results for college graduates are similar to those for the general public, with a few differences (see Figure 7). Unlike the general public, college graduates display no decline in variance on the GSS omnibus scale (in fact, kurtosis declines) or in attitudes toward racial integration or women's family roles; there is also no increase in kurtosis for racial attitudes, nor any decline in alphas for attitudes toward women's public roles. These differences reflect the fact that the general public has gravitated toward a liberal consensus on racial integration and gender that college graduates had already reached at the onset of the time series. By contrast, college graduates' feelings toward poor people did not increase in variance over the period, though, as for the full sample, kurtosis declined, indicating movement toward bimodality. (We were surprised to find that college graduates' responses to the NES abortion measure became *less* bimodal, though no less dispersed.)

Young People.   Perhaps a polarizing trend, like an earlier trend toward liberalism (Davis 1992), may be found in cohort succession, the force of which is felt only as members of younger cohorts replace their elders. To test this possibility, we look for opinion polarization among people who were between the ages of 18 and 29 at the time of the survey administration. The question here is whether there has been a trend toward greater polarization among successive cohorts of men and women entering adulthood between the early 1970s and the early 1990s.

Differences between young people and the general public are numerous but inconclusive (see Figure 6). Responses of men and women under 30 do not display the reduced variance in the GSS omnibus scale found in the full sample, but they *do* exhibit declining dispersion and constraint in the NES omnibus scale. Signs of polarization visible in the general public's attitudes toward conservatives and toward the poor, and increased variance and constraint on the GSS abortion scale, are absent from data on younger respondents. Other indicators, however, point to somewhat *more* polarization among young people. Responses (which, unlike those of older Americans, grew more negative) to the African-American feeling thermometer among young people became more dispersed. Also in contrast to the general public, young people displayed no decline in variance in attitudes toward aid to minorities, no trend toward peakedness in racial attitudes, and no significant decline in constraint in views on women's public roles and crime.

Summary.   Lacking evidence of substantial polarization in the general public's social attitudes from the early 1970s to the middle 1990s, we analyzed separately data from voters, political activists, college graduates, and young people, to see if polarization was more marked among attentive publics or the young. This exercise revealed intriguing patterns, but identified no group that had experienced substantially greater polarization than the public at large. Overall, results reinforce the conclusion drawn from analyses of the full sample: increased unity with respect to gender roles, support for racial integration, and the control and punishment of crime; polarization with respect to abortion and, to a lesser extent, feelings toward the poor; and no systematic change with respect to other issues.

Polarization as Between-Group Difference

Could it be that perceptions of societal polarization reflect a deepening gulf between one or more highly visible pairs of social groups? Does our malaise reflect a situation in which "the social groups into which the society is dividing are less and less capable of understanding and talking to one another" (Piore 1995:8)? In this section we explore change over time in opinion dissensus associated with gender, race, age, educational level, religion, self-defined political ideology, party affiliation, and region.

For each pair of contrasting groups, we plot the mean value over time of each group's response to each opinion scale or item. We then regress the absolute value of the difference in means against time (year) to establish a slope and test for trends. We regard a positive slope combined with a coefficient for year significant at $P \le .10$ as evidence of increasing between-group polarization. Figures are presented only for variables for which intergroup differences displayed a significant trend (Figures 8–13). . . .

This comparison is just one part of the story, however. Polarization is of interest because of its potential impact on intergroup conflict and opportunities for political mobilization. Therefore we must also attend to the distribution of opinion *within* each group. Even if differences between two groups have increased, the likelihood that such differences will lead to conflict, as opposed to inaction or to the subordination of one group to the other, depends on each group's capacity to mobilize (Simmel [1908] 1955). One part of this capacity is the degree of unity within the group, as indicated by *kurtosis*. Effective intergroup polarization represents both a deepening of dissensus *between* two groups and a strengthening of consensus *within* each group.

Page and Shapiro (1992) document the phenomenon of "parallel publics": subgroup opinions on most issues change in the same direction over time as members of each group assimilate the same new information and ideas, a process that leads to generally stable group differences (reflecting variation in interests or values) across changing levels of mean response. We shall ask, first, if significant change in some between-group differences has occurred within this overall context of stability, and, second, if parallelism characterizes internal consensus (as tapped by *kurtosis*), as well as substantive opinion.

Age. We compared the attitudes of men and women less than 35 years old to those of respondents more than 45 years old. This classification permits the onset of the series to capture the most celebrated generational divide—the counterposition of the 1960s generation and their elders—while the end of the series distinguishes adequately between the baby boomers (and surviving preboomers) and their successors.

In the wake of the 1960s, some observers expected age to become a defining axis of political conflict in postindustrial societies (see, e.g., Gorz 1973, on youth as a class). But Davis's work (1992) reports a decline in the association of youth with liberalism in the 1980s (see also Page and Shapiro 1992:304), so we expected to find declining age polarization, and indeed we did. Difference in means between age groups increased for no measures and declined significantly for 12 of 18. . . .

Educational Attainment. Conservative polemicists, from Dan Quayle to William Bennett (1992), have dwelt on a supposed gulf in values between the "intellectual elite" and everyone else. Bloom (1987) locates the origins of this divide in higher-educational reforms of the 1960s. If he is right, then attitudes of college graduates and others should diverge, as graduates who attended college after the 1960s reforms replace their more conservative predecessors.

One finds more substantial warrant within sociology to expect that the educational divide might increasingly structure opinion. New-class theory (Gouldner 1979) viewed higher education as a major determinant of political orientation. Collins (1979) argued that college graduates are an important status group, possessing shared interests and a common culture. Evidence for education's increasing salience can be found in research on marital selection, which finds educational homogamy increasing as other bases of spousal choice decline (Kalmijn 1991).

Surprisingly, then, significant trends toward opinion *convergence* between college graduates and people with no more than a high school education were observed for 9 of 18 measures, with divergence on none (Figures 8a–8b). Between the 1970s and the early 1990s, opinions of college graduates and the less schooled became more similar with respect to the GSS omnibus scale, feelings toward conservatives, and attitudes toward women's roles (NES and GSS), abortion (GSS only), race, sex education, and legal restrictions on divorce. Like the "generation gap," then, the "education gap" (at least in attitudes toward social issues) seems to have reflected the peculiar social and demographic configuration of the 1970s rather than an emergent trend.

80   Paul DiMaggio, John Evans, and Bethany Bryson

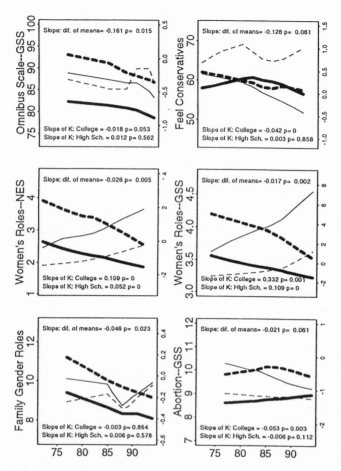

Figure 8a. Between-group polarization, education; *x*-axis = year. Thick lines and
large numbers are means, thin lines and small numbers are kurtosis. Solid line
indicates college graduates, broken line indicates those with high school–level
education or less.

Gender. Political observers have noted a growing "gender gap" in electoral behavior since 1980. Do differences in voting patterns reflect divergence in social attitudes as well? Previous research has demonstrated
gender differences in many values and attitudes (Beutel and Marini 1995).
Shapiro and Mahajan (1986:42), using data from the 1960s to the
mid-1980s, report growth in gender differences in evaluations of "policies
involving the use of force" and, to a lesser extent, in attitudes toward "regulation and public protection, matters of compassion, and traditional values."
We find slim evidence of a growing gender gap (Figure 9). Men's and

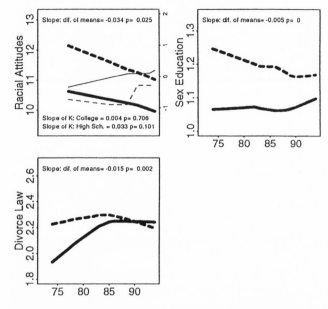

Figure 8b. Between-group polarization, education; *x*-axis = year. Thick lines and large numbers are means, thin lines and small numbers are kurtosis. Solid line indicates college graduates, broken line indicates those with high school–level education or less.

women's scores on the NES omnibus scale diverge significantly; but the actual increase is tiny and the result was not repeated for any of the scale components. By contrast, we observed convergence (largely complete by 1985) in opinions on crime and justice and sex education, and persistence of moderate, stable gender differences in other social attitudes.

Race. Racial divisions in social attitudes, as in other matters, are well established. Hochschild (1995) and Page and Shapiro (1992:298) document striking differences though the latter note some convergence in attitudes toward racial and moral issues in the 1980s. Extending analyses through the mid-1990s, we find a notable decline in racial polarization, with significant convergent trends in feelings toward liberals, conservatives, and the poor; views on aid for minorities, on crime and justice, and on abortion (GSS only); and scores on the NES omnibus scale. On no scale or item did black/white differences increase (Figures 10a–10b).

This convergence is consistent with Wilson's expectation (1978) that growth in the African-American middle class would increase similarity between African Americans and Whites and expand diversity within the Black population. Indeed, on issues related to race and class, opinion diversity

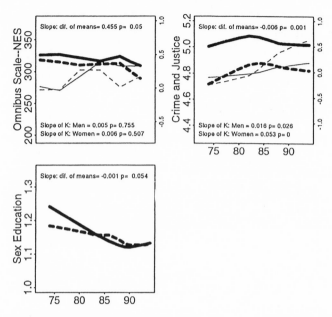

Figure 9. Between-group polarization, gender; x-axis = year. Thick lines and large numbers are means, thin lines and small numbers are kurtosis. Solid line indicates men; broken line indicates women.

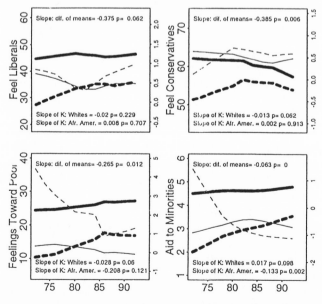

Figure 10a. Between-group polarization, race; x-axis = year. Thick lines and large numbers are means, thin lines and small numbers are kurtosis. Solid line indicates Whites; broken line indicates African-Americans.

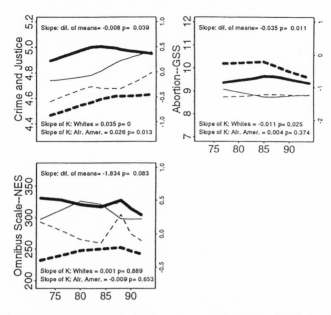

Figure 10b.   Between-group polarization, race; *x*-axis = year. Thick lines and large
numbers are means, thin lines and small numbers are kurtosis. Solid line indicates Whites; broken line indicates African-Americans.

among African Americans has grown substantially, even as group means
have moved in the same direction as those of Whites. We find marked
declines in kurtosis in feeling thermometers for Blacks and the poor and for
attitudes toward government assistance to minorities. Polarization *within* the
African-American community may make it more difficult for Blacks to maintain united fronts in political struggles, as those on either end of the opinion
spectrum can credibly defy efforts to present any position as representing the
group as a whole.

These findings are notable for three reasons. First, they provide circum-
stantial support for our contention that information on *intra*group polarization is useful in assessing the political implications of *inter*group differences
in opinion: one can argue impressionistically that African Americans have
had more difficulty mobilizing politically during the 1990s, in part due to
the internal division reflected in these data. Second, these findings suggest
that the "parallelism" visible in directional opinion change may not always
characterize change in intragroup distributions. Third, they make us more
cautious than we might otherwise be in interpreting polarization in the
general population's attitudes toward the poor and toward government assistance for minorities as a simple displacement of conflict over racial integration (on which opinions have now converged) by a homologous division of
opinion over symbolic racial issues.

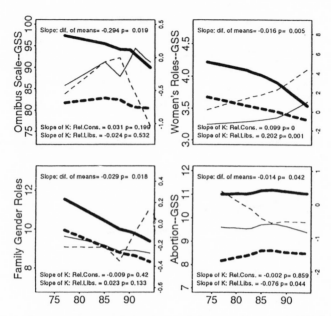

Figure 11a. Between-group polarization, religion; x-axis = year. Thick lines and large numbers are means, thin lines and small numbers are kurtosis. Solid line indicates religious conservatives; broken line indicates religious liberals.

Religion. Few bases of political opposition have received as much recent attention as the clash between the Religious Right—politically oriented evangelical Protestants perceived to be allied on many issues with conservative Roman Catholics and Orthodox Jews—and the secular and liberal religious worlds (Evans 1996; Wuthnow 1988). Although research on congregations (Ammerman 1987) has demonstrated much attitude heterogeneity among conservative Protestants, it remains to be seen whether the political mobilization of conservative faith communities has increased polarization between their members and other Americans, as reflected in public opinion data.

We compared members of conservative Protestant denominations and Roman Catholics who reported attending services almost weekly or more to members of religiously liberal Protestant denominations, Jews, and the religiously unaffiliated.[13] (Because NES did not collect detailed data on religion until 1992, we used only GSS measures.) Remarkably, given a frequent equation of conservative faith communities with "the Religious Right," differences between religious conservatives and religious liberals *declined* during the 1970s and 1980s, with significant convergence on seven of nine attitude measures (Figures 11a–11b). The groups' opinions became more

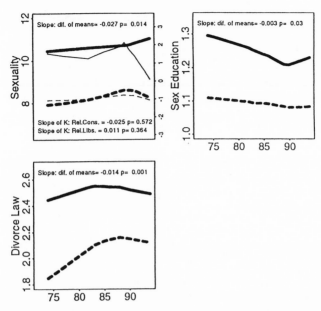

Figure 11b. Between-group polarization, religion; x-axis = year. Thick lines and large numbers are means, thin lines and small numbers are kurtosis. Solid line indicates religious conservatives; broken line indicates religious liberals.

similar not just on such issues as women's roles, on which polarization declined more generally, but also on such "hot-button" moral issues as abortion, sexual conduct, sex education, and legal restrictions on divorce. Only attitudes toward crime, where a tiny difference vanished by 1980, and school prayer, where a large difference persisted, evaded this trend. . . .

The attitudes of religious conservatives and liberals on women's roles converged dramatically. On most other issues, very large differences became modestly, but significantly, smaller. On sex education, for example, the views of religious conservatives became more liberal. On abortion and sexual conduct, convergence reflected a shift of religious liberals toward more conservative positions—accompanied, in the case of abortion, by significant internal polarization.

We also separated church-attending members of evangelical Protestant denominations from churchgoing Roman Catholics and replicated the comparison to religions liberals for each. The major conclusion was confirmed: in no case (either group, any variable) did a divergent trend appear. Significant convergence appeared between both groups and religious liberals in attitudes toward women's public roles, sex education and divorce law. Catholics became more similar to religious liberals in their views on abortion, family gender roles, and sexuality. Evangelicals and religious liberals became more similar in their scores on the GSS omnibus scale (figures available on request).

Given the prevailing political wisdom, how can we explain these results? Although liberal Protestants remain more highly educated than members of other faith communities, college attendance increased during the past several decades among religiously conservative Protestants and Roman Catholics, which might be expected to moderate differences on issues such as racial intolerance in which education is central (Hunter 1987; Wuthnow 1988). Moreover, evangelical denominations have attracted new members in recent years: it may be that these converts share traditional views on such issues as abortion and school prayer, but not the conservative views on race and gender that characterized religious conservatives in the beginning of our time series.

Region. The effects of southern residence on opinion are well documented (Ellison and Musick 1993). Although evidence points to a decline in southern racial intolerance, the emergence of a strongly Republican "solid South" in presidential (and, increasingly, statewide) politics suggests that regional differences in other attitudes may have increased. We found no evidence of regional polarization in our data, however. Differences between southerners and other Americans declined with respect to the NES omnibus scale and attitudes toward women's public roles (GSS), government aid to minorities, and sex education, and fluctuated or remained stable for other measures.[14]

Ideology. Polarization may appear to increase if political identities become linked to more distinctive social attitudes: for example, if liberal identifiers move to the left as conservative identifiers move to the right. To see if this is the case, we compare respondents who describe themselves as "liberal" or to those who say they are "conservative."

With one exception, we find no polarization (Figure 12). Throughout our time series, consistent with the notion of "parallel publics," the social opinions of conservative and liberal identifiers moved in tandem, actually becoming more similar on feelings toward the poor, government aid to minorities, and women's public roles.

The exception, once again, is abortion, on which liberal and conservative opinion has diverged according to both GSS and NES measures. The pattern is striking: no change (NES) or modest pro-life change (GSS) among conservatives; larger pro-choice movement among liberal identifiers (see also Hout 1995). During this process, liberal opinion (about as divided as that of conservatives in 1977) became increasingly unified (higher k), while conservative opinion grew more internally polarized.

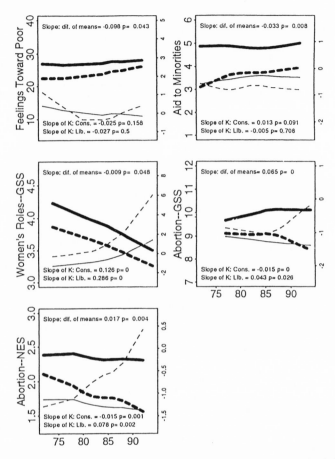

Figure 12. Between-group polarization, ideology; *x*-axis = year. Thick lines and large numbers are means, thin lines and small numbers are kurtosis. Solid line indicates political conservatives; broken line indicates political liberals.

Party Identification. Finally, we compare the social attitudes of those who call themselves Republicans to those who say they are Democrats. Evidence of increased political partisanship in congressional voting (*Congressional Quarterly* 1994) may reflect increased divergence among party identifiers. Yet the moderating effects of parties' efforts to build electoral coalitions [see Mueller (1983) on median-voter theory] should prevent the members from drifting too far apart.

During the past two decades, the mechanisms that attract parties to the political center appear to have broken down. In striking contrast to other groups, Republicans and Democrats display significant polarizing trends

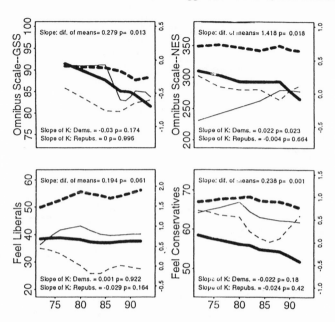

Figure 13a.   Between-group polarization, party identification; x-axis = year. Thick
lines and large numbers are means, thin lines and small numbers are kurtosis.
Solid line indicates Democrats; broken line indicates Republicans.

with respect to attitudes on 8 of 17 social issues (see . . . Figures 13a–13b).
Democrats' and Republicans' views diverged on both the GSS and the NES
omnibus scales. Polarization on feeling thermometers toward liberals, conservatives, and the poor, and on attitudes toward crime and justice, suggest
that Republican use of wedge issues may have had an effect. Increased
divergence on attitudes toward abortion and divorce law may reflect the
movement of conservative Roman Catholics and southern evangelicals from
the Democratic party to the Republican party.

Democrat and Republican opinions on most issues changed in parallel:
divergence occurred when the *rate* of change was greater for one party than
for the other. For example both groups' scores on the GSS omnibus scale
grew more liberal, but Democrats' did so at a faster rate.

There were only two deviations from parallelism. Democrats' views on
crime and justice became a bit more liberal while Republicans' remained
conservative. As usual, however, abortion attitudes deviated most dramatically from the norm. Whereas in the 1970s Republicans were less opposed
to abortion than Democrats, the groups moved in opposite directions, cross-
ing in the mid-1980s and diverging thereafter. At the same time, Republicans

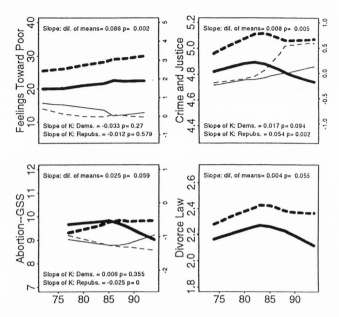

Figure 13b. Between-group polarization, party identification; x-axis = year. Thick lines and large numbers are means, thin lines and small numbers are kurtosis. Solid line indicates Democrats; broken line indicates Republicans.

divided more sharply over abortion (as indicated by declining *k*; patterns are similar for the GSS and the NES items but only significant for the GSS).

Conclusions. Having found little evidence of polarization in distributions of opinion of the public or selected subsamples, we examined trends in social-attitude differences between paired subgroups. Evidence of intergroup polarization was strikingly absent with one exception. Between the 1970s and 1990s opinions of Americans of different ages and educational levels converged markedly, as did views on many issues of Blacks and Whites and of religious conservatives and religious liberals. Differences between men and women were largely stable. Attitudes of liberals and conservatives grew more similar on three items, but diverged on attitudes toward abortion. The two abortion items and the anomalous male/female trend in the NES omnibus scale were the *only* cases of significant divergence in our comparisons of attitudes of groups based on age, education, gender, race, religion, region, and political ideology. By contrast, we found *46 instances of significant convergent trends.* The evidence, then, points to dramatic *depolarization* in intergroup differences.

Only when we turn to political party divisions do we find evidence of polarization: striking divergence of attitudes between Democrats and Republicans. In traditional pluralist theory, social conflict emerges from struggles between groups in civil society. Political parties, seeking support from the vital center, take the rough edges off of such conflicts. Our findings—that the social attitudes of groups in civil society have converged at the same time that attitudes of party identifiers have polarized—raise troubling questions about the role of political parties in a pluralistic society.

These results also confirm the utility of looking together at *inter*group differences and *intra*group polarization. Certain patterns of change in the latter (e.g., the greater bimodality of opinions of African Americans on aid to minorities and feelings toward the poor, and in conservative and Republican views on abortion) suggest that the phenomenon of parallel publics, supported for central tendencies, may not hold for change in within-group distributions. When intergroup differences mask intragroup division, attention to the latter suggests why divided groups may have trouble mobilizing around issues (like abortion for Republicans) that seem to separate them from others.

Summary of Findings

1.   We find no support for the proposition that the United States has experienced dramatic polarization in public opinion on social issues since the 1970s. Variance in most attitudes has not increased; neither has bimodality of response. Nor have most attitudes grown more constrained by ideology or (except for party affiliation) group identity.

2.   If attitude polarization entails increased variance, increased bimodality, and increased opinion constraint, then only attitudes toward abortion have become more polarized in the past 20 years, both in the public at large and within most subgroups. Abortion attitude measures behave differently than measures of opinion on any other issue, underscoring the exceptional character of the abortion debate. To generalize from the abortion controversy to other issues, or to view it as evidence of more deepseated polarization, is profoundly misleading.

3.   Partial polarization (in some measures but not others) has occurred in a GSS omnibus scale (bimodality only for voters and college graduates); in attitudes toward conservatives (bimodality for the general public, voters, college graduates, and political activists) and liberals (dispersion for activists); and in feelings toward the poor (dispersion and bimodality for the general public and voters, increased dispersion for people under 30 and increased bimodality for college graduates) and toward African Americans (greater dispersion for people under 30). Despite an overwhelming trend

toward convergence in support of racial integration, these results indicate some polarization on issues imbued with racial symbolism (see Jackman 1994).

4. Most scales and items display no increase in any measure of polarization for any subgroup. Americans have become more unified in their attitudes toward racial integration, crime and justice, and, especially, women's roles. Dispersion and bimodality in attitudes toward sexuality and feelings toward African Americans and liberals have remained largely stable.

5. Between-group differences in social attitudes have steadily declined. Although many remain great in absolute terms, social-attitude polarization by age, education, race, religious faith, region, and (except for abortion) political ideology, declined between the 1970s and the 1990s. Only the gap between Republicans and Democrats grew, suggesting that the party system, which has conventionally been expected to moderate social divisions, has been exacerbating them.

6. Polarization is measurable, multidimensional, and interesting. The findings that the public has polarized around the abortion issue and (to a lesser extent) in its views of the poor, but has become more unified in support for racial integration, the rights of women to participate in public life, and tough stands on crime and justice are intuitively plausible. The fact that measures of spread, bimodality, and constraint do not move in tandem (and in some cases move in opposite directions) indicates that polarization is multidimensional.

CONCLUSIONS

Why Do We Perceive More Polarization Than There Is?

How do we explain the sharp gulf between *perceived* polarization in public discourse and *observed* stability (or convergence) in distributions of public opinion? One set of explanations might revolve around problems of survey method. For example, Converse (1992) suggested that there are "liberal" items and "conservative" items (survey questions on issues about which one or the other side feels strongly) and that surveys that overrepresent one side will fail to pick up movement on the other. Because our measure addressed many issues of interest to both sides of the political spectrum, we doubt that this influenced our findings.

It is also possible that surveys adapt too late to changing political currents to capture polarization. Surveys often try to probe attitudes about timely issues on which there is reason to expect opinion to vary, and items with low variance are more likely than those with high variance to be dropped. Thus focusing only on questions that have been asked for many years (as one must to study change) may introduce two kinds of bias: *overestimation* of polarization, when items on which polarization declines are dropped and those with high variance are retained, and *underestimation*, because our items do not tap opinions on issues that became politicized in the late 1980s (e.g., public support for the arts). The stability of the GSS series through 1994, and the fact that NES and GSS measures tell the same story, make us doubt that these factors affected our results.

It is, of course, entirely possible that people perceive polarization that has not, in effect, occurred. This could be the case for many different reasons:

1.   Perhaps change has occurred not in what people believe but in the intensity with which they believe it. The (GSS and NES items effectively tap cognitive diversity in opinion, but, except for the feeling thermometers, they are less useful for measuring intensity of affect (Schuman and Presser 1981, chap. 9; Krosnick and Abelson 1994).

2.   Perceptions of greater conflict may reflect a historical amnesia that perceives the past as less divided than it was. Moreover, our time series may begin at the conclusion of a period of political polarization, from the early 1960s to the early 1970s [Nie et al. 1976:143; Page and Shapiro 1992:9; but Glenn (1974) reports no change from the early 1950s to the late 1960s]. In any case, to say that the U.S. public is not *more* polarized than it was in the 1970s is not to say that it is particularly united.

3.   Views expressed in the media may have become polarized. Hunter points to this when he writes of polarization of "institutionalized and articulated moral visions" (1994:vii) rather than of public opinion itself. The extent to which conservative views are included in public debate, and the range of permissible right-wing opinion, appears to have increased in the 1980s, with the emergence of conservative policy institutes, talk radio, and conservative religious media (Messer-Davidow 1993).[15]

4.   Polarization may be *perceived* to increase even when it does not, if public positions are taken in a harsher, more disputatious manner. An evident decline in many aspects of cultural authority (DiMaggio and Bryson 1995) may be reflected in weakened inhibitions on public utterances of many kinds.

5.   Normative consensus may coexist with factual disagreement. For example, social attitudes of African Americans and Whites have converged; but when one looks not at what Blacks and Whites believe to be *just and appropriate*, but rather at what they believe to be *factually true*, one sees sharp divisions (Hochschild 1995).

6.　Heightened partisanship and electoral volatility may reflect moral or affective dissensus. Large declines in confidence in institutions (Lipset and Schneider 1987) and in other measures of social cohesion (Putnam 1996) may increase perceived polarization even if confidence is not polarized, a topic about which we know little [but see Fox and Firebaugh (1992) on trends in gender differences in confidence in science].

7.　Apparent polarization may reflect changes in resources available for mobilization by different groups. For example, a decline in mobilization of trade unionists and an increase in mobilization of religious conservatives may alter political agendas without shifting underlying sentiments.

8.　Changes in the level at which actors mobilize may also alter perceptions. Local communities have long been sites of acrimonious controversy over race, schools, and morality (Coleman 1957), but conflicts over such issues that are organized nationally may receive more attention.

9.　Shifts in the relative importance of forms of political participation that tend to increase the extent of "representation bias" (Converse, Clausen, and Miller 1965; Verba et al. 1995)—that is, a decline in the importance of voting or letter writing and an increase in the importance of cash contributions or protest—may render political conflict more apparent.

10.　Increased partisanship may reflect institutional changes that reduce party organizations' discipline over divisive candidates and officeholders (Polsby 1983). Or divisive social rhetoric may reflect strategies of the parties themselves.

11.　If citizens vote on the basis of identities that are only loosely coupled to policy preferences—for example, race, religion, region—they may support candidates on the basis of shrill symbolic appeals without sharing such candidates' polarized issue preferences.

12.　Political volatility may reflect not shifting opinions, but shifting issue frames (Gamson 1992; Schuman and Presser 1981; Sniderman, Tetlock, Carmines, and Peterson 1993). Shifting frames can alter political agendas by altering the relative salience of differing attitudes even when the attitudes themselves remain stably distributed.

This discussion raises more questions than it resolves. Our purpose is to suggest directions of inquiry that might explain the paradox of widespread belief that social-issue politics have become more polarized even though opinion data demonstrate that social attitudes have not. . . .

By developing a theoretically grounded set of operational definitions, applying that approach to the substantively important issue of distributional changes in U.S. social attitudes between the early 1970s and the mid-1990s, and suggesting theoretical applications, this discussion may inspire further research on the measurement and consequences of distributional properties of public opinion. . . .

ACKNOWLEDGMENTS

For helpful discussions and advice, we are grateful to Larry Bartels, Jennifer Hochschild, Jill Kiecolt, Ellen Messer-Davidow, Victor Nee, Tom Smith, Paul Starr, Howard Taylor, Bruce Western, two *AJS* reviewers, and those in attendance at presentations at the Russell Sage Foundation, the 1995 American Sociological Association meetings (Session on Public Opinion), Bryn Mawr College, Smith College, the Princeton Sociology Department's Culture and Inequality Workshop, and the Eastern Sociological Society's 1996 meetings. Support for data analyses from Princeton University is gratefully acknowledged. Direct correspondence to Paul DiMaggio, Department of Sociology, Princeton University, Princeton, New Jersey 08544.

NOTES

1. Princeton Survey Research Associates, Newsweek Poll, released June 28, 1995, recovered through Public Opinion Online, Roper Center at the University of Connecticut (question identification, USPSRNEW.062895, RO3). We are grateful to Herbert Abelson of Princeton's Survey Research Center for providing this information.

2. Former Senator Warren Rudman, interviewed by Daniel Schorr on National Public Radio, broadcast on Saturday, August 12.

3. Empirical studies of opinion polarization reduce it to between-group differences. Students of economic inequality have done useful work [see, esp., Esteban and Ray (1994) on income polarization], though their solutions are incomplete and not entirely transferable to opinion polarization.

4. Such balance, when it is observed, is as likely to reflect question framing (including effective efforts by item designers to maximize response variance) as polarization (Schuman and Presser 1981; Schuman 1986; Sigelman and Presser 1988:336).

5. Variables derived from the GSS are scales. Those derived from the NES— except for the omnibus scale—are single items. Therefore, alphas (which measure association among items on a scale) are reported for GSS but not for NES variables. All variables are scaled so that the more conservative or rightist position receives a higher rating. This policy has one unfortunate consequence—that the NES feeling thermometers for attitudes toward liberals, Blacks, and poor people are rescaled to make "100" into "0" and vice versa, whereas the feeling thermometer for conservatives, by contrast, retains its scale. Although we recognize that this treatment of the thermometer variables is potentially confusing and potentially unfair (nothing in most versions of conservatism dictates racial antipathy), we consider these evils subordinate to the good of retaining a single ideological direction for all measures.

6. At the beginning of the time series the introduction to the question referred

to "blacks and other minority groups"; after 1988, it referred only to "blacks." In 1980, the term "even if it means giving them preferential treatment" was added, but after 1980 it was removed.

7. The two middle categories of the abortion question were altered in 1980. Before 1980, the options were to permit an abortion "if the life or health of the mother is threatened" and to permit an abortion "if the mother will find it difficult to care for the child." From 1980 on, the second option has been "only in case of rape, incest, or when the woman's life is in danger" and the third became "only in case of rape, incest, or danger to the woman's life, but only after the need for the abortion has been clearly established." Furthermore, beginning in 1980, the question was reworded to underscore that the options were about the treatment of abortion by law, rather than by custom or informal norms. In 1980 both versions of the question were asked and the new version was found to increase slightly the polarization of response.

8. The split ballot resulted in very low Ns for some subgroups for the omnibus and racism scales, which could only be tallied for one of three ballots. Consequently, getting adequate samples of college graduates, religious conservatives, and African Americans on these two scales required pooling the 1988 and 1989 samples and the 1990 and 1991 samples.

9. This enables us to chart change in polarization over time, but at the cost of moderately confounding the measurement of opinion spread and bimodality with within-domain attitude constraint.

10. South is a combination of the South Atlantic, East South Central, and West South Central census regions.

11. Each item was rescaled to an equivalent range to avoid arbitrary inconsistencies in the weight of each scale component. The alternative, normalization, was rejected because its point is to standardize variables with respect to precisely the distributional properties that are the foci of this study.

12. To be sure, one can find evidence of liberalization of attitudes toward abortion during this period, e.g., in responses to the NES abortion question. On the other hand, one can find evidence of fluctuation in views, for example in responses to the GSS-derived scale. We suspect that the relatively unusual vulnerability to question frame and wording reflected in responses to GSS and NES abortion items indicates the sophistication or uncertainty of many people's views on this unsettled (and unsettling) topic.

13. Conservative Protestant denominations were identified on the basis described in Smith (1990a); Catholics were included because of previous work indicating that observant Catholics are similar to conservative Protestants in their social views (ibid.). Because the GSS did not distinguish among Reform, Conservative, and Orthodox Jews before 1988 and because the number of Orthodox Jews in GSS samples thereafter is negligible, Jewish respondents are coded as "liberal" (again following Smith 1990a). We excluded members of what Smith calls the "Protestant moderate" denominations in order to sharpen the contrast between the two groups and thus provide the polarization hypothesis with a fairer test. In initial analyses, we compared religious conservatives to everyone else. Surprised by the absence of

evidence of polarization, we then conducted the analyses reported here (comparing them only to religious liberals and the nonreligious), but we still found no polarization.

14. A significant decline in differences in racial attitudes is not reported, as it may be artifactual. Similar comparisons of easterners and westerners, respectively, to persons from other sections also failed to find any instances of opinion polarization (results available upon request).

15. We are indebted to Robert K. Merton for this suggestion.

REFERENCES

Ammerman, Nancy T. 1987. *Bible Believers: Fundamentalists in the Modern World.* New Brunswick, NJ: Rutgers University Press.

Arnold, R. Douglas. 1990. *The Logic of Congressional Action.* New Haven, CT: Yale University Press.

Bennett, William J. 1992. *The De-Valuing of America: The Fight for Our Culture and Our Children.* New York: Summit.

Berry, Jason. 1993. "Bridging Chasms of Race and Hate." *St. Petersburg Times,* August 12, 1993, p. 6D.

Beutel, Ann M., and Margaret Mooney Marini. 1995. "Gender and Values." *American Sociological Review 60:*436–48.

Blau, Peter. 1977. *Inequality and Heterogeneity.* New York. Free Press.

Bloom, Allan. 1987. *The Closing of the American Mind: How Higher Education Has Failed Democracy and Impoverished the Souls of Today's Students.* New York: Simon & Schuster.

Chafetz, Janet Salzmans, and Helen Rose Fuchs Ebaugh. 1983. "Growing Conservatism in the United States? An Examination of Trends in Political Opinion between 1972 and 1980." *Sociological Perspectives 26:*275–98.

Coleman, James S. 1957. *Community Conflict.* New York: Free Press.

Collins, Randall. 1979. *The Credential Society: An Historical Sociology of Education.* New York: Academic Press.

Congressional Quarterly. 1994. "1994 Party Unity Votes." *52*(December 31):3658–59.

Converse, Philip E. 1964. "The Nature of Belief Systems in Mass Publics." Pp. 206–61 in *Ideology and Discontent,* edited by David E. Apter. New York: Free Press.

———. 1992. "Comment on 'Changeable Weather in a Cooling Climate . . . ' by James A. Davis." *Public Opinion Quarterly 56:*307-10.

Converse, Philip E., Aage R. Clausen, and Warren E. Miller. 1965. "Electoral Myth and Reality: The 1964 Election." *American Political Science Review 59:*321–36.

Davis, James A. 1992. "Changeable Weather in a Cooling Climate atop the Liberal Plateau: Conversion and Replacement in 42 General Society Survey Items, 1972–1989." *Public Opinion Quarterly 50:*261–306.

Davis, James A. and Tom W. Smith. 1991. *General Social Surveys, 1972–1992: Cumulative Codebook.* Chicago: National Opinion Research Center.

————. 1992. *The NORC General Social Survey: A User's Guide.* Newbury Park, CA: Sage.

DiMaggio, Paul, and Bethany P. Bryson. 1995. "Americans' Attitudes towards Cultural Authority and Cultural Diversity." General Social Survey Topical Report Series, no. 27. NORC, Chicago.

Ellison, Christopher G., and Mark A. Musick. 1993. "Southern Intolerance: A Fundamentalist Effect." *Social Forces* 72:379–98.

Esteban, Joan-María, and Debraj Ray. 1994. "On the Measurement of Polarization." *Econometrica* 62:819–51.

Evans, John. 1996. "'Culture Wars' or Status Group Ideology as the Basis of U.S. Moral Politics?" *International Journal of Sociology and Social Policy* 16:15–34.

Fox, Mary Frank, and Glenn Firebaugh. 1992. "Confidence in Science: the Gender Gap." *Social Science Quarterly* 73:101–13.

Gamson, William A. 1992. *Talking Politics.* New York: Cambridge University Press.

Glenn, Norval D. 1974. "Recent Trends in Intercategory Differences in Attitudes." *Social Forces* 52:395–401.

Gorz, Andre. 1973. *Socialism and Revolution.* New York: Anchor.

Gouldner, Alvin. 1979. *The Future of the Intellectuals and the Rise of the New Class.* New York: Continuum.

Guinness, Os. 1993. *The American Hour: A Time of Reckoning and the Once and Future Role of Faith.* New York: Free Press.

Hochschild, Jennifer. 1995. *Facing Up to the American Dream.* Princeton, NJ: Princeton University Press.

Hout, Michael. 1995. "Abortion Politics in the United States, 1972–1994: From Single Issue to Ideology." Working Paper, University of California, Berkeley, Survey Research Center.

Hunter, James Davison. 1987. *Evangelicalism: The Coming Generation.* Chicago: University of Chicago Press.

————. 1991. *Culture Wars: The Struggle to Define America.* New York: Basic Books.

————. 1994. *Before the Shooting Begins: Searching for Democracy in America's Culture War.* New York: Free Press.

Jackman, Mary R. 1994. *The Velvet Glove: Paternalism and Conflict in Gender, Class, and Race Relations.* Berkeley: University of California Press.

Jackman, Mary R., and M. J. Muha. 1984. "Education and Intergroup Attitudes: Moral Enlightenment, Superficial Democratic Commitment, or Ideological Refinement?" *American Sociological Review* 49:751–69.

Judd, Charles M., and Michael A. Milburn. 1980. "The Structure of Attitude Systems in the General Public: Comparisons of a Structural Equation Model." *American Sociological Review* 45:627–43.

Kalmijn, Matthijs. 1991. "Status Homogamy in the United States." *American Journal of Sociology* 97:496–523.

Kiecolt, K. Jill. 1988. "Recent Developments in Attitudes and Social Structure." *Annual Review of Sociology* 14:381–403.

Krosnick, Jon A., and Robert P. Abelson. 1994. "The Case for Measuring Attitude Strength in Surveys." Pp. 177–203 in *Questions about Questions: Inquiries into the Cognitive Bases of Surveys,* edited by Judith M. Tanur. New York: Russell Sage Foundation.

Lipset, Seymour Martin, and William Schneider. 1987. "The Confidence Gap during the Reagan Years, 1981–1987." *Political Science Quarterly 102*:1–23.

Messer-Davidow, Ellen. 1993 "Manufacturing the Attack on Liberalized Higher Education." *Social Text 36*:40–80.

Mueller, Dennis C. 1983. *Public Choice II.* Cambridge: Cambridge University Press.

Nie, Norman H., Sidney Verba, and John R. Petrocik. 1976. *The Changing American Voter.* Cambridge, MA: Harvard University Press.

Page, Benjamin I., and Robert Y. Shapiro. 1982. "Changes in Americans' Policy Preferences, 1935–1979." *Public Opinion Quarterly 46*:24–42.

———. 1992. *The Rational Public: Fifty Years of Trends in Americans' Policy Preferences.* Chicago: University of Chicago Press.

Piore, Michael J. 1995. *Beyond Individualism: How Social Demands of the New Identity Groups Challenge American Political and Economic Life.* Cambridge, MA: Harvard University Press.

Polsby, Nelson. 1983. *Consequences of Party Reform.* New York: Oxford University Press.

Putnam, Robert D. 1996. "The Strange Disappearance of Civic America." *American Prospect* no. 24, pp. 34–49.

Schuman, Howard. 1986. "Ordinary Questions, Survey Questions, and Policy Questions." *Public Opinion Quarterly 50*:432–42.

Schuman, Howard, and Stanley Presser. 1981. *Questions and Answers in Attitude Surveys: Experiments on Question Form, Wording, and Content.* New York: Academic Press.

Schuman, Howard, Charlotte Steeh, and Lawrence Bobo. 1985. *Racial Attitudes in America: Trends and Interpretations.* Cambridge, MA: Harvard University Press.

Shapiro, Robert Y., and Harpreet Mahajan. 1986. "Gender Differences in Policy Preferences: A Summary of Trends from the 1960s to the 1980s." *Public Opinion Quarterly 50*:42–61.

Sigelman, Lee, and Stanley Presser. 1988. "Measuring Public Support for the New Christian Right: The Perils of Point Estimation." *Public Opinion Quarterly 52*:327–37.

Simmel, Georg. [1908] 1955. *Conflict,* translated by Kurt H. Wolff and Reinhard Bendix. New York: Free Press.

Smith, Tom W. 1990a. "Classifying Protestant Denominations." *Review of Religious Research 31*:225–45.

———. 1990b. "Liberal and Conservative Trends in the United States since World War II." *Public Opinion Quarterly 54*:479–507.

Sniderman, Paul M., Philip E. Tetlock, Edward G. Carmines, and Randall S. Peterson. 1993. "The Politics of the American Dilemma." Pp. 212–36 in *Prejudice, Politics, and the American Dilemma,* edited by Paul M. Sniderman, Philip E. Tetlock, and Edward G. Carmines. Stanford, CA: Stanford University Press.

Verba, Sidney, Kay Lehman Schlozman, and Henry E. Brady. 1995. *Voice and Equality: Civic Voluntarism in American Politics.* Cambridge, MA: Harvard University Press.

Wilson, William Julius. 1978. *The Declining Significance of Race.* Chicago: University of Chicago Press.

Wuthnow, Robert. 1988. *The Restructuring of American Religion: Society and Faith Since World War II.* Princeton: Princeton University Press.

Wyszomirski, Margaret Jane. 1994. "From Accord to Discord: Arts Policy During and After the Culture Wars." Pp. 1–46 in *America's Commitment to Culture: Government and the Arts,* edited by Kevin V. Mulcahy and Margaret Jane Wyszomirski. Boulder, CO: Westview.

Yang, Yonghe, and N. J. Demerath III. 1996. "What American Culture War? A View from the Trenches as Opposed to the Command Posts and the Press Corps." Manuscript. University of Massachusetts, Amherst, Department of Sociology.

5

Religious Affiliation, Commitment, and Ideology among U.S. Elites

TIMOTHY SHORTELL

The relationship between religion and political attitudes is typically studied by examining differences in political views among affiliational groups. Affiliational groups are thought of as aligned along an ideological continuum, from liberal to conservative (Hayes 1995; Kellstedt, Green, Guth, and Smidt 1994; Pyle 1993; Shortell 1995). A number of historical factors have combined to create distinct affiliational subcultures. Membership in an affiliational group, then, leads to adherence to particular political views.

It is clear that all members of an affiliational group do not hold identical views. Some members are more likely than others to be in agreement with the predominant views in the subculture. Those who are more invested socially and psychologically in the subculture would be more likely to share these predominant views. Religious commitment should amplify affiliational differences.

Is there evidence in the literature of coherent ideological blocs defined by religious affiliation and commitment? An early review of empirical research on religiosity and political views yielded evidence of both positive and negative findings (Wuthnow 1973). Of the 266 studies reviewed, 39 percent found a positive association between some measure of religiosity and some measure of conservatism, 46 percent of the studies showed no relationship, and 15 percent found a negative relationship. The likelihood of finding a positive relationship is influenced by the operationalization of both religiosity and conservatism. Of the sixty-nine studies that used church attendance as a measure of religious commitment, only 30 percent found a positive relationship to conservatism.

The relationship between the religion variable and conservatism also depends on which dimension of conservative ideology is measured. "Social" conservatism tended to be most clearly related to religiosity, with 45 percent of the studies employing such a variable showing a positive association. "Political" conservatism was positively related to religious commitment in 36 percent of the studies. "Economic" conservatism was positively related to the religion variable in only 19 percent of the studies reviewed.

Pyle (1993) has reported that moderate Protestants and Fundamentalists are less likely than Catholics to support government economic assistance measures, a central aspect of economic ideology. Liberal Protestants were not significantly different from Catholics on this issue. On the other hand, Pyle showed a positive relationship between biblical literalism and support for assistance measures.

Kellstedt et al. (1994) have demonstrated consistent differences in political opinion and voting among Christian affiliations. Evangelical Protestants are most conservative on all issues in data from the spring of 1992, but the largest differences are on abortion, women's rights, and support for Israel. Catholics and mainline Protestants appear to be similar, though Catholics are significantly more conservative on abortion and slightly less so on health care policy. Secularists align at the liberal end of the continuum across the board. Data from fall 1992 find Evangelicals substantially more conservative on all issues. The differences between mainline Protestants and Catholics became more prominent. The Catholics are more liberal on all items except abortion. Once again, the secularists are farthest to the left.

Kellstedt et al. (1994) suggest that the composition of voting blocs is changing. Blocs defined primarily by affiliation are being replaced by blocs defined by theological view. Conservative Catholics are joining with conservative Evangelicals and Fundamentalists in support of candidates who advocate a socially conservative agenda. Liberal Catholics are more likely to vote with secularists and Jews, supporting candidates with a more liberal platform.

Most studies of affiliational differences focus on the *content* of ideology. Miller (1996) has suggested that the *structure* of ideology itself might vary among groups. That is, affiliational groups may encourage distinctive attitudes because the context in which a particular attitude is formed is differently structured; one group might see an issue in the context of personal morality, while another might see it as an issue of social policy. Examining General Social Survey (GSS) data, he makes three predictions: members of conservative Protestant groups will tend to associate more specific issues with morality than other groups; Jews will be most likely to differ among the common U.S. affiliations, particularly in the area of morality; and conservative Protestants will tend to see abortion and homosexuality as moral issues, whereas Jews will tend to see them as social issues.

Implicitly acknowledging the importance of commitment, Miller restricts his analysis to the more active participants in each affiliational group (at least monthly attendance for Christians and at least annual attendance for Jews). His analysis suggests that there are structural differences in ideology. Conservative Protestants, moderate Protestants, and Catholics were similar; these groups viewed abortion and homosexuality as moral issues, loading on a component with pornography, marijuana use, and premarital sex. Liberal and Black Protestants exhibited the same morality dimension, but saw economic issues differently. Jews, as predicted, were most distinctive. Abortion was seen as an issue of women's rights. Homosexuality and premarital sex loaded on the same component, different from the morality one containing the pornography and marijuana items.

Miller's hypothesis about the difference between conservative Protestants and the other Christian affiliations was not supported by the data; his hypotheses about the Jewish-Christian differences were. The data support Miller's claim that structural differences exist between affiliational groups. The GSS data, however, are not exhaustive of the ideological domain and are not, for that reason, a good place to look for empirical evidence of the structure of ideology for these groups. Differences between conservative Protestants and the other Christian groups, for example, may be obscured by the relatively limited number of attitudinal items available in this data.

THE DIMENSIONS OF AMERICAN IDEOLOGY

The Center for the Study of Social and Political Change (CSSPC) at Smith College, directed by Stanley Rothman, has conducted a large-scale study of U.S. elites, gathering data on the political beliefs of leaders of the corporate, cultural, and legal sectors. Using these data, Lerner, Nagai, and Rothman (1996) suggest that American ideology is defined by four major dimensions: collectivist liberalism, expressive individualism, system alienation, and regime threat.

The first dimension organizes attitudes toward economics and welfare state issues. A conservative orientation would favor less governmental action in the economic realm, while the liberal position would favor a more activist state. The second dimension concerns individual morality and social norms. Lerner et al. label the conservative end point "traditional puritanism" and the liberal one "expressive individualism." The third dimension discussed by Lerner et al. is one's orientation to social institutions and the status quo. The conservative view is one of loyalty, a belief that the present system is working well. The liberal sees the status quo as fundamentally flawed and in need of reform. The authors' final dimension:

taps into the degree to which a person feels threatened by the outside world, whether it be on the international sphere (and hence a strong anti-communist response), or by the violation of system norms (and thus a strong reaction against perceived leniency toward criminals). (Lerner et al. 1996:26)

Using a slightly different organizing idea, a recent study using public opinion data (Shortell 1995) suggests that two major axes organize American ideology. One is defined by public policy issues, such as military spending and health care policy, and the other by morality and social norms. And as noted above, the ideological space has also been defined along political, economic, and social dimensions (Wuthnow 1973). Thus, notwithstanding some minor differences, there is substantial agreement that the structure of American ideology separates issues of the public sphere from issues of personal and moral conduct. The CSSPC data, because of the breadth of the issues included, represent the most sophisticated treatment of the varied dimensions upon which ideological views vary. The effects of religion, if present, ought to be manifest in these data.

THE PRESENT STUDY

In light of the complexity of the relationship between religious affiliation, religious commitment, and ideology, the present study addresses several questions. Are there ideological differences among liberal Protestants, moderate Protestants, conservative Protestants, Catholics, Jews, and those of no affiliation? Are differences manifest in terms of content only, or of content and structure? How important is strength of religious commitment in determining differences between groups?

Social science has two classical approaches to ideology. One view derives traditionally from classical Marxist theory, defining ideology as the false consciousness that results from capitalist production. This view has been used to explain why the working class holds political views contrary to its class interest, for example. The other view defines ideology as the structure of social consciousness particular to any given societal group or class, and resulting from a multitude of social factors. The latter definition is used here. Empirically, ideology is defined as the principal-components statistical model of twenty attitudinal items. Also, in this study "liberal" and "conservative" positions are identified with reference to contemporary public opinion literature and popular political discourse, rather than classical political theory.

Several specific expectations with respect to the *content* of ideology can be identified: (1) liberal Protestants will be more conservative on economic issues than the other affiliational groups, and more devout liberal Protestants will be most conservative; (2) conservative Protestants will be more conservative with respect to individual morality than the other groups, and the difference between more and less devout conservative Protestant will be largest on this dimension; (3) conservative Protestants will be more conservative on issues regarding threats to the status quo than the other groups; (4) Catholics will be less conservative on economic and political issues than on social ones, and the differences between the more and less devout among Catholics is also likely to be larger on the social dimension of ideology; and (5) Jews are likely to be less conservative on economic, political, and social issues.

Following Miller (1996), several predictions about the *structure* of ideology can be identified: (1) conservative Protestants will see more issues as relating to personal morality, and this will be manifest in two effects: (a) the morality component will account for a larger percentage of the variance than the political or economic components, and (b) a larger number of issues will load on the component containing items about abortion, adultery, homosexuality, and women's roles; and (2) the component structure for Jews will be most distinctive; in particular, items about abortion, adultery, homosexuality, and women's roles will not load on the same component.

METHOD

Data

The CSSPC data were used for the present study. The data were collected between 1979 and 1985. The sample includes 200 high-ranking government bureaucrats, 242 upper- and middle-management personnel from four Fortune 500 companies, 134 congressional aides, 114 federal judges, 95 officers of national unions and trade associations, 150 corporate lawyers who were partners at large firms, 238 journalists and editors of print and television news organizations, 152 field grade officers from the armed services, 96 writers, producers, and directors of top-grossing contemporary films, 158 public interest lobbyists, 178 leaders of religious organizations, including universities and seminaries, religious publications and media, and religious bodies such as National Council of Churches, and 104 writers, producers, and executives of prime-time television series. Each subsample was a random sample taken from a larger list of members of that group. An attempt was made, given the many practical constraints of a study of this nature, to construct representative samples. The total sample size is 1861.

Religious groups were defined by self-reported affiliation. Protestant denominations were grouped into three categories, conservative, moderate, and liberal, according to the scheme employed by Roof and McKinney (1987). Roman Catholics and Jews were the fourth and fifth groups.[1] Those who reported no affiliation or agnosticism were included as a comparison group. This left a sample size of 1011.

Frequency of attendance at religious services was used as an indicator of strength of religious commitment. The original four-point Likert-type scale was dichotomized, with weekly or almost weekly attendance defined as "more devout" and less frequent attenders labeled "less devout." With this categorization, 38 percent of the total sample—58 percent of those with a religious affiliation—is considered more devout.

Analysis

First, working with the proposition that the structure of ideology is the same for all groups, an attempt was made to simplify the ideological structure suggested by Lerner et al. (1996). Lerner et al. used twenty-eight belief items in their analysis, and calculated principal factors. The present study retained twenty of those items, and used principal-components analysis. Lerner et al. make a convincing case in support of their use of principal factors. The present study, however, makes use of principal components because it is more common and less restrictive, and as such, suitable to an initial attempt to establish differences among religious groups. The items are given in Table 1.

In order to produce a principal-components solution common to the entire sample, factor scores were calculated with the regression method (Norusis 1994). These scores were used as dependent variables in ANOVAs with religious affiliation (conservative Protestant, moderate Protestant, liberal Protestant, Catholic, and Jew) and strength of commitment (less devout, more devout) as factors.

Next, adopting the proposition that the structure of ideology varies among affiliational groups, separate principal-components solutions were calculated for each affiliational group. An attempt was made to replicate the common solution for each group; that is, the five-component solution was calculated for each group and compared to the common solution.

RESULTS

Five dimensions emerged from the common principal-components analysis. There are only a few minor differences in the structure of the present

Table 1. Attitudinal Items Included in the Principal-Components Analysis

Variable	Item
BusReg	Less government regulation of business would be good for the country.
Law > $	The American legal system mainly favors the wealthy.
CapFair	The American private enterprise system is generally fair to working people.
Abort	It is a woman's right to decide whether or not to have an abortion.
GayTeach	Lesbians and homosexuals should not be allowed to teach in public schools.
Envir	Our environmental problems are not as serious as people have been led to believe.
Revol	The U.S. needs a complete restructuring of its basic institutions.
PubOwn	Big corporations should be taken out of private ownership and run in the public interest.
Adltry	It is wrong for a married person to have sexual relations with someone other than his or her spouse.
GaySex	It is wrong for adults of the same sex to have sexual relations.
CIA	It is sometimes necessary for the CIA to protect U.S. interests by undermining hostile governments.
FP > Bus	The main goal of U.S. foreign policy has been to protect U.S. business interests.
USSR	We should be more forceful in our dealings with the Soviet Union even if it increases the risk of war.
Poverty	In general, people are poor because of circumstances beyond their control rather than lack of effort.
BlPov	In general, Blacks don't have the motivation or willpower to pull themselves out of poverty.
Bl > Wh	Almost all the gains made by Blacks in recent years have come at the expense of Whites.
MilPow	It is important for America to have the strongest military force in the world, no matter what it costs.
WomWork	A woman with young children should not work outside the home unless it is financially necessary.
Socism	The U.S. would be better off if it moved toward socialism.
Crime	There is too much concern in the courts for the rights of criminals.

study and Lerner et al. (1996). The first (PC I) includes items concerning foreign and domestic threats to the status quo; it is identified as "regime threat." The second dimension (PC II) includes items about the present U.S. economic system; it is identified as "capitalism." The third dimension (PC III) is made up of items concerning individual morality and social norms; it is identified as "expressive individualism." The fourth dimension (PC IV) contains items relating to the desirability of massive economic restructuring; it is identified as "socialism." The final dimension (PC V) includes two items about race issues; it is identified as "race" (this represents attitudes on two racial issues, not racial identity). The structure of the common analysis is given in Table 2.

To tease apart the effects of affiliation and commitment, two-way ANOVAs were calculated for the principal-component dimensions of re-

Table 2. Principal-Components Structure of Attitudinal Items, Common Analysis[a]

Regime Threat	Capitalism	Expressive Individualism	Socialism	Race
USSR	Law > $	Abort	PubOwn	BlPov
Crime	CapFair	GaySex	Socism	Bl > Wh
MilPow	FP > Bus	Adltry	Revol	
CIA	Poverty	WomWork		
Envir	*BusReg*	GayTeach		
BusReg				
		% Var		
15.1	8.8	7.2	5.9	5.4

[a] Italicized items load on more than one component. Only items with loadings greater than or equal to .40 are included. Total variance accounted for: 42.4%. $N = 1009$.

gime threat, capitalism, and expressive individualism, and for "self-described ideology" (respondents' answers placing themselves on a liberal-to-conservative continuum). No differences were found for socialism and race—they were thus excluded from this analysis.

On regime threat, there is a significant main effect for affiliation ($F = 8.21$, $p < .05$), but not for commitment. The three Protestant groups, themselves alike, were more conservative on this dimension than either Catholics or Jews (see Table 3).

Table 3. Analysis of Variance for Regime Threat by Religious Affiliation and Strength of Commitment

Source	df	SS	MS	F	p<
Overall Test	7	3914.56	434.95	4.21	.05
Main Effects					
Affiliation	4	3394.33	848.58	8.21	.05
Commitment	1	2.42	2.42	0.02	n.s.
Interaction					
Affil × Commit	4	347.24	86.81	0.84	n.s.
Within	765	79084.31	103.38		
Total	774	82998.87			

Affiliation

[mean/(n)] Commitment	Jew	Cons. Prot.	Mod. Prot.	Lib. Prot.	Cath.	Total
Less devout	102.92	96.56	95.56	97.48	100.26	99.90
	(137)	(14)	(58)	(56)	(56)	(321)
More devout	100.35	96.66	98.03	97.17	100.12	98.94
	(24)	(52)	(85)	(62)	(231)	(454)
Total	102.54	96.64	97.03	97.32	100.15	99.34
	(161)	(66)	(143)	(118)	(287)	(775)

Table 4.   Analysis of Variance for Capitalism by Religious Affiliation and Strength of Commitment

Source	df	SS	MS	F	p<
Overall Test	7	2859.23	317.69	3.26	.05
Main Effects					
Affiliation	4	2047.25	511.81	5.25	.05
Commitment	1	1.69	1.69	0.02	n.s.
Interaction					
Affil × Commit	4	697.93	174.48	1.79	n.s.
Within	765	74561.04	97.47		
Total	774	77420.27			

			Affiliation			
[mean/(n)]		*Cons.*	*Mod.*	*Lib.*		
Commitment	*Jew*	*Prot.*	*Prot.*	*Prot.*	*Cath.*	*Total*
Less devout	102.64	99.48	97.28	96.10	100.29	100.16
	(137)	(14)	(58)	(56)	(56)	(321)
More devout	99.06	99.61	100.20	97.04	99.68	99.38
	(24)	(52)	(85)	(62)	231)	(454)
Total	102.11	99.58	99.02	96.60	99.99	99.70
	(161)	(66)	(143)	(118)	(287)	(775)

Table 4 provides the results of the ANOVA for the capitalism dimension. Again, there is a significant main effect for affiliation, but not for commitment. Jews are least conservative on capitalism, and liberal Protestants are most conservative. Conservative Protestants, moderate Protestants, and Catholics fell between the two other groups, all at about the midpoint.

The results of the comparisons for expressive individualism are given in Table 5. Both affiliation and commitment are significantly related to this ideological dimension. The interaction is also significant. The more devout of all faiths were more conservative than the less devout of all faiths. The difference between more and less devout Catholics was enormous—about ten points, or one standard deviation; this difference among liberal Protestants was minimal. For moderate and conservative Protestants and for Jews, this difference was substantial. Less devout Jews were least conservative and more devout Catholics were most conservative on this dimension.

Affiliation is significantly related to self-described ideology, as indicated in Table 6. There is no significant effect for commitment. Jews identified as least conservative. Moderate Protestants and Catholics identified somewhat more conservative than Jews, but still on the liberal side of the scale. Liberal Protestants were at about the midpoint. Only conservative Protestants identified as conservative in political view. In sum, with the important exception of the expressive individualism dimension, these analyses indicate that religious affiliation itself is more significant than religious commitment in deter-

Table 5. Analysis of Variance for Expressive Individualism by Religious Affiliation and Strength of Commitment

Source	df	SS	MS	F	p<
Overall Test	7	19578.62	2175.40	28.03	.05
Main Effects					
Affiliation	4	3704.67	926.17	11.93	.05
Commitment	1	6276.42	6276.42	80.87	.05
Interaction					
Affil × Commit	4	1098.64	274.66	3.54	.05
Within	765	59376.20	77.62		
Total	774	78954.82			

			Affiliation			
[mean/(n)]		Cons.	Mod.	Lib.		
Commitment	Jew	Prot.	Prot.	Prot.	Cath.	Total
Less devout	105.63	101.32	101.70	103.15	102.15	103.69
	(137)	(14)	(58)	(56)	(56)	(321)
More devout	97.09	94.40	96.10	101.01	92.56	94.83
	(24)	(52)	(85)	(62)	231)	(454)
Total	104.36	95.87	98.37	102.03	94.43	98.50
	(161)	(66)	(143)	(118)	(287)	(775)

Table 6. Analysis of Variance for Self-described Ideology by Religious Affiliation and Strength of Commitment

Source	df	SS	MS	F	p<
Overall Test	7	212.86	23.65	9.51	.05
Main Effects					
Affiliation	4	140.77	35.19	14.15	.05
Commitment	1	3.61	3.61	1.45	n.s.
Interaction					
Affil × Commit	4	12.32	3.06	1.23	n.s.
Within	765	1902.56	2.49		
Total	774	2115.42			

			Affiliation			
[mean/(n)]		Cons.	Mod.	Lib.		
Commitment	Jew	Prot.	Prot.	Prot.	Cath.	Total
Less devout	5.41	3.93	4.05	4.14	4.30	4.69
	(137)	(14)	(58)	(56)	(56)	(321)
More devout	4.67	3.60	4.27	3.97	4.17	4.12
	(24)	(52)	(85)	(62)	231)	(454)
Total	5.30	3.67	4.18	4.05	4.20	4.35
	(161)	(66)	(143)	(118)	(287)	(775)

Table 7. Principal-Components Structure of Attitudinal Items for Nonaffiliated Respondents[a]

PC1	PC2	PC3	PC4	PC5
CapFair	Crime	PubOwn	GayTeach	Bl > Wh
Poverty	*MilPow*	Socism	Abort	Womwork
Law > $	CIA	Revol	GaySex	*MilPow*
BusReg	USSR	*BusReg*	Envir	
FP > Bus	Adltry		BlPov	

		% Var		
13.1	9.9	7.5	6.8	6.1

[a] Italicized items load on more than one component. Only items with loadings greater than or equal to .40 are included. Total variance accounted for: 43.5%. *N* = 229.

mining political views. For expressive individualism, both aspects of religiosity, and their interaction term, had significant effects.

The next step in the analysis was to calculate the principal-components structure for each of the affiliational groups. There is evidence of differences in the structure of ideology among the groups, which means that some of the issues in question load onto different components for the different groups. For the unaffiliated, the first principal component is similar to the capitalism component in the common analysis. Regime threat is the second component, and has picked up the adultery item. Socialism is the third component. The final two components are considerably different than those in the common solution. The two items about race loaded on different components. The two items about homosexuality and the abortion item loaded on the same component, but it also included the environmentalism and Black poverty items, and lost the item about women working. The five components accounted for 43.5 percent of the variance. The component structure is given in Table 7.

Among Jewish respondents, regime threat is the first component. Two items from the capitalism dimension in the common analysis ended up on the regime threat component here. Socialism was the second component, and it picked up the two remaining capitalism items. Attitude toward capitalism, then, is not a distinct ideological dimension for Jews. The two items about homosexuality and adultery loaded on the same component, with the addition of the item on Black poverty. Abortion loaded on a different component. Explained variance for the five components is 45.9 percent; the component structure is given in Table 8.

The first component for conservative Protestants includes most of the expressive individualism items and two of the capitalism items. It accounts for almost 19 percent of the variance. Regime threat is the second compo-

Table 8. Principal-Components Structure of Attitudinal Items for Jews[a]

PC1	PC2	PC3	PC4	PC5
Crime	Socism	GaySex	Womwork	Bl > Wh
USSR	PubOwn	GayTeach	Envir	Abort
MilPow	Revol	BlPov	*FP > Bus*	
BusReg	Poverty	Adltry		
Law > $	*FP > Bus*			
CapFair				
		% Var		
13.7	11.3	8.1	6.8	6.0

[a] Italicized items load on more than one component. Only items with loadings greater than or equal to .40 are included. Total variance accounted for: 45.9%. *N* = 161.

nent, with the addition of the Black poverty item. The fourth component also has a regime threat character. Taken together, the five components account for 51.9 percent of the variance. Component structure is given in Table 9.

The first component for moderate Protestants has a regime threat quality. It includes some of the regime threat items in the common analysis but with the addition of the adultery, socialism, foreign policy, and one of the homosexuality items. It accounts for more than 16 percent of the variance. The second component is a mixture of regime threat, capitalism, and socialism items. The two race items loaded on the same component, picking up the foreign policy and poverty items. The abortion item did not load with the other expressive individualism items. The five components together account for 47.9 percent of the variance. Component structure is given in Table 10.

For liberal Protestants, a regime threat item is the first component. It

Table 9. Principal-Components Structure of Attitudinal Items for Conservative Protestants[a]

PC1	PC2	PC3	PC4	PC5
GayTeach	USSR	FP > Bus	Envir	Bl > Wh
Abort	CIA	Poverty	Crime	*Adltry*
Adltry	*BusReg*	*PubOwn*	*BlPov*	*PubOwn*
Law > $	*CapFair*	MilPow	Revol	
WomWork	*BlPov*	Socism		
CapFair		GaySex		
		BusReg		
		% Var		
18.9	11.1	7.7	7.6	6.5

[a] Italicized items load on more than one component. Only items with loadings greater than or equal to .40 are included. Total variance accounted for: 51.9%. *N* = 66.

Table 10. Principal-Components Structure of Attitudinal Items for Moderate Protestants[a]

PC1	PC2	PC3	PC4	PC5
USSR	CIA	Bl > Wh	Womwork	Abort
Crime	PubOwn	FP > Bus	GayTeach	Revol
Adltry	Law > $	BlPov	*GaySex*	MilPow
BusReg	*Poverty*	*Poverty*		
Socism	CapFair			
FP > Bus	Envir			
GaySex				

		% Var		
16.6	9.4	8.9	6.9	6.0

[a] Italicized items load on more than one component. Only items with loadings greater than or equal to .40 are included. Total variance accounted for: 47.9%. *N* = 143.

includes the USSR, military power, and crime items, but also the homosexuality items. It accounted for more than 15 percent of the variance. The second component includes the capitalism items, and picked up the Black-White item. The expressive individualism items did not load on a single component, suggesting a difference in the way liberal Protestants think about these issues. The five components together account for 47.5 percent of the variance. Component structure is given in Table 11.

Capitalism was the first component for Catholics, accounting for about 13 percent of the variance. Regime threat was the second component, picking up one of the homosexuality items. Expressive individualism was the third component. Three items did not load on any of the components. Taken

Table 11. Principal-Components Structure of Attitudinal Items for Liberal Protestants[a]

PC1	PC2	PC3	PC4	PC5
USSR	Law > $	BlPov	CIA	PubOwn
GayTeach	CapFair	Socism	WomWork	FP > Bus
GaySex	Poverty	Adltry		Abort
MilPow	BusReg	Envir		
Crime	Bl > Wh	Revol		
	FP > Bus			

		% Var		
15.3	10.5	8.5	7.0	6.2

[a] Italicized items load on more than one component. Only items with loadings greater than or equal to .40 are included. Total variance accounted for: 47.5%. *N* = 118.

Table 12.   Principal-Components Structure of Attitudinal Items for Catholics[a]

PC1	PC2	PC3	PC4	PC5
Poverty	GayTeach	GaySex	USSR	Socism
Law > $	Crime	Adltry	*BusReg*	PubOwn
FP > Bus	CIA	Abort	*FP > Bus*	
CapFair	Envir	Womwork		
Bl > Wh				
BusReg				
		% Var		
13.3	9.3	7.7	6.2	5.7

[a] Italicized items load on more than one component. Only items with loadings greater than or equal to .40 are included. Total variance accounted for: 42.3%. $N = 287$.

together, the five components accounted for 42.3 percent of the variance. Component structure is given in Table 12.

DISCUSSION

As the results of the present analysis show, the relationship between affiliation, commitment, and ideology is far from simple. Ideology is a multi-dimensional phenomenon, varying in both content and structure among various social and religious groups. The effect of religion is different for the various ideological dimensions. Some of the dimensions showed a consistent affiliational pattern, but some did not. A stronger religious commitment is not always associated with greater conservatism. The more devout appeared to be more conservative on expressive individualism, but not on regime threat or capitalism. On socialism and race, there was no effect for affiliation or commitment.

The effect of the religion variables was strongest on the ideological dimension concerning issues of individual morality. On this dimension, those with a stronger commitment tended to be more conservative than those with a weaker commitment. The effect of commitment was greatest for Catholics. Although, as a group, Jews tended to be more liberal than Christians, the interaction shows that the less devout of whatever affiliation tended to be less conservative than the more devout. Merely identifying with a religious group does not always entail holding conservative attitudes about morality.

Many, though not all, of the expected results were supported by the data. With respect to differences in the content of ideology, the data showed that liberal Protestants were more conservative than the other affiliations on capitalism, and that the more devout of this group were most conservative of all. Although conservative Protestants were more conservative on expressive individualism than other Protestants, Catholics proved to be just as conservative. More devout Catholics were the most conservative of all. The difference between more and less devout conservative Protestants was largest on this dimension, as was expected. Indeed, there were no differences between the more and less devout of this affiliation on the other dimensions. Contrary to expectations, no significant differences among Protestants were found on regime threat. More devout moderate Protestants were most conservative and less devout moderate Protestants were least conservative, but all the Protestant groups, more and less devout, were similar. Catholics and Jews were least conservative on this dimension.

Catholics were at the midpoint of the scale on capitalism and regime threat, but farther to the right on expressive individualism. As with conservative Protestants, the difference between the more and less devout Catholics was largest on this dimension. Jews were least conservative on all the dimensions, though the more devout were more conservative than the less devout on all three dimensions.

The data suggest the possibility that groups differ in terms of ideological content and structure. It was expected that expressive individualism would be the most important dimension for conservative Protestants. It was the first component, accounting for almost 19 percent of the variance. No other group placed as great an emphasis on individual morality, at least as measured by explanatory power of the individual components. The expressive individualism component did not, however, include many more items for conservative Protestants than it did in the common analysis. Two capitalism items were included, but the item about homosexual relations loaded on a different component.

Jews tended to see the capitalism dimension differently than the other groups; it did not emerge as a separate dimension for this group. Items about homosexuality and adultery loaded on the same component, but women's rights and abortion loaded on different components. This suggests that Jews also see expressive individualism differently than the other affiliational groups. Their perspective, in this regard, is similar to those with no affiliation.

The effect of commitment does not appear to amplify the effect of affiliation, as the socialization hypothesis would suggest. Commitment yielded a significant independent effect only on expressive individualism. There were affiliational differences on three of the five ideological dimensions, but these differences do not form a clear pattern. Conservative Protestants were most conservative only on the regime threat dimension, though they self-identified as most conservative. Liberal Protestants were most conservative on the capitalism dimension and Catholics were most conservative on expressive individualism.

Lerner et al. (1996) found ideological differences among occupational groups. Traditional elites, such as business and military, tended to be most conservative along all dimensions. New cultural elites, including media and public interest, tended to be least conservative. The effect of occupation may be confounding the religion effects. Because of the uneven distribution of religious affiliations among occupational groups, however, it is impossible to control for occupation in the present data. It would form a profitable area for future research.

Gender is also a probable confounding variable. The relatively small number of women in the sample made it difficult to control for gender. The CSSPC is collecting a new wave of data from a sample of elites, with better gender balance, so it will be possible to examine the effect of gender on the religion-ideology relationship.

Kellstedt et al. (1994) suggest that old political alliances based on affiliational groups are being replaced by new ones based on ideology. Conservatives from many Christian affiliations are joining together in political activity. The results from the present study hint that the ideological motivation for this realignment is social conservativism, particularly attitudes toward abortion and homosexuality. These issues seem to have taken a more central role in public political discourse in the 1990s. Whether or not this dimension has created a long-term shift in political allegiances remains to be seen, since the realignment does not seem to extend beyond the issues associated with expressive individualism.

The pattern of differences evidenced for expressive individualism does not hold on the other ideological dimensions. The current political oppositions, then, might be subject to further shifts, as other issues come to the fore. In the aftermath of the 1996 elections, both parties might be looking for a new strategy, based on economic issues rather than the divisive social ones. The possible emergence of a third party adds more uncertainty. The data in the present study suggest that new alliances might be based on affiliational groups. Protestants may come into opposition with Catholics, Jews, and secularists if the new voting blocs are defined by economic issues, for example.

NOTE

1.   According to Davidson (1994), in the late 1970s, liberal Protestants made up about 32 percent of the American elites. Moderate Protestants constituted another 21 percent, and conservative Protestants 7 percent. Thus, about 60 percent of American

elites identified as Protestant. Catholics made up 16 percent and Jews just 5 percent. Davidson points out that, despite some gains by other groups, America's elites are predominantly liberal Protestant.

REFERENCES

Davidson, James D. 1994. "Religion among America's Elite: Persistence and Change in the Protestant Establishment." *Sociology of Religion* 55(4):419–40.

Hayes, Bernadette C. 1995. "The Impact of Religious Identification on Political Attitudes: An International Comparison." *Sociology of Religion* 56(2):177–94.

Kellstedt, Lyman A., John C. Green, James L. Guth, and Corwin E. Smidt. 1994. "Religious Voting Blocs in the 1992 Election: The Year of the Evangelical?" *Sociology of Religion* 55(3):307–26.

Lerner, Robert, Althea K. Nagai, and Stanley Rothman. 1996. *American Elites.* New Haven, CT: Yale University Press.

Miller, Alan S. 1996. "The Influence of Religious Affiliation on the Clustering of Social Attitudes." *Review of Religious Research* 37(3):219–32.

Norusis, Marija J. 1994. *SPSS Advanced Statistics.* Chicago: SPSS.

Pyle, Ralph E. 1993. "Faith and Commitment to the Poor: Theological Orientation and Support for Government Assistance Measures." *Sociology of Religion* 54(4):385–401.

Roof, Wade Clark, and William McKinney. 1987. *American Mainline Religion.* New Brunswick, NJ: Rutgers University Press.

Shortell, Timothy. 1995. "A Comparison of The Dimensions of Ideology of Mainline Protestants, Born Again Christians and Catholics in the United States: Some Preliminary Findings." Jahnige Center Research Reports, Smith College, Northampton, Massachusetts, number 1 (http://socsci.smith.edu/jweb/paper1.htm).

Wuthnow, Robert. 1973. "Religious Commitment and Conservatism: In Search of an Elusive Relationship." In *Religion in Sociological Perspective,* edited by Charles Glock. Belmont, CA: Wadsworth.

II

CULTURE WARS WITHIN INSTITUTIONS

6

Culture Wars?
Insights from Ethnographies of Two Protestant Seminaries

JACKSON W. CARROLL and PENNY LONG MARLER

Late- or postmodernity has fostered competing religious and moral visions in American society. Two recent and widely discussed works, Robert Wuthnow's *The Restructuring of American Religion* (1988) and James Davison Hunter's *Culture Wars* (1991), discuss these competing visions. Among the important issues involved are questions of the sources of truth and interpretive authority. In this chapter, we present case studies, based on extensive ethnographic research over a three year period, of the culture of two U.S. theological schools. In these schools, one liberal Protestant and the other conservative Protestant, questions of truth and interpretive authority are articulated and negotiated in strikingly different ways. Indeed, since these are institutions that educate religious elites, the cases offer important insights into broader cultural dynamics.

In *The Restructuring of American Religion,* Robert Wuthnow (1988) analyzes religious responses to social change in the post–World War II period. In particular he considers shifting symbolic boundaries in U.S. religious institutions. Responses to social change have encouraged ideological conflict, competition, and resource mobilization of special purpose groups within and across traditional denominational boundaries as liberal moral visions clash with more conservative conceptions. The result is what James Davison Hunter (1991) has called a "contemporary culture war."

In Hunter's view (pp. 43–44), the battle lines form around "orthodoxy," with its commitment to an external, transcendent authority, and "progressivism," with its finger on the pulse of the modern *zeitgeist,* especially the "spirit of rationalism and subjectivism." These competing moral visions, Hunter claims, lie at the heart of the present cleavage in American culture. They, in turn, are fundamentally religious in character; that is, they are based on "systems of faith" which make "claims to truth about the world" (ibid., 56).

Both Hunter and Wuthnow observe that, to the extent that clearly differentiated moral visions exist, they do so especially in the public rhetoric and actions of elites who play important roles in shaping the debate on either side. The most influential of these elites, however, are not the university intellectuals, but middle elites, so-called "knowledge workers," including the clergy and religious administrators of all denominations and faiths.

In this chapter, we use data gathered for another purpose to shed light on the culture wars thesis, especially the issue of the sources of truth and interpretive authority in the two visions. The data are from a three-year ethnographic study of two Protestant theological seminaries aimed at assessing the role of a seminary's culture in the formation of students.[1] The data allow us to look at the "seedbeds" (the literal meaning of the word *seminarium*), where the perspectives of religious middle elites are nurtured and formed, for clues about the shape and function of their moral visions. Because one of our schools stands within conservative or evangelical Protestantism and the other within liberal or mainline Protestantism, our data should shed some light on the culture wars thesis. As Hunter notes, these two Protestant streams are major contributors to the disparate moral visions that lie behind the culture wars.

The data were collected by teams of two researchers at each of the two schools. The researchers spent thirty or more days a year for three years (1989–1992) at each school living in dormitories, attending classes and faculty gatherings, eating with students and faculty, participating in campus events, and visiting students in local church and student fieldwork settings. They also conducted lengthy focused interviews with students who began their programs in 1989, and with the majority of the faculty of each school.[2]

We begin with a series of vignettes from each school, drawn from our ethnographies. The vignettes provide insight into the ways that questions of truth and interpretive authority are articulated and negotiated in each context. Then we link ethnographic insights to literature on the sources of these moral visions. Finally, we revisit the question of "culture wars" in American religion.

EVANGELICAL THEOLOGICAL SEMINARY:
TRUTH AS OBJECTIVELY GIVEN

Chapel services at Evangelical Theological Seminary (hereafter ES) are held three days a week. Today, the preacher is one of the younger New Testament professors and a popular figure on campus. The service is well-attended.

The pews of the attractive but plainly adorned chapel are arranged in a fan-shape and face the dais, the central feature of which is the pulpit. The Dean of the Chapel, the preacher, and three well-dressed students sit on the platform.

The service begins with a hymn sung to an organ accompaniment: "My faith has found a resting place, Not in device or creed; / I trust the Everliving One, His wounds for me shall plead. / I need no other argument, I need no other plea, / It is enough that Jesus died, and that he died for me." As the hymn concludes, the Dean of the Chapel welcomes the worshippers and announces that "Joseph will now lead us in prayer." Joseph, a student dressed in coat and tie, moves to the lectern and begins to pray, punctuating his prayer repeatedly with the phrase, "Father I pray. . . . "

The Dean stands again to introduce the next parts of the service. He comments on the preacher and then turns to one of the students, a young woman with long, dark hair and wearing a black dress. He instructs, "Now Sue, you come and sing for us." Accompanied by a tape, she sings a popular Christian song, the pivotal line of which is: "I wonder would I know you now." Sue has a low, breathy voice that enhances the romantic tone of the song. A male student reads the scripture from I Corinthians 15, with its central focus on the reality of Christ's Resurrection.

The preacher, Robert Williams, has an animated, nervous manner. All eyes are riveted on him. Apologizing for beginning his sermon with a personal story, which he usually avoids, he says that his heart beats faster when he speaks of the Resurrection. That is because he is obsessed with death; he dreams about it regularly and wakes up terribly upset. So, he says, he likes to think that God rose for him. He likes to think that so that he can sleep at night. But he hopes that his audience can hear the lie in those words. The Resurrection, Williams says, was done not for his sake but for God's sake, and his whole happiness is in that. He continues to speak of the reality of the Resurrection and how it and the whole gospel way of thinking are so antithetical to the way that we think. Then he returns once more to his central point (what follows is a close paraphrase of Williams's words):

> The point is this: Denying the possibility of the Resurrection would mean something horrendous to God. God would be a liar. If God is a liar, you can't get God's benefits. . . . It robs the gospel of its power. It's not enough for me, when I wake up sweating, to know that I have the prospect of a risen soul, a spiritual high, or a thousand years of Christ's reign like the Jehovah's Witnesses. The issue is the right doctrine about God. If we preach wrong, your faith is futile, and the end is the grave. . . . Dear preachers: please remember that preaching precedes application. The only way is sound biblical preaching.

In a concluding prayer, Williams prays: "Father, thank you for raising Jesus from the dead. Apart from the empty tomb, I would be drowning my sorrows in success, substances and self-help. Help us, that we may not misrepresent you or give you false hopes."

The Normative Core

The sermon theme and the rather austere worship style that gives central place to biblical preaching are not unusual at ES. The school is non-denominational, with over seven hundred students (including certificate and part-time students as well as those in degree programs) and approximately twenty-six full-time faculty.[3] Students are mostly White and the majority are male (approximately 70 percent). Asian-Americans, especially Koreans, constitute a growing ethnic minority. There is a small number of African-American students. Approximately 50 percent of the 103 students who entered in 1989 were enrolled in the Master of Divinity degree program, preparatory to ordination as ministers. Just over 20 percent of the 103 expressed an intention to become pastors. Counseling, teaching, evangelism, missions, and youth ministry were some of the other vocational choices. Students come from a variety of mainline and evangelical Protestant denominations.

The school views itself as guarding "the essentials of the Reformation faith," while allowing "freedom in the formulation of the non-essentials." Its Mission Statement declares that the school is united around "the twin convictions . . . of the abiding truth of God's written Word and the centrality of Christ's saving work." "Provided these principles are honored, differences in denominational outlook and theological formulation are welcome," the Statement affirms.

The first article of the Mission Statement emphasizes the scriptural core: "To encourage students to become knowledgeable of God's inerrant Word, competent in its interpretation, proclamation, and application in the contemporary world." Other articles accentuate academic excellence, training in ministry skills, student spiritual growth, maintaining an evangelical presence in society, and developing a vision for God's redemptive work throughout the world. At the center, however, defining the school's normative core or "orthodoxy" is the commitment to sound interpretation of an inerrant scripture, using the original languages. One faculty member refers to this as "industrial strength exegesis." Students refer to this commitment as that which makes the school "solid," a word they used numerous times in speaking of their choice of ES.

Experience Is Not Enough

Prospective students hear this central message loud and clear when they visit the campus at a "Discover ES Weekend." Old Testament professor,

David Burns, has been asked to give students a taste of the academic life of the school. His lecture is titled, "How to Misinterpret the Twenty-Third Psalm and Other Famous Passages," and it reflects a course that he teaches on the "Uses and Abuses of the Bible."

His point of departure is a popular evangelical book, *A Shepherd Looks at the Twenty-Third Psalm,* that has sold over a million copies. While the book is well intentioned, says Burns, and many have been blessed by it, it is, nevertheless, an example of "world-view confusion." It uses one's own world-view and experience to interpret the text and fails to understand that the text was written from a very different world-view. The Psalm, he argues, is not primarily about sheep and shepherding, and the question is whether the author's experience as a shepherd gives him interpretive expertise when the Psalm moves beyond references to sheep and shepherding. Burns tells the prospective students that he is not trying to impugn the author's motives, but emphasizing that good intentions in biblical interpretation are not enough. He concludes:

> The concern of ES is for careful, accurate interpretation. Languages are crucial. Our real goal is to make scripture applicable in a very proper way so that it will guide belief and action.

Right Thinking and Solidity

Faculty teaching styles reinforce the school's commitment to right thinking based on accurate scriptural interpretation and Reformed theology. Pedagogy is generally didactic. Lecturing is the preferred mode, especially for those in the Divisions of Biblical Studies and Christian Thought.[4] In an interview, James Rivers, Professor of Theology, says that his goal in lectures is

> not a question just of laying out doctrines and getting [students] to learn them. It's more a question of replicating in themselves the habits of thought that you find in the scripture. Undoubtedly [this does] yield a . . . set of doctrinal crystals. . . . But it's a way of thinking that needs to be replicated, [one] that needs to be brought into contact with our modern world.

"Getting Things Straight"

Rivers's comment makes an important point about ES. Students are not "force fed" the core message of the culture. While the normative core is presented with considerable vigor and clarity, students are encouraged to negotiate a stance toward it. And negotiate they do! Students have enormous theological energy. As one listens to dormitory discussions, deliberations at mealtime in the cafeteria, exchanges in hallways outside classrooms, one hears students engaged in a process that our research team came to call "getting things straight"—vigorous arguments with each other as they sharpen their understanding of God, the nature of the church, the obligations of Christians in the world, how Scripture should be studied, and other topics such as women's ordination, millennialism, the right way to do evangelism, or the place of music and art in the Christian life. At one lunchtime forum that featured a professor speaking about believer's baptism, more than sixty students showed up. A bulletin beard in a hallway outside the cafeteria is called "Iron Sharpens Iron" and is the venue for lively exchanges. On it students place signed position papers, responses to other students' statements, clippings from the media, and cartoons—most of which are arguments for or against some doctrinal or ethical position. A typical board may include an article damning abortion, a discussion (pro and con) of the Robert Mapplethorpe exhibit showing at a nearby art museum, a theological rationale for women's ordination, and another arguing the need for women to be submissive to their husbands on biblical grounds.

Student efforts to "get things straight" aim both at gaining clarity about core commitments that the school's culture upholds and also negotiating a position on issues within the culture where legitimate differences of opinion are allowed.

As to core commitments, in addition to those previously noted, world missions and evangelization get considerable emphasis; and, although it is not stated in the school's official documents, a right-to-life stance on abortion gets widespread support. One faculty member commented that opposing abortion "has become the social badge of honor [for Evangelicals]. It defines you culturally and institutionally as an Evangelical [much as] inerrancy has done."

Diversity

Areas on which there can be legitimate differences include: the role of women in the church, including women's ordination; the use of inclusive language; some aspects of charismatic theology, including whether the Holy Spirit continues to perform "signs and wonders" beyond the end of the Apostolic age; and whether there are avenues to God's truth in addition to careful interpretation of scripture.

A particularly spirited exchange occurred over a poster placed on the "Iron Sharpens Iron" board by a student group, Partners for Biblical Equality (PBE). The group supports male-female equality, including the ordination of women, from an evangelical perspective. PBE members are particularly opposed to those who use certain biblical texts (interpreted as culture-bound and therefore nonbinding) to place women in subordinate, submissive roles.

The controversial poster used a drawing based on a verse from the prophet Joel, "and your sons and daughters shall prophesy," to challenge traditionalist opposition to the ordination of women. The poster caused so much acrimony that it had to be placed under glass on another bulletin board to prevent defacement.

The debate was also about the place of art and images as media for communicating truth. In an ensuing discussion in a student publication, one student contends that such images present a story, not an argument; therefore, they should not be used to argue the cause of important questions. "Will 'art' replace verbal articulation, or dance replace debate?" he asks. His opponent asserts the opposite: "the importance of communicating beyond words, and the cruciality of perceiving beyond the printed page. . . . [T]he power of an image can bypass our 'literary defenses' and pierce to our hearts." A faculty member agreed with the first student in a subsequent article entitled, "A Word is Worth A Thousand Pictures."

The Reform of Evangelicalism

To what end is all of this theological and ethical energy directed? One answer is that it is in the service of forming students, "replicating in [them] the habits of thought that you find in the scripture," as Rivers puts it. There is also another agenda. Many faculty members are concerned to combat the "acids of modernity." While this may seem consistent with Hunter's 'culture wars' thesis and in continuity with fundamentalist-modernist battles of the past, such assumptions miss an important point: The battle in which ES faculty members are engaged is not only with "secular humanists" or mainstream denominations that have adapted to modernity. Another important contest is with *fellow Evangelicals* who have taken modernity into their bosoms in an uncritical, atheological accommodation to the culture. Their opposition includes the sentimental, individualist, popular evangelical piety that many students exhibit, expressed for example in praise choruses and highly personalistic prayers. In particular, however, they oppose the sell-out to modernity of many Evangelical church and parachurch leaders who have adopted modern technology and marketing techniques to engineer growing churches at the cost, in the faculty's view, of attention to truth. Also, Dr. Kenneth Coates, one of the younger faculty members, notes that he and his colleagues opposed what they see as a shift of models of pastoral leadership away from an "older model: the pastor as the broker of truth," to models that emphasize "the pastor as therapist" or the "pastor as the manager." Agreeing with Coates, Dr. Rivers says, "What you have is these manager types who are presiding over the Evangelical world who don't know how to replenish it and who have no vision as to where it should be going."

All of these groups, he and many of his colleagues contend, exhibit what they call "self-ism," a kind of subjectivization characteristic of modernity that idolatrously places the self and its needs at the center of things, usurping the proper place of God.

Getting the Message

Do students get this message? Based on our data, most do. While not "clones" of the ES's culture, most are formed or reinforced by the school's core commitments. With echoes from Burns's lecture to prospective students, these are the words of a student speaker at the school's commencement:

> Shame on us if the world is more studious and industrious than those committed to the Gospel. How can such a precious message be handled with mediocrity? The Christian minister must be a diligent student. . . . We live in a world that believes that what is sinful is normal and what is righteous is strange. But our Lord commands us to proclaim the Gospel. Without the Gospel promise that God will be with us, this commission would lead us to despair. God has called us to a ministry of the Word.

His words were met with loud "Amens" from fellow students.

Students also seem to get the message about "self-ism." Many come to be critical of therapeutic and technocratic models of ministry. Whether they will be "seduced" by these models after leaving the school, we cannot say. Most students, however, do not reject the expressions of piety connected with popular Evangelicalism. Rather, as one graduate told us, they learn to appreciate the more classical, Reformed styles of piety and discipline while continuing to enjoy the popular styles.

Some students, however, pay a price for their engagement with this culture and its definition of truth. A few find what they call "the one right answer" approach of some of the faculty more than they can take. They either leave, or find ways of minimizing the culture's impact, quietly reinterpreting some of its core elements in ways that enable them to survive. Women students pursuing ordination are at times discouraged and hurt by the attitudes of some fellow students and several faculty members who strongly oppose women's ordination, often on biblical grounds. One woman, the only one in a particular class, was asked by a male student why she was taking the course, since she was likely to end up "having babies" instead of using what the course taught.[5] Similarly, one of the small number of African-American students at the school commented that "I am at ES because [it] has a high regard of Scripture and because I felt that it was the most intellectually and doctrinally diverse of conservative, evangelical schools." But, he added, "I only wish that more of [them here] would . . . open their eyes and see that the real world is not a White, middle-class suburb."

The disenchantment and pain felt by such students are palpable, but they are a minority. Most, including those who are not happy with their experience, are strongly influenced by the moral vision they encounter in ES's culture.

MAINLINE SEMINARY: MANY VOICES, ONE FAITH

The fine, filtered sunlight of a winter midmorning plays across the refectory floor. On a large center stage diverse actors jump and twirl to a cacophony of sounds. The central figure is a Black man in bright African robes. As he careens around the perimeter, this young professor exposes a well-muscled calf in energetic kicks. The dance is also punctuated by drumbeats and the responsive chants of two African students in their own tribal dress. Behind them, several Korean women in intricately embroidered silks gently sway to the lilting strains of harp and *ching*.

The congregation leans slightly forward as this dramatic invocation entitled, "Primeval Chaos," concludes with a responsive reading. "And God saw everything that God made, and behold, it was very good." Then, there is silence. And slowly, the rich, baritone chords of an American Black spiritual begin. The worship order hails the "good creation."

Suddenly, the scene shifts. The liturgy recounts the story of Babel: how the people of the earth set out to build a tower to the heavens to "make a name for ourselves" and how the Lord decided to "confuse their language, that they may not understand one another's speech." The liturgist, a Korean faculty member, instructs the congregation to shout in their native languages—spoken or signed: "Babel! Babel! Babel! Babel! A name for ourselves! A name for ourselves! A name for ourselves!"

All quiets as an African-American student begins to sing, "Sometimes I feel like a motherless child." Her song is followed by the Korean Han dance. A jet-haired, pink figure moves slowly and purposefully to an Oriental tune from a cassette recorder. The woman's face is impassive; her flowing arms and hands are delicate, yet strong and fraught with meaning. The worship order says that "Han" means sorrow and pain.

The final scene is Pentecost. And the liturgy states that, in this event, the "good creation" is reunited. The Scriptures are read aloud: "And there appeared to them tongues as of fire, distributed and resting on each one of them . . . and [they] began to speak in other tongues." Everyone is told to call out, "Christ is Lord." First in English; next in other dialects or "voices" including African dialects, Korean, Spanish, beating drums, clanging cymbals, and the motions of American Sign Language; and finally, all together.

"In the last days it shall be, God declares, that I will pour out my Spirit upon all flesh, and your sons and your daughters shall prophesy, and your young men shall see visions, and your old men shall dream dreams . . . ," the people read. After reciting the Lord's Prayer in many voices, worship ends with these sung words: "We are one in the spirit; we are one in the Lord. . . . And we pray that our unity may one day be restored. And they'll know we are Christians by our love, by our love. . . . " As the final note dies, each person—standing or sitting—holds the hand of the nearest neighbor.

Social diversity is imaged, experienced, and reimaged in the opening ritual of an "Issues Retreat" at Mainline Seminary (hereafter, MS) in early 1992: through African and Korean dress, music, and dance; in African-American spirituals; in the clash of many languages spoken and unspoken; through the choice of biblical images and themes emphasizing chaos and Spirit more than order and Law, heterogeneity more than homogeneity, action more than passive reception, and conventional roles turned upside-down like "daughters prophesying" in the context of a place for everyone, young and the old; and finally, in the reversal of power in the worship itself—no White male and only one White female lead despite the fact that the school is majority White, and the upper administration and faculty are majority White males.

Images of Diversity and Inclusivity

MS has a total enrollment of nearly four hundred, 60 percent of whom are in the Master of Divinity program leading to ordination. The remainder are enrolled in the Master of Religious Education (4 percent), Master of Theological Studies (11 percent), and Doctor of Ministry (12.5 percent) programs or are part-time "special students" who are not pursuing a degree (12.5 percent). Although MS is an official seminary of a particular mainline denomination, about 25 percent of the student body claims affiliation with another denominational group. Three-quarters identify with another mainline denomination; the rest are made up of Black Baptists and other Evangelicals.

While denominational diversity at MS is permitted, racial and gender diversity are explicitly encouraged. The most vivid image of such diversity is found on the faculty. Of twenty-four full-time faculty in 1992, nearly 30 percent were women and a little over 20 percent were Black or Hispanic.

Compared to the faculty, the student body is much more homogeneous. Although there have been significant gains among women, Blacks, Asians, and Hispanics in recent years, a 1992 enrollment study self-consciously highlights the schools' growing female and Black constituency. In 1982, 24 percent of all Master of Divinity students were women and 6 percent were Black. By 1992, the largest degree program at MS realized a four percentage point increase in the number of women (28 percent) and a seven percentage point increase in the number of Blacks (13 percent). The presence of a small number of Asian and Hispanic students brought the total of non-White Master of Divinity students to 15 percent. And even though seminary officials proudly marked this milestone, the statistical inventory was—as always—qualified by, "But we're not there yet."

In MS's catalogues and publicity material since the mid-1960s, there is a recurring picture. It is a rectangular grid composed of irregular boxes, all bounded by a stark white border. The pictures in the grid tend to shift as the constituency of the student body changes. In the 1989 catalogue, the grid appears opposite the school's "Mission and Ministry" statement. Upper left box: the largest square contains a shot of a married White male student in a white sweater, leaning forward over a book. Upper right: an attractive single White female in a dark sweater stares ahead intently; her arm rests on an open notebook. Middle left box: a baby-faced White male in a cable-stitched sweater vest puts finishing touches on a clay figurine. Middle right: an African man in native headdress poses in front of a library stack. Lower left box: a Korean student smiles warmly; he is dwarfed by a large, carved seal bearing the word "oikoumene." Lower right: a middle-aged White female takes notes in a large classroom. We have labeled this institutional image of social representation and proportionality, "matrix pluralism."

Images of diversity and inclusivity are not only embodied and publicized at MS, they are also dramatized and discussed. At the closing of New Student Orientation, the film "Places in the Heart" was shown. The movie traces the struggle of traditionally powerless persons—a woman, children, a blind man, and a Black man—against traditionally powerful White men in a small southwestern town. The film closes with a surrealistic Eucharist celebration set in a white-steeple-and-clapboard church. At the table are Ku Klux Klan members and the Black field hand they ran out of town; a bank president with the widowed woman, two children, and the blind brother he victimized; and finally, the Sheriff who was accidentally killed by a young Black man, and the young man himself, who was consequently lynched. In small group discussion afterwards, some students protested that the presence of Klan members defiled the ritual; most, however, talked about the last scene as an image of "true inclusivity" that is only accomplished through Christ. It is what one third-year student reminiscing about her time at MS

called "the vision of the kingdom [of God] as the perfectly inclusive, perfectly diverse unity" over against "the kingdom on earth" where "our human
structures always fail."

The Authority Of Experience

On a Monday evening in April, 1992, forty students gather around a
display of black-and-white angular drawings taped to a chalkboard. The
class, "Contemplative Drawing: A Path to the Fuller Self," is a popular
offering that meets a two-hour requirement in Religion and the Arts for all
Master of Divinity students. Carol Kane, an energetic and attractive professor, reviews student attempts to draw a chair with the aid of a viewfinder
and says, "What's important here? There are relationships to the bounding
edges of the format. There is the concept of shared edges, and there is the
relative relationship of the parts." One student complains about how hard it
is "to hold a viewfinder and draw at the same time; and then, to deal with
the layers of negative space." The technique, Dr. Kane explains sympathet-
ically, pushes you to engage the "whole brain."

The discussion turns to the creativity and pain of art as "birthing." Leaning
forward on the lectern, Dr. Kane intones: "The patriarchal church denies
birthing images; creativity requires birthing." A woman sitting close to the
front raises her hand and speaks authoritatively, "People resisting the arts are
patriarchal and patronizing." Another woman chimes in, "I took [the course]
'Women and Spirituality,' and we learned that Hildegaard envisioned an
egg. The men said, "You can't do that!" So they sent a male scribe to
illustrate her visions. In response she did her own illustration. They denied
her vision. . . . "

Referring to a reading by Matthew Fox, Dr. Kane draws parallels between
a more organic and cosmological way of viewing the world and the artistic
act. A Black woman responds, "I feel good about the expression of a holistic
worldview, especially the creation piece, you know; you are the creation
and the creator. There's no need for a hierarchy to tell you what to do."

Dr. Kane moves to application: "Okay, so you recognize this creative
ability in yourself and yet you know the world is full of problems. What do
you do as leaders of churches?" Another African-American woman responds, "You bring people in to be co-creators; that way, they're included."
With sudden animation Dr. Kane responds: "That's an approach! I've always
thought you could open up fellowship halls in churches and have opportunities for poor, indigent street people to come in and make something with
their hands. That's what I call 'power with'. . . . " A young White male adds,
"That reminds me of an empowerment model of counseling; I'm learning
that here, too."

How things are taught at MS matters almost as much as what is taught. Experiential learning is valued, and the action-reflection or "praxis" approach is favored. For example, a student panel discussion in a "Global Mission" class began with personal experiences of racism; moved to a discussion of what the Bible says about racism; then to a presentation of what the school's denomination and the World Council of Churches say about racism versus what they actually do; and ended with an invitation for students to act. Sign-up sheets for information about strategies to protest apartheid in South Africa were provided. In fact, action-reflection through art, drama, journaling, field trips, internships, and even social protest is valued so highly that more didactic presentations in large classes draw negative reviews. Talking about the required classes for the Master of Divinity degree, one student noted, "You really can't do a whole lot when you've got ninety people in the room in terms of hearing other voices and being sensitive, [you have to] really struggle to hear other opinions and learn to respect them. You can't."

And as in Carol Kane's class, *what* is taught supports the importance of reflection and action. With a few exceptions, phenomenological perspectives such as feminist theology, Black theology, process theology, social and anthropological theories, and third-world liberation theology are favored. Contextual and political sensitivities are heightened, and the use and abuse of power becomes a common theme. Consequently, traditional, external authority—namely, the patriarchal church and Eurocentric male truth—is frequently questioned. Especially telling is a 1990 classroom discussion about the Bible. In response to Dr. Diane Carpenter's query "Why don't MS students carry Bibles?" a United Church of Christ woman in Urban Ministry noted, somewhat wistfully, "If we found it authoritative, we would bring it with us." A United Methodist pastor added, "It's a question of which translation to carry; it's a political decision." She continued, "[Anyway] in worship I want to feel more than intellectualize." "It [intellectualizing] is 'White male,' patriarchal, and hierarchical. Some of us find it a burden," another mainline Protestant pastor—White male himself—insisted.

Oppression and intolerance are the gravest sins at MS, and the most sought-after remedy is the liberation and empowerment of traditionally marginalized groups. Still, most students and faculty would not reduce salvation to liberation. A Black South African pastor and visiting professor put it this way:

God has not withdrawn from human beings. Because God still talks, you have to relate the good news of the Gospel to the situation of oppression in South Africa. Liberation and salvation are not the same. Salvation relates to the calling of God. [But] nobody has salvation who can allow the organized oppression in South Africa. [Instead] salvation *leads to* liberation.

The primary vehicle for liberation and empowerment at MS is the group. Groups are allowed, even encouraged, to proliferate on campus. A large number are official, which means they have submitted a budget to the Seminary Council. Over a three-year period they included a woman's covenant group; an Evangelical association; Black seminarians; a Korean fellowship; a "liberation resources" center; a spiritual life committee; seminarians for gay, lesbian, and bisexual concerns; and a social action group, among others. More informal groups included: a Marx reading group; two feminist-womanist reading groups; a liturgics group; a gospel choir; a men's choir; and temporary groups organized around events such as a March for the Homeless and a National Organization for Women's Pro-Choice March. In addition, there are a number of impromptu groups, most in the dormitories, including in-room Bible studies and small-group worship services in the "Lovett Prayer Room"—a carpeted room bounded by a low bench with a central, oriental-style table always littered with candles and spent matches.

Among other things, campus groups provide a base for acting on issues which directly affect their members. For example, Black seminarians mobilized for removal of a White "Nefertiti doll" on exhibition at the campus. One woman described it this way:

> We had a Mexican stand-off because he [the Old Testament professor] told us that the doll wasn't coming out of the window. . . . And we had to regroup and replan our strategies. [At the next meeting] I made my little statement that the doll had to go and then this Black guy, this brother, got up and said the same thing. And so [the professor] said, you know, well, how do you propose to do that or something like that. So this guy came off with, "by any means necessary," you know. Some Malcolm X sounding thing, so we again had this impasse. We took the issue up with the Dean of Students, and it became a discussion for the faculty meeting and so forth. And we were very adamant about that, and the doll was out of the showcase in about two weeks.

While diverse, more homogeneous, student-run groups are effective forums for reflection and action, seminary-organized, inclusive groups enjoy less success. Students frequently complain about their "lack of real power" as "token" representatives on faculty and staff-led committees. And the Seminary Council which previously included representatives from students, faculty, administration, and staff dissolved in 1990–1991 in favor of an entirely student-run group. Also, required and assigned "Covenant" groups—while meaningful for a number of mainline Protestant students, particularly pastors—are referred to as "legislated spirituality" by others.

The Price of Inclusivity

Doug is Black, ex-Navy, and an Episcopalian. He works in the campus post office, lives in Seminary housing, is an official campus escort for visitors and prospective students, and a popular disc jockey for student parties. Talking with one of the authors about "campus taboos" over breakfast in a local pastry shop, he observed:

> I think if I stood up and said I supported the right of the Klan to exist, somebody would shoot me. Because that is not "politically correct." It speaks to the other side of the liberation theology issue that nobody wants to deal with. This is a "love your enemies" side of liberation theology.
>
> Unfortunately what happens when something gets to be a taboo is that if I, as a male, stand up and say that feminism is oppressive, I am told essentially, "You had better shut up." It is a function of my being male. . . . Sometimes celebration of maleness is not something you can do at MS. But celebration of femaleness, you can do that. . . . I think of myself as male, and I think I have an incredible sensitivity. As a matter of fact, I spend a lot of time covering that up. . . . Female friends of mine—and this is symbolic of Black theologians who say White people can't understand the suffering of Blacks—they say "well you can't really understand because you are not a female."
>
> After a while, it [all] really starts to eat away at your esteem. It is another form of oppression. If you are getting your esteem and your sense of wholeness from standing on my throat—none of us benefits, anymore than if I get my esteem from standing on yours. . . . I don't know the whole truth, you don't know the whole truth—truth is found in community.

Sam Rogers commutes a couple of times a week from a suburban church. Sam is confessedly "more conservative" than a lot of students; he describes another taboo, but very similar dynamics:

> I have felt real held back at some times. I think part of [my holding back] is the desire to keep dialogue and diversity at the expense of real proclamation of the gospel of Jesus Christ. And I would say, evangelical proclamation. I think it was [uncomfortable] for me at the very first. But I think because I have become more comfortable with my identity, with who I am, I don't feel intimidated at all. But I have to admit there are times . . . well, just, boldness is sometimes quenched.
>
> But, then, there have been times when there [has] been [a] very powerful sense of Christ's presence in worship. So, I think there is a certain grace in diversity. Yet, at times, a sort of self-absorbed hypocrisy really—in the diversity that you are not allowed. You can't accept the Evangelical. As long as you are a liberal activist-oriented person, it is okay, we will include you. But if you tend to be more charismatic or evangelical or towards those shades of Christianity, there is a little less acceptance, I think. I like to be challenged by somebody; even a Fundamentalist can challenge me in ways that a Unitarian/Universalist can't.

Karen James is what MS calls a "semi-commuter" student. She stays on-campus a couple of nights a week, and then travels to her church field. She is widowed, has a daughter in college, and is the new pastor of a mainline Protestant church. Karen's on-campus experience has been educative in ways she did not expect.

> I think I have come to a greater understanding of the pain of the Black community. When I came here I loved the community. Everybody seemed to be working together. Loving each other. I thought, "This is what the whole world should be." And we had our first class in Black liberation theology. And all of a sudden, I saw the anger. It was very painful, and I thought, why are they doing this at the seminary? Here we had the model. We were working together, and they are destroying it.
>
> And then suddenly, it wasn't until last year, I suddenly realized that this was the safe place to let all of that out . . . that we could be trusted to absorb that pain and help them to work it through. And then, in our own sense, grow also. . . . So I came full circle with that.

At MS there is continuous negotiation between the value of diversity for a truly inclusive community and the strains that inequity, suspicion, and even anger and confusion produce. Intolerance of the intolerant, by which is meant conservatives or traditionalists, is one fracture line. Reimaging the role and relationship of oppressors, by which is meant White males, is another fracture line. Coming to terms with the anger of the traditionally oppressed, which typically includes everyone except White males (but especially Blacks and women), constitutes still another fracture line. And finally, growing tension revolves around the institution's relationship to the sponsoring denomination and its mandate to educate pastors for local churches. Roy Anders, a second career student who is also a pastor, talks about holding the balance at MS:

> It's such a diverse place. We've got everyone from Southern Baptists to Unitarians. And I guess I have learned to appreciate a little bit the diversity of MS and how God's grace can work in that diversity. [It's] kind of neat. Probably two of the furthest people apart theologically in the entire group would be my roommate and I. And I usually find reality somewhere in between the way he perceives what is going on and the way I perceive what is going on.
>
> In many ways, students at MS have divorced life experiences from their perspectives. For example, you could just go storming off beating your fists against the desk and never see what was really happening to people in your local congregation—or that they just don't care to see it that way. I think there is grace in that pull for me: that people in my churches are far more conservative than I am and people here at school are far more liberal than I am, and it's important to learn from both of them. I figured that's what the Lord had in mind all along.

SOURCES OF THE TWO MORAL VISIONS

In Table 1, we summarize the dominant themes (contents and styles) of the moral vision embodied in each culture. We emphasize *dominant* themes, reminding the reader that the actual situation is less polar and more nuanced than the table implies.

The contrasting visions of truth, especially those emphases highlighted in Table 1, have an obvious affinity with the moral visions at the heart of Hunter's culture wars thesis. Each, in its own way, is a response to the Enlightenment and modernity, though each also is rooted in much earlier ways of understanding truth in the Christian tradition and in relation to theological formation (Kelsey 1992). These modern versions of the two visions were crystallized in the chaotic and expansive late nineteenth and early twentieth centuries: the orthodox vision in the fundamentalist movement; the progressive in the social gospel movement (Abell 1943). Although the movements failed in the 1920s, the core of these two visions lingered in the neo-Evangelical movement, of which ES is a direct heir, and in Protestant liberalism, the legacy of MS (Szasz 1982; Marsden 1980; Hutchison 1976; Hopkins 1940; Johnson 1940; White and Hopkins 1976).

ES's orthodox vision views truth as "out there," or more accurately, as "back there," instantiated in an inerrant Scripture. The task of the Christian—especially the theological scholar and the pastor—is to interpret the biblical text accurately so that it can be applied to issues of personal and social life. Before any application, however, there must be sound biblical preaching, based on careful exegesis using the original languages. The goal is to uncover the truth of the text while attempting to discipline the influence of the interpreter's own culture. Reason, especially "redeemed reason," as one ES faculty member puts it, and which includes common sense, is essential to the process. Thus, the primary avenue to truth is cognitive and rational, a style exhibited in the preferred didactic pedagogy.

As the various incidents from our data illustrate, the role of experience in the interpretive process is less clear. Even if not totally ruled out, it clearly is secondary to hard rational-cognitive work, as in Burns's lecture on interpreting Psalm 23. Likewise, preference for rational-cognitive approaches to truth lies behind the preferred pedagogical style and informs the debate over the use of art and other images as media of communication.

The battle against "self-ism," whether in the popular evangelical charismatic piety of the students or in the therapeutic and technocratic practices of many evangelical pastors and parachurch leaders, also reflects the school's view of truth. Popular Evangelicalism's sell-out to this subjective approach to truth strikes at the heart of the Reformed view of God as transcendent and of truth as objectively given.

Table 1. Cultural Contents and Styles

School	Dominant Epistemology	Interpretive Authority	Favored Pedagogy	Locus of Cultural Action	Formation Goal	Cultural Paradox
Evangelical	Cognitive-rational "getting it straight"	Scripture (external)	Didactic, Lecture	The individual	Orthodoxy	"One answer" vs. awareness of "other answers"
Mainline	Affective/behavioral "doing it right"	Experience (internal)	Experiential, Action-Reflection	The group	Orthopraxy	"Inclusivity" but "on whose terms?"

In ES's vision one can see the legacy of Reformed Puritan orthodoxy. There is also a connection between its interpretive strategy and Scottish "common sense" realism, which not only influenced earlier conceptions of science, but found strong theological expression at Princeton Theological Seminary in the late nineteenth and early twentieth centuries. Pregiven categories of reason, including one's common sense, resonate with the sensory world, making scientific knowledge of it possible. They also help to discipline cultural biases in the interpretation of Scripture (May 1976; Marsden 1980; Wells 1986).

Rather than viewing science as a strategy for unearthing given truths, MS's progressive vision embraces science as part and parcel of the unfolding truth.[6] For progressives, the truth is inherent in human beings and the natural order, and human experience is valued. As in the opening illustrations, this perspective is reflected at MS in the *structure* of worship (social diversity and inclusiveness) as well as the *content* of worship (chaos and creation, struggle and liberation). Similarly, it is supported both by *what* is taught (liberation and process theologies) and *how* it is taught (action and reflection).

For progressives, the truth is "in here"—inherent in human beings and the natural order, and "out there"—a state that the world is moving toward. Human judgment and experience are to be trusted. Advances of reason over the course of human experience are seen as positive steps toward ultimate purpose and truth. Consequently, traditional institutions and the beliefs that undergird them are subject to revision in the light of contemporary experience and/or the current standards of scientific advance; and, in contrast to the orthodox scheme, with its emphasis on individual initiative, the progressive position emphasizes social responsibility (May 1967, 1976; Nisbet 1980).

The late nineteenth century roots of these positions can be stated simply: for the orthodox, the problem with society is flawed individuals—the remedy, change individuals; for progressives, the problem is flawed social structures—the remedy, change structures. As a MS student observed, "truth is in community." Consequently, the seminary encourages group formation, and group action is the preferred channel for change. These smaller, homogeneous groups, however, are often in tension with the larger, heterogeneous community ideal. And the burden of social responsibility rests heaviest on those "in charge," i.e., White mates in general and the institution's administration in particular.

Because advances of reason are seen as positive steps toward ultimate truth in the progressive scheme, traditional institutions are always subject to revision in the light of contemporary experience. This characteristic is the source of liberalism's peculiar, ongoing negotiation of modernity. Keeping pace with and integrating "the modern" is difficult enough. The greatest challenge, however, has been adjusting to dramatic change in scientific self-understanding. Such has been the case in the latter half of the twentieth century.

THE CHALLENGE OF LATE-MODERNITY

If we can trace fundamental elements of two distinct, early twentieth century moral visions to the present-day cultures of the two schools, do we assume that these visions remain unaffected by subsequent cultural changes? No. In fact, our research indicates that both schools are significantly challenged by the late-modern situation. Anthony Giddens notes that late- or postmodernity is characterized by the subjectivity of truth claims and the necessity of self-evaluation and self-correction (Giddens 1991:15–17).[7] This being the case, the older progressive impulse which tends toward subjectivity and self-reflexivity—the "truth in here" and trust of individual human experience—finds new legitimation in the late-modern context. At the same time, the values and norms of older liberal institutions themselves are challenged.

MS reflects this late-modern shift. The culture explicitly promotes questioning of accepted liberal traditions. Passionate encounters across the boundary lines of MS's social matrix are the necessary refining fires for a late-twentieth century progressive faith. Out of the chaos of social diversity, there is confidence that a new creation, a new birth, will occur: the truly diverse, truly inclusive Kingdom of God. It is nineteenth century post-millennialism turned inside out: liberal values and institutions are unmasked, and the liberation or emancipation of the self becomes the starting point for the liberation of social structures (the world). As with the older vision, however, self-liberation only occurs in (diverse, inclusive) community. What strains against this subjective freedom and experimentation is suspicion of the very institutions that first opened the door to variety—MS itself and the mainline denomination that it serves.

It is clear that late- or postmodern subjective understandings of truth strike directly at the heart of the objective, foundational claims about truth put forward at ES. Late-modernity presents a special threat to its theological and moral vision. Yet, there is a paradox here that the climate of subjectivist truth reveals. Because late-modernity recognizes and takes seriously subjective claims to truth, the orthodox vision (including its emphasis on the Bible and the historic Evangelical emphasis on the authority of the conversion experience) also gains a right to speak that it did not have before. It does so, however, precisely as *one among many subjective claims to truth*. This paradoxical result was recognized by Kenneth Coates, ES's young theology professor, at the conclusion of a course exploring options in modern theology. He granted that postmodernity has given Evangelicals tools for critiquing the culture of modernity. Nevertheless, he acknowledges that "the postmodern vision extends the modern and makes it difficult for us to hang on to the rootedness of the Evangelical vision." Thus, for Evangelicals, late- or postmodernity is a two-edged sword.

CULTURE WARS?

What do our findings reveal about the culture wars thesis? Our brief summaries of the two schools' cultures clearly give some support to Hunter's depiction of the two warring moral visions at the heart of American culture. Furthermore, they support his contention that the two moral visions are grounded in religious or faith traditions that, in turn, make claims to truth about the world. They also give some insight into the formative process of middle elites such as clergy and other religious leaders.

But do our data support the thesis that these two visions lead to a culture war? With only two cases, we cannot provide a definitive answer, but we venture to respond with a qualified no. To be sure, the potential for warfare is present in the two visions, and battles have occurred over such issues as right-to-life versus choice, homosexual rights, the role of women, and the role of the church in society, to name but a few.

At the same time, however, our experiences in the two schools lead us to believe that, for the most part, the more intense battles are internal to each culture.[8] As we have suggested, ES's primary warfare is not with mainline Protestants or even with secular humanists. It is rather against the excesses of popular Evangelicalism and especially what they perceive as the idolatry of those Evangelicals who have sold out to the "self" movement and to therapeutic and technocratic models of the church.

Likewise, MS is not at war with Evangelicalism. In fact, in the name of diversity and inclusiveness, the school supports and encourages a self-consciously evangelical group on campus. The most noticeable warring occurs along the boundary lines of the social matrix over issues of race and gender. Yet these are very functional brushfires; through them, the culture acts out its commitment to liberation. In a sense, handling these skirmishes prepares MS's students for the big battle—that is the reform of its denomination, the church more generally, and the world.

Indeed, because ES's and MS's battles are more internal to each culture and because the visions themselves are so diametrically opposed, the two groups seem mainly to talk past each other. There is little real face-to-face engagement. For the most part, they seem unconcerned with the other's existence. That hardly makes for war!

Furthermore, we are not content with Hunter's characterization of the conflict in such sharp, bipolar terms. Our data do make clear that two different visions exist, but it must be remembered that we studied only two schools, and we selected them in part to provide sharply contrasting cultures. Had we chosen to study other theological schools we would have found more moderate, middle-ground positions.

Moreover, in the schools, there was not consensus about either vision. Rather we found students and faculty who, if they were brought together, would find considerable common ground. Indeed, Hunter recognizes the existence of the middle: "In truth, most Americans occupy a vast middle ground between the polarizing impulses of American culture" (1991:43). We do not doubt that some of the emerging elites—graduates of these two schools—will find themselves leading some of the special purpose groups that conduct the culture wars. Most, however, will likely focus their energies within their own subcultures or find common ground in the middle.

In sum, we would argue that the presence and persistence of these very different theological and moral visions create a situation where the majority on either side are less at war than at cross purposes. A main effect is misunderstanding and tension within and between the two cultures which feed "culture skirmishes."

Is some kind of rapprochement possible? Our data provide a small but tantalizing hint. These two theological and moral visions were forged in and by a White Protestant hegemony. Both are significantly challenged by cultural visions outside the pale. At MS, and increasingly at ES, students encounter and dialogue with other racial and ethnic groups. That cross-cultural contact, particularly at MS, is already reshaping the way students view the world. In particular, we speculate that African-American churches may provide a viable middle way that bridges the gulf between these disparate visions. The Black church holds generally to the truth "out there" approach that characterizes both ES's culture and the orthodox vision that Hunter describes. It combines this perspective, however, with a strong commitment to social justice like that found in the vision at MS. It does so in part by also taking seriously the truth "in here" approach, drawing from the African-American experience of oppression as an interpretative principle.

We do not mean to suggest that the Black church is simply a synthesis of the two positions we have described. Rather, it offers a third way, one that itself is not without internal conflicts. Nevertheless, it may be that this group, joined by others of the middle who are uncomfortable with either extreme, will win the right to have a major voice in defining how the public culture is shaped.

NOTES

1.   The study has been funded by grants to Hartford Seminary by the Pew Charitable Trusts and the Spencer Foundation. In addition to the authors of this paper, Barbara G. Wheeler and Daniel Aleshire have also been principal researchers for the project. Wheeler and Carroll, whose background is in liberal Protestantism, carried out the fieldwork at the Evangelical seminary. Marler and Aleshire, whose background is in conservative Protestantism, undertook the fieldwork at the mainline Protestant school. A forthcoming book, tentatively entitled *Being There: Culture and Formation in Two Protestant Theological Schools,* will report the full results of our work. The authors are grateful for their contributions to this paper. While we have disguised the actual names of the two schools, we wish to express our deep gratitude to the students, faculty, and administrators for their gracious hospitality and willing assistance during our fieldwork. We also wish to thank Hartford Seminary, where both authors were previously faculty members, for its continuing support.

2.   Field notes and interview transcripts have been entered into a freeform database (ASKSAM) which permits a variety of ways of accessing data.

3.   The average student body size (full- and part-time) of Evangelical theological schools in 1991–1992 was 518, and the average full-time faculty size was 18.6. (Source: Association of Theological Schools data, further classified by school type.)

4.   Experiential pedagogies are more likely to be used by faculty members in the Division of the Ministry of the Church.

5.   Many faculty members and students, however, are supportive of women students and give women visible roles in public events such as chapel services.

6.   Eighteenth-century Wesleyan perfectionism, Transcendentalism, and nineteenth-century Darwinian evolutionary thought lie behind this moral vision (Hutchison 1976).

7.   Older notions of causal-linear objectivity and grounded truth were initially challenged by quantum theory in the 1930s, verified in the early 1960s, and extended by chaos theory more recently (Bernstein 1985; Prigogine and Stengers 1984). The underlying discovery that the observer substantially affects the observed reinforced an emerging consensus among feminist and third-world scholars that Enlightenment truth was really Eurocentric, male truth (Huyssen 1990).

8.   Coser (1956:67ff.) maintains that the more intense hostility is expressed toward those with whom one is close rather than toward those who are at a distance.

REFERENCES

Abell, A. 1943. *The Urban Impact on American Protestantism. 1865–1900.* Cambridge, MA: Harvard University Press.

Bernstein, R. J. 1985. *Beyond Objectivism and Relativism: Science, Hermeneutics, and Praxis.* Philadelphia: University of Pennsylvania Press.

Coser, L. 1956. *Functions of Social Conflict.* New York: Free Press.

Giddens, A. 1991. *Modernity and Self-Identity: Self and Society in the Late Modern Age.* Stanford, CA: Stanford University Press.

Hopkins. C. 1940. *The Rise of the Social Gospel in American Protestantism 1865–1915.* New Haven, CT: Yale University Press.

Hunter, James Davison. 1991. *Culture Wars: The Struggle to Define America.* New York: Basic Books.

Hutchison, William R. 1976. *The Modernist Impulse in American Protestantism.* Oxford: Oxford University Press.

Huyssen, A. 1990. "Mapping the postmodern." Pp. 234–77 in *Feminism/Postmodernism,* edited by L. Nicholson. New York: Routledge.

Johnson, E. F. 1940. *The Social Gospel Re-Examined.* New York: Harper and Brothers.

Kelsey, D. H. 1992. *To Understand God Truly: What's Theological about a Theological School.* Louisville, KY: Westminster/John Knox.

Marsden, George M. 1980. *Fundamentalism and American Culture: The Shaping of Twentieth-century Evangelicalism, 1870–1925.* Oxford: Oxford University Press.

May, H. F. 1967. *Protestant Churches and Industrial America.* New York: Harper and Row.

———. 1976. *The Enlightenment in America.* Oxford: Oxford University Press.

Nisbet, R. 1980. *History of the Idea of Progress.* New York: Basic.

Prigogine, I., and I. Stengers. 1984. *Order out of Chaos: Man's New Dialogue with Nature.* New York: Bantam.

Szasz, P. 1982. *The Divided Mind of Protestant America, 1880–1930.* Tuscaloosa: University of Alabama Press.

Wells, D. F. 1986. "An American Evangelical Theology: The Painful Transition from Theoria to Praxis." Pp. 83–93 in *Evangelism and Modern America,* edited by G. Marsden. Grand Rapids, MI: Eerdmans.

White, R. C., and C. Hopkins. 1976. *The Social Gospel: Religion and Reform in Changing America.* Philadelphia: Temple University Press.

Wuthnow, Robert. 1988. *The Restructuring of American Religion: Society and Faith Since World War II.* Princeton, NJ: Princeton University Press.

7

Culture Wars and the Party System:
Religion and Realignment, 1972–1993

TED G. JELEN

In recent years, several analysts have argued that political cleavages based on race, ethnicity, or economic class are giving way to a new alignment of American public opinion, based primarily on cultural issues involving questions of personal morality. This "culture war" is thought to pit the religiously "orthodox" against "progressives" (Hunter 1991) or the religious against the not-so-religious (Kellstedt, Green, Guth, and Smidt 1994a, 1994b). In this morally dualistic polity, "family values" are regarded as the dominant axis of political conflict (Hammond, Shibley, and Solow 1994; Reed 1994), and the degree of religiosity is thought to supersede sectarian divisions based on doctrine or denominational preference (Guth and Green 1993; Kellstedt et al. 1994a, 1994b). The politicization of issues of personal morality is thought to result from the major cultural changes (in sexual morality, personal decorum, drug use, and other issues) that took place in the 1960s and 1970s. This can be expressed as the "culture wars" hypothesis: a belief that American political discourse increasingly exhibits a dualistic structure, with competing political factions organized around issues of moral traditionalism or life-style conservatism.

Controversy exists concerning the level at which the culture war might take place. Davis and Robinson (1996) have shown that American public opinion does not exhibit the dualistic structure that one might expect in a culturally polarized polity. In response, Hunter (1996) has argued that public opinion is an inappropriate place to look for cultural conflict. Hunter proposes a Durkheimian perspective, in which the moral visions underlying public discourse assume "a reality larger and independent (in the sense of disembodied) from those who give it expression" (p. 246).

Hunter is surely correct in suggesting that political discourse is not reduc-

145

ible, in a sociological sense, to the constituent individuals who might be carriers of a particular perspective. A lack of attitude constraint or consistency among mass publics is not necessarily decisive evidence against a broad view of social phenomena. Nevertheless, if the metaphor of a culture war is based in some sort of social reality, and is not simply a metaphysical ghost, the dualistic discourse of which Hunter writes must be manifested in some concrete social actor(s).

To the extent that the culture war constitutes a relatively permanent change in the American political culture, we might anticipate that such a cleavage would be manifested in American political institutions. That is, absent revolutionary changes in the practice of American politics,[1] a new alignment of social and political conflict might be expected to emerge in familiar political arenas of American politics. One such arena is the party system. Indeed, if indeed anything approaching a culture war exists in the United States, it should be observable in the structure of political parties. Not only are parties the principal means by which public opinion is translated into public policy, but the party system in the United States (for both legal and cultural reasons) exhibits a stubborn dualism (see Duverger 1954). If the culture war is, in any sense, a political battle (it would be quite implausible to argue that it is not), the party system provides an excellent setting in which the battle can be waged. Indeed, political parties are perhaps the most important means by which the opinions of ordinary citizens are connected with broader social realities.

Recent analyses of the "Christian Right" (certainly an important component of any traditionalist coalition in a culture war) indicate that it has become an important faction within the Republican party. Culturally and theologically conservative Christians have adapted to the pragmatic style of political activity in the United States (Moen 1992, 1994) and have come to be quite active within the Republican party (Rozell and Wilcox 1995, 1996; Wilcox 1996). Within a number of state party organizations the Christian Right has come to be quite influential, and it has become the dominant faction in several (see Rozell and Wilcox 1995).

This chapter examines empirical evidence relating to the culture wars hypothesis at the level of the "party in the electorate" (Sorauf 1976). Are the parties in fact realigning among the religiously observant, so that the party system is becoming a morally traditionalist Republican party, and a more secular, progressive, Democratic party (see Layman 1996)? Is partisan change related to the values of cultural traditionalism? Are these effects (if they exist at all) uniform across religious groups?

Despite changes in socioeconomic status across generations, Roman Catholics remain among the most loyal members of the Democratic coalition (Kellstedt et al. 1994b; Kenski and Lockwood 1989). Conversely, previous research has shown that evangelicalism has been having an increasing effect on partisanship and voting behavior. There is substantial evidence that White Evangelicals are shifting to the Republican party, and that such voters are among the most loyal members of the Republican electorate (see Kellstedt et al. 1994a, 1994b). Moreover, unlike other political manifestations of religious belief, this apparent realignment does not appear to be fragmented by the effects of religious particularism (Jelen 1991). The party system appears to aggregate the preferences of a theologically diverse group of evangelical Protestants.

The empirical analyses that follow are intended to address two questions. First, to what extent can the apparent realignment of White Evangelicals be attributed to the social conservatism of such voters? Does the increasing Republican share of the evangelical vote support the culture wars thesis? Second, is a shift to the Republican party that is based on the increased salience of social issues an ecumenical phenomenon? That is, are non-Evangelicals who share conservative attitudes on social issues being recruited into the Republican coalition? Does the scope of the culture war extend beyond the ranks of Evangelical Protestants?

DATA AND METHOD

Data for this study were taken from the NORC General Social Surveys (GSS), 1972–1993. These data are quite appropriate for several reasons. First, the series begins in 1972, a year regarded by many as a watershed for the political mobilization of cultural conservatives (see Lopatto 1985). Second, the study has been administered virtually every year since 1972, a feature that enables researchers to combine years (in a manner to be described below) to obtain a large number of cases for rather precisely defined subgroups (e.g., Evangelical Christians who attend religious services at least once a week). Finally, the GSS contains a number of questions regarding "social" or life-style issues, which are of primary interest here.

For purposes of this study, the GSS has been divided into four periods: 1972–1976 (the Nixon-Ford administration), 1977–1980 (the administration of Evangelical Jimmy Carter), 1981–1985 [the first Reagan administration, which Moen (1992, 1994) has argued corresponds to the "expansionist period" of the New Christian Right], and 1986 to the present (which Moen characterizes as the "institutional period" of the Christian Right).[2] This procedure permits monitoring attitudinal changes over the span of two decades, while providing an adequate number of cases at each observation point.

I limit the current analyses to White Christians. Moreover, in order to assess the impact of religious socialization, attention is confined to respondents who report attending religious services at least once a week. Church attendance is a behavioral measure of religious salience, as well as exposure to religious communications (Wald, Kellstedt, and Leege 1993). It is less likely that religious values will have a strong effect on those whose religious commitments are intermittent or casual (Kellstedt 1989).

The principal independent variable in this study is religious preference, measured by denominational affiliation (for the precise coding scheme, see Smith 1990). While the use of denominations to measure religious variables may not be an ideal strategy, denominational preference is the only religious variable measured across the entire GSS.[3] Respondents are divided into Evangelical Protestants, Mainline Protestants, and Roman Catholics.

I use two general dependent variables in this chapter. First are attitudes toward several different "social issues"; these include attitudes toward traditional sexual morality, homosexuality, abortion, tolerance toward nonconformists (see Wilcox and Jelen 1990), pornography, and school prayer. I also examine both "public feminism," tapping attitudes toward gender roles in public settings such as politics, and "private feminism," which measures gender role attitudes in family settings [see Jelen (1988); and Wilcox and Jelen (1991), for theoretical and empirical analyses of the different forms of feminism]. The second dependent variable is the respondent's party identification, as it is affected by religious preference and issue attitudes.

FINDINGS

The first, and perhaps most important finding, is that there is *no general tendency* for the religiously devout among any denominational family to become more conservative on social issue attitudes for the period under consideration. As I have shown elsewhere (Jelen 1996), such attitudes are quite stable across frequent church attenders among all three religious groups examined here. There is a tendency for Catholics and Mainline Protestants to become more permissive with respect to sexual morality over time, but there is no corresponding change among White Evangelicals. Similarly, Catholics have become more liberal on the issue of homosexuality during the past two decades. On both public and private feminism, there has been a liberalizing trend across all denominational groupings, and religiously observant Protestants of both Evangelical and Mainline denominations have become somewhat more conservative on the issue of abortion. Evangelicals tend to be more conservative than other White Christians, but except on the issues of homosexuality and sexual morality, most religious groups move in the same direction. There is also no general trend to be

Table 1. Mean Consistency Scores, by Denomination and Period

1972–1976	1977–1980	1981–1985	1986–1993
	Evangelicals		
.39	.40	.41	.39
	Mainline Protestants		
.38	.33	.41	.39
	Roman Catholics		
.38	.40	.41	.39

Source: Compiled by author from General Social Surveys.

observed, since, on some issues (abortion, pornography) changes have taken place in a conservative direction, while in others (feminism, tolerance, homosexuality, sexual morality) the trend has been generally liberal. Thus, there is no general conservative mobilization of religiously observant Christians.

Moreover, there does not appear to have been any tendency for any religious group to take more consistently conservative positions across social issues. Table 1 contains the results of an analysis of the internal consistency of issue positions taken by individuals. This was done by recoding issue positions on abortion, tolerance, public feminism, pornography, homosexuality, sexual morality, and school prayer to a common direction and range. The next step was to compute standard deviations across these issues for each respondent. The lower the score, the greater the internal consistency (in a liberal-conservative sense) of an individual's belief system (see Jelen 1990). The entries in Table 1 are the mean consistency scores for each religious group, over the four time periods under consideration.

As Table 1 indicates, the coherence of belief systems is virtually constant across religious traditions, and over time. The consistency scores only range from .38 to .41. Substantively, this finding means that there is no tendency for respondents to regard these diverse social issues as part of a single package or *gestalt*. Hunter (1991) argues that the culture war is characterized by an increasingly coherent dualistic social structure, in which progressives are pitted against traditionalists across a number of different issues. However, the evidence presented here suggests that there has been no increase in the tendency of mass publics to perceive two coherent "sides" to cultural conflict. The consistency scores in the most recent period are not significantly lower than those of the earlier period.[4]

However, there has been a Republican shift among all three religious groups during the past two decades. The shift has been most pronounced among Evangelicals (Kellstedt et al. 1994a, 1994b) and Catholics, although Catholics retain their Democratic allegiance throughout the period (Kellstedt

Table 2. Mean Party Identification Scores, by Denomination and Period[a]

1972–1976	1977–1980	1981–1985	1986–1993
	Evangelicals		
2.94	2.80	3.18	3.51**
	Mainline Protestants		
3.44	3.22	3.52	3.69*
	Roman Catholics		
2.14	2.30	2.34	2.69**

[a] Higher scores indicate greater Republican identification. *, difference between 1972–1976 and 1986–1993 significant at .05; **, difference between 1972–1976 and 1986–1993 significant at .01.
Source: Jelen (1996:61).

and Noll 1990; Kenski and Lockwood 1989). Across all four time periods, Mainline Protestants are the most Republican group of regular church attenders, Catholics the most Democratic. For both groups of Protestants, there was a very slight shift in the direction of the Democrats during the Carter administration. (See Table 2.)[5]

However, it is not clear that the general shift to the Republican party is the result of the increased salience of cultural issues among the religiously devout. When a similar analysis was conducted among White Christians who do not regularly attend religious services (data not shown), there was a significant shift to the Republicans among the postwar, boomer, 1970s, and Reagan cohorts as well. Thus, churchgoing White Christians do not appear to be particularly distinctive in their partisan leanings, but seem to be part of a large national trend.

To what extent does the shift to Republicanism reflect the increased salience of "cultural" or "social" issues among religiously devout White Christians? Since there has been no general increase in social issue conservatism over the past two decades, the increase in Republican identification among White, church-attending Christians can only be attributed to a renewed attention to "family values" or "moral traditionalism" if the relationship between these issues and party identification has increased over time. In other words, the culture wars hypothesis can be correct if respondents perceive an increased relevance of cultural values to partisanship over time. Of course, such a change would support the notion that religiously based political mobilization is in large part a defensive reaction to social trends and government policies that render it difficult to maintain a religiously based "traditional" life-style (see Reed 1994).

This possibility is tested in Table 3, which contains the relationships (product-moment correlations) between issue positions and party identifications over time for each religious tradition.

Table 3 suggests that, prior to the Reagan administration, issues of tradi-

Table 3. Correlations between Social Issue Positions and Partisanship Over Time, by Denomination (Frequent Church Attenders Only)

	1972–1976	1977–1980	1981–1985	1986–1993
		Evangelicals		
Sexual morality	−.03	−.01	−.07	−.08*
Homosexuality	−.04	−.03	−.09	−.11**
Private feminism	—	.09	.04	.04
Public feminism	.08	.09	.01	−.10*
Abortion	.00	.08	−.12**	−.08*
Tolerance	−.07	−.07	−.19**	−.13*
Pornography	.02	.02	−.03	−.09*
School prayer	−.12*	.04	−.11*	−.03
		Mainline Protestants		
Sexual morality	.01	.08	.01	−.04
Homosexuality	.01	.05	−.01	−.23**
Private feminism	—	−.04	.02	−.11*
Public feminism	.01	.07	−.11*	−.14*
Abortion	−.06	−.06	.06	−.1**
Tolerance	−.05	−.01	−.02	.02
Pornography	−.03	−.02	.09	−.11*
School prayer	−.16*	−.02	.06	.11
		Roman Catholics		
Sexual morality	.03	−.00	.03	−.04
Homosexuality	−.02	.09	.04	−.03
Private feminism	—	−.07	−.04	.08
Public feminism	−.05	.01	−.02	−.04
Abortion	−.01	.02	.05	.03
Tolerance	−.09*	−.19**	−.11*	−.11*
Pornography	.02	.03	.04	−.08*
School prayer	.12*	−.03	.03	−.01

*, significant at .05; **, significant at .01.
Source: Jelen (1996:61).

tional morality were not generally related to partisanship among frequent church attenders. One interesting exception is that the issue of school prayer seems to have been salient to all religious groups during the Nixon-Ford era, although, among Catholics, support for school prayer is related to a Democratic party identification. However, none of the other coefficients attains statistical significance among either group of Protestants.

Among Evangelicals, the issues of abortion, school prayer, and tolerance toward nonconformists come to affect partisanship sometime during Ronald Reagan's first term. For Evangelicals, then, a realignment in a Republican direction is well under way during the early 1980s (during the period Moen has described as one of strong mobilization on the part of the Christian

Right; see also Nesmith 1994). During the most recent period, Republican identification among Evangelicals is significantly related to conservative positions on abortion and tolerance, as well as on issues of public feminism, sexual morality, and homosexuality. While the magnitude of these coefficients is quite moderate, all are statistically significant, and in the expected direction.

By contrast, social issue attitudes (with the exception of public feminism) are not significantly related to partisanship among Mainline Protestants until the most recent period. For this group, the "cultural" component of a pro-Republican realignment does not occur until late in the 1980s. In this most recent period, conservative positions on both forms of feminism, as well as on homosexuality, abortion, and pornography are associated with Republican identification among Mainline Protestants. Indeed, the coefficients are slightly stronger for Mainline Protestants than for Evangelicals.[6]

What this suggests, of course, is that the culture wars thesis has become increasingly credible with the passage of time among American Protestants. In the early stages of the mobilization of the Christian Right, the cultural component of partisan realignment appears to have been confined to Evangelicals. As time has passed, the partisan effects of traditional values on issues of sexual morality and life-style have penetrated the Protestant Mainline. To this extent, the assertion that it is the *extent* of religiosity rather than the *type* of religiosity that has political relevance (Kellstedt et al. 1994a, 1994b) seems plausible.

However, the hypothesis that the parties are realigning around an axis of cultural conflict must be qualified by the responses of Roman Catholics. With the aforementioned exceptions of school prayer in the early 1970s and of pornography in the most recent period, the only social issue that exhibits a significant relationship with party identification is tolerance toward nonconformists. In one sense, this is not surprising, since issues of intellectual freedom have long been quite salient to American Catholics (see Jelen 1995; Wilcox and Jelen 1990; McNamara 1992). However, since the partisan effects of tolerance are virtually constant for the past two decades, it is unlikely that tolerance can account for partisan change among American Catholics. Thus, it is difficult to maintain that Catholics (even those with high levels of religious observance) are likely to be a component of an orthodox, traditionalist, Republican coalition.[7]

It is possible to perform a simpler test of the hypothesis relating religiosity to party identification. Table 4 contains the relationships (product-moment correlations) between church attendance and party identification for the most recent period. As these data suggest, the relationships between religious observance and partisanship are strong, significant, and positive for both groups of Protestants. This suggests that the more religious (as mea-

Table 4. Correlations between Church Attendance and
Party Identification, by Denomination (1990–1993)

Evangelicals	Mainline	Catholics
.14**	.13**	−.05

**, significant at .01.
Source: Compiled by author from General Social Survey.

sured behaviorally) are generally more Republican than their less devout counterparts. However, among Catholics, the relationship between attendance and identification with the Republican party is reversed (religiously observant Catholics are slightly more likely to identify as Democrats) and statistically insignificant (Leege 1996).

CONCLUSION

Earlier manifestations of the Christian Right, such as the Moral Majority and Pat Robertson's 1988 presidential campaign, were rendered ineffective in part because of the effects of religious particularism (Green 1995; Jelen 1991, 1993; Wilcox 1992). That is, differences in theology or denominational affiliation inhibited the formation of morally traditionalist political coalitions. In its most recent manifestation [what Rozell and Wilcox (1996) have termed the "Second Coming"], Christian Right leaders such as Ralph Reed (1994) have sought to minimize the effects of religious particularism and to form genuinely ecumenical political coalitions. Indeed, Reed (the executive director of the Christian Coalition) has sought to deemphasize specifically religious appeals, in favor of more secular arguments about "rights" (see especially Moen 1994), and to include Catholics in an ecumenical traditionalist political movement.

How well have religious conservatives done in institutionalizing cultural conflict within the Republican party? While the data presented here suggest that the increased political salience of issues involving traditional morality cannot be the complete story, there is also evidence that the observed Republican shift among observant White Christians contains elements of a values-based realignment. While issue positions have been relatively stable among regular church-attending Evangelicals, Catholics, and Mainline Protestants, the effects of these issue positions on partisanship have varied across time and across religious tradition.

The political mobilization of Evangelicals based on social issues appears to have begun during the early years of the Reagan administration. While Carter's candidacy in 1976 appears to have occasioned increased turnout among Evangelicals, an increase in the relationship between conservative positions on social issues and party identification (and presidential voting) appears to have coincided with the rise of the Christian Right. With respect to Mainline Protestants, the partisan salience of social issues occurred more slowly. The relationship between conservative positions on "family values" and underlying partisanship did not occur until the very end of the 1980s.

However, a culture wars realignment, based on the mobilization of religious and social conservatives, remains incomplete, since an increase in the relationship between moral-cultural conservatism and Republican identification has not occurred among religiously devout Roman Catholics. While churchgoing Catholics do tend to take conservative positions on some social issues (especially on abortion), Catholic social conservatives are no more Republican than their more liberal counterparts. While the data do suggest that Catholics are becoming more Republican (although they remain the most Democratic group of White Christians), these partisan shifts are not related to an increased salience of moral traditionalism.

The nonmobilization of Roman Catholics around traditional moral values is an important finding. Most analysts who argue for a value-based realignment (Falwell 1980; Hunter 1991; Reed 1994) suggest that Catholics are an important component of a traditionalist political coalition. Roman Catholicism is the single largest denomination in the United States, and the Church's centralized, hierarchical structure suggests that the Church has substantial political resources (see especially Segers 1995). The failure of even culturally conservative Catholics to mobilize around a traditionalist Republican party represents an important question mark for the future of religiously based politics in the 1990s. Indeed, it may well be that the future political success of the "orthodox," "religious" side in the culture war depends in the recruitment of Roman Catholics to an increasingly traditionalist Republican party.

Explaining the partisan inertia of Roman Catholics, of course, is well beyond the scope of this study. Devout Roman Catholics are about as likely to take conservative positions on social issues as are their Protestant counterparts. Moreover, Catholics are, as a group, becoming more Republican, although they remain the most Democratic group of White Christians. However, these two trends appear to be unrelated. The institutionalization of the culture war into the American party system appears to be limited by the resistance of a large group of Catholics to culturally based realignment. This further suggests that elections in America are unlikely to be contested on the terrain of the culture war as long as this formidable group of potential soldiers remains unrecruited.

ACKNOWLEDGMENT

A version of this paper was presented at the annual meeting of the Social Science History Association, November 16–19, 1995, Chicago.

NOTES

1. It might be noted that not all analysts are willing to grant this assumption. For example, James Davison Hunter has entitled a subsequent volume about the culture war *Before The Shooting Begins* (1994).

2. Experimentation with subdividing the most recent period (e.g., second Reagan term, Bush administration, first year of Clinton presidency) makes little difference in bivariate analysis.

3. The American National Election Studies suffer from the same limitation prior to the 1980s.

4. Experimentation with the cutting points for the time periods does not measurably alter these results.

5. The source of this change among all three religious groups appears to a combination of period effects and generational replacement (see Abramson 1976, 1979; Converse 1976, 1979; Claggett 1981). That is, younger cohorts enter the electorate more likely to identify as Republicans than their elders, and move more easily in a Republican direction (see Jelen 1996).

6. The relatively late cultural mobilization of traditionalist Mainline Protestants may also account for the surge in the importance of "family values" in explaining presidential vote in 1992 reported by Hammond, Shibley, and Solow (1994).

7. Very similar results obtain when presidential vote is used as the dependent variable. See Jelen (1996).

REFERENCES

Abramson, Paul. 1976. "Generational Change and the Decline of Party Identification in America: 1952–1974." *American Political Science Review 70*:469–78.

———. 1979. "Developing Party Identification: A Further Examination of Life-Cycle, Generational, and Periodic Effects." *American Journal of Political Science 23*:78–96.

Claggett, William. 1981. "Partisan Acquisition versus Partisan Intensity: Life Cycle, Generation, and Period Effects, 1952–1976." *American Journal of Political Science 25*:193–214.

Converse, Philip E. 1976. *The Dynamics of Party Support: Cohort Analyzing Party Identification*. Beverly Hills, CA: Sage.

———. 1979. "Rejoinder to Abramson." *American Journal of Political Science* 23:97–100.

Davis, Nancy J., and Robert V. Robinson. 1996. "Religious Orthodoxy in American Society: The Myth of a Monolithic Camp." *Journal for the Scientific Study of Religion* 35:229–45.

Duverger, Maurice. 1954. *Political Parties*. New York: Wiley.

Falwell, Jerry. 1980. *Listen, America!* Garden City, NY: Doubleday.

Green, John C. 1995. "Pat Robertson and the Latest Crusade: Religious Resources and the 1988 Presidential Campaign." *Social Science Quarterly* 74:157–68.

Guth, James L., and John C. Green. 1993. "Salience: The Core Concept?" Pp. 157–74 in *Rediscovering the Religious Factor in American Politics,* edited by David C. Leege and Lyman A. Kellstedt. Armonk, NY: M.E. Sharpe.

Hammond, Phillip E., Mark A. Shibley, and Peter M. Solow. 1994. "Religion and Family Values in Presidential Voting." *Sociology of Religion* 55:277–90.

Hunter, James Davison. 1991. *Culture Wars: The Struggle to Define America*. New York: Basic Books.

———. 1994. *Before the Shooting Begins: Searching for Democracy in America's Culture War*. New York: Free Press.

———. 1996. "Response to Davis and Robinson: Remembering Durkheim." *Journal for the Scientific Study of Religion* 35:246–48.

Jelen, Ted G. 1988. "The Effects of Gender Role Stereotypes on Political Attitudes." *Social Science Journal* 25:353–65.

———. 1990. "Religious Belief and Attitude Constraint." *Journal for the Scientific Study of Religion* 29:118–25.

———. 1991. *The Political Mobilization of Religious Beliefs*. New York: Praeger.

———. 1993. *The Political World of the Clergy*. Westport, CT: Praeger.

———. 1995. "Catholicism, Conscience, and Censorship." Pp. 39–50 in *Judeo-Christian Traditions and the Mass Media: Religious Audiences and Adaptations,* edited by Daniel A. Stout and Judith M. Buddenbaum. Newbury Park, CA: Sage.

———. 1996. "Religion and Public Opinion in the 1990s: An Empirical Overview." Pp. 55–68 in *Understanding Public Opinion,* edited by Barbara Norrander and Clyde Wilcox. Washington, DC: CQ Press.

Kellstedt, Lyman A. 1989. "The Meaning and Measurement of Evangelicalism: Problems and Prospects." Pp. 3–21 in *Religion and Political Behavior in the United States,* edited by Ted G. Jelen. New York: Praeger.

Kellstedt, Lyman A., John C. Green, James L. Guth, and Corwin E. Smidt. 1994a. "It's the Culture, Stupid: 1992 and Our Political Future." *First Things* 42(April):28–33.

———. 1994b. "Religious Voting Blocs in the 1992 Election: The Year of the Evangelical?" *Sociology of Religion* 55:307–26.

Kellstedt, Lyman A., and Mark Noll. 1990. "Religion, Voting for President, and Party Identification, 1948–1984." Pp. 355–79 in *Religion and American Politics,* edited by M. A. Noll. New York: Oxford University Press.

Kenski, Henry C., and William Lockwood. 1989. "The Catholic Vote from 1980 to

1986: Continuity or Change?" Pp. 109–37 in *Religion and Political Behavior in the United States,* edited by T. G. Jelen. New York: Praeger.

Layman, Geoffrey. 1996. "Parties and Culture Wars: The Manifestation of Cultural Conflict in the American Party System." Ph.D. dissertation, Indiana University, Bloomington.

Leege, David C. 1996. "The Catholic Vote in '96: Can It Be Found in Church?" *Commonweal 123*(September 27):11–18.

Lopatto, Paul. 1985. *Religion and the Presidential Election.* New York: Praeger.

McNamara, Patrick H. 1992. *Conscience First, Tradition Second: A Study of Young Catholics.* Albany: SUNY Press.

Moen, Matthew C. 1992. *The Transformation of the Christian Right.* Tuscaloosa: University of Alabama Press.

———. 1994. "From Revolution to Evolution: The Changing Nature of the Christian Right." *Sociology of Religion 55:*345–57.

Nesmith, Bruce. 1994. *The New Republican Coalition: The Reagan Campaign and White Evangelicals.* New York: Lang.

Reed, Ralph. 1994. *Politically Incorrect: The Emerging Faith Factor in American Politics.* Dallas: Word.

Rozell, Mark, and Clyde Wilcox, eds. 1995. *God at the Grassroots: The Christian Right in the 1994 Elections.* Lanham, MD: Rowman-Littlefield.

———. 1996. "Second Coming: The Strategies of the New Christian Right." *Political Science Quarterly 111:*271–94.

Segers, Mary C. 1995. "The Catholic Church as a Political Actor." Pp. 87–130 in *Perspectives on the Politics of Abortion,* edited by T. G. Jelen. Westport, CT: Praeger.

Smith, Tom W. 1990. "Classifying Protestant Denominations." *Review of Religious Research 31:*225–45.

Sorauf, Frank J. 1976. *Party Politics in America.* Boston: Little, Brown.

Wald, Kenneth D., Lyman A. Kellstedt, and David C. Leege. 1993. "Church Involvement and Political Behavior." Pp. 121–38 in *Rediscovering the Religious Factor in American Politics,* edited by David C. Leege and Lyman A. Kellstedt. Armonk, NY: M.E. Sharpe.

Wilcox, Clyde. 1992. *God's Warriors: The Christian Right in the Twentieth Century.* Baltimore: Johns Hopkins University Press.

———. 1996. *Onward Christian Soldiers? The Religious Right in American Politics.* Boulder, CO: Westview.

Wilcox, Clyde, and Ted G. Jelen. 1990. "Evangelicals and Political Tolerance," *American Politics Quarterly 18:*25–46.

Wilcox, Clyde, and Ted G. Jelen. 1991. "The Effects of Employment and Religion on Women's Feminist Attitudes," *International Journal for the Psychology of Religion 1:*161–71.

8

Civility or the Culture Wars in Politics and Religion:
Case Study of Oliver North in Virginia

MARGARET S. HREZO and MELINDA BOLLAR WAGNER

Theology teaches us what ends are desirable and what means are lawful, while Politics teaches what means are effective.
—C. S. Lewis, *God in the Dock*

Politics is what we do "when metaphysics fails."
—Benjamin Barber, *Strong Democracy*

In a nutshell, we believe we must systematically attempt to rebuild our civilization on the biblical foundations on which we were originally built. We believe God is calling all local Christians to participate in this holy endeavor. . . . We have no other option.
—Coalition on Revival letter and brochure, February 26, 1990

What is the place of conservative Christianity in American society? As mainstream culture and conservative Christian culture negotiate their relationship with each other, is "civility" increasing, or are the "culture wars" between the "orthodox" and the "progressives" becoming increasingly more strident? In 1983, James Davison Hunter found that the hard edges of evangelicalism had been "culturally edited" to make them more palatable: "While the doctrinal creed of conservative Protestantism has remained largely unchanged by the encounter with modernity, the cognitive style has changed" (1983:99). Evangelical religion had become more "civil" (ibid., 87). Melinda Wagner's (1990) study of Christian schools also found a good deal of accommodation to American popular culture in progress in the education arena. Yet, in 1991, Hunter's *Culture Wars* posited a widening chasm between orthodox and progressive perspectives. He characterizes orthodoxy as "commitment to an external, definable, and transcendent authority"; progressives are those who tend "to resymbolize historic faiths according to the

159

prevailing assumptions of contemporary life" (ibid., 44–45). Hunter says "it is arguable that the complexity and the stridency of the antagonism between orthodox and progressive voices has sharply increased" (ibid., 143).

Many of the most vocal Evangelicals themselves frame what they are doing in the language of war. James Dobson, an evangelical child psychologist who heads the large and wide-ranging Focus On the Family enterprise, says "We are in a civil war of values and the prize to the victor is the next generation—our children and grandchildren." Presidential hopeful Patrick Buchanan says, "There is a culture war. . . . This war is for the soul of America" (both quoted in Wagner 1997). At the September 8–10, 1995, convention of the Christian Coalition held in Washington, D.C., Pat Robertson reaffirmed the organization's goal of having "a significant voice in one of the political parties by 1994" and came very close to admitting the goal of dominating a major party (Edsall 1995). Ralph Reed's speech at that occasion explained that the coalition wants more power in the GOP than "the AFL-CIO or the radical feminists have over the Democratic Party. The question is not who we will endorse [for president] but who will endorse our agenda" (Broder 1995).

Anthropologists, political scientists, sociologists, and political pundits increasingly ask two questions concerning the implications for American politics of the politicization of conservative Christianity: (1) In the political arena, will conservative Christians make compromises with the surrounding culture or will they grow ever more strident? (2) Will conservative Christians win with either strategy? The 1994 Virginia Senate race provides an interesting case study of the importance of civility if the Christian Right is to be influential.

THE 1994 VIRGINIA SENATE RACE

Most Virginians did not look forward to the 1994 Senate race. The incumbent, Charles Robb, had been governor of Virginia and began his Senate career as one of the most respected of a group of moderate young Democrats who were expected to curb the "excessive liberalism" of Democratic politics and provide a solid base of Democratic support on important social issues. He was one of the "great hopes" of the Democratic party. Increasingly, however, he had to combat both allegations of moral misconduct—attendance at parties where drugs were taken, drug use, and marital infidelity—and general citizen dissatisfaction with incumbent Democratic politicians and with President Clinton. Oliver North carried the albatross of a felony conviction for lying to Congress about the Iran-Contra affair. Marshall Coleman, although considered honest, never seemed a viable candidate to most Virginians. North spent $20,000,000 on his campaign, about 80 percent of which came from sources outside the Commonwealth. Robb spent $5,000,000 (70 percent from outside sources). When the votes were counted, Robb had 46 percent to North's 43 percent. Coleman trailed far behind with 11 percent of the vote.

Why did North lose? Does his loss tell us anything useful about the agenda or the strengths and limits of the power of the Christian Right, or whether the road to be traveled is paved with civility or culture wars? North was supported by the Christian Coalition, which had assisted him greatly in winning the Republican nomination. The home base of the Christian Coalition is in Virginia and the organization is influential in the Commonwealth's politics. In particular, it played an important role in North's nomination. The *Christian Coalition Voter Guide* handed out at the polls election day showed North agreeing with its positions in every area—including education, an issue that ultimately favored Robb. In 1993, the Coalition's support was a key ingredient in the election of George Allen as governor and Jim Gilmore as attorney general of Virginia. Conservative Protestants make up at least 25 percent of the population of sixty-one of Virginia's counties and 50 percent or more of at least twenty-six counties. Exit polls suggested that 67 to 80 percent of fundamentalist and evangelical Christians who voted supported Oliver North (Wilcox, Rozell, and Coker 1995:16).

On the other hand, 20 to 30 percent of these Christians did not support North. North lost in Lynchburg, the home of Jerry Falwell and Liberty University. He barely carried Virginia Beach, the center of the Christian Coalition. Two of the three counties where 75 to 100 percent of church adherents are conservative Protestants voted for Robb. Five of the twenty-three counties in which 50 to 74 percent of church adherents are conservative Protestants voted for Robb. Thus 27 percent of conservative Protestant counties went for Robb. Six of the seven Virginia counties where 50 percent or more of the church adherents are Black Protestants voted for Robb. Table 1 shows in detail the religious orientation of the Virginia counties that voted for Chuck Robb.

We would argue that the causes of North's defeat go beyond his personal liabilities and the fact that, by a 51 to 40 percent margin, voters believed North had "morally done the wrong thing" in the Iran-Contra affair (see Sabato 1995:2). The Commonwealth's voters certainly had no greater faith in Robb's moral integrity. The roots of Oliver North's defeat lie in the tension inherent in the Christian Right's ideology and in the exigencies of American party politics. The 1994 Virginia Senate race offers a compelling example of the strengths and weaknesses of the Christian Right and of its attempts to reconcile the tension between the demands of the world and the demands of God, between politics as the search for power and politics as a meeting ground for the human and the transcendent.

Table 1 All Virginia Counties Carried by Robb and Their Religious Affiliation

Location	County	Population Unclaimed Certain Denom. (%)[a]	Church Adherents Conservative Prot. (%)	Church Adherents Black Prot. (%)
Coalfield	Wise	50–74	50–74	
	Dickenson	75–100	75–100	
	Buchanan	75–100	75–100	
	Russell	50–74	50–74	
University	Montgomery	50–74		
Central	Albemarle	50–74		
	Nelson		50–74	
	Amherst	50–74		
	Buckingham			
Southside	Southampton			50+
	Greensville			50+
	Brunswick			50+
	Sussex			50+
	Surry			50+
Tidewater	Northhampton			50+
	Charles City			
	James City			
	Caroline	50–74	50–74	
	King and Queen		50–74	
	Westmoreland			
Nova (Northern Va.)	Fairfax	50–74		

[a] Certain denominations report membership figures to the Association of Statisticians of American Religious Bodies (ASARB). But unclaimed is not the same as unchurched: an unclaimed person may well attend a church that does not report to the ASARB. Such churches include independent Baptist churches, nondenominational charismatic churches, independent Pentecostal churches, and snake-handling churches. Church tends to be important in many of these counties, particularly in the coalfields. Virginia's independent cities are not included in this table; religious affiliations for each of the independent cities were not available.
Source: Church data are derived from Bradley et al. (1992); election data are from the *Roanoke Times and World News* and the Commonwealth of Virginia State Board of Elections.

A RIGHT ORDERING OF MEANS AND ENDS: THE CITY OF GOD

The most basic questions raised by the Christian Right relate to the dichotomy between realist and idealist approaches to politics. The issues inherent here are well-focused by Lewis (1970) and Barber (1984) in the opening quotations. For the realist, politics is what we do when metaphysics fails. And metaphysics fails all the time. The Good is either unknowable or does not exist. At best we create justice as a kind of human artifice to smooth over the harsher aspects of the struggle for power. The just will always suffer at the hands of the unjust. Life, in Hobbesian terms, is "a restless desire for power after power, that ceaseth only in death" (1962:80). Realists view human beings as organisms in an environment who seek to satisfy their passions and appetites. Even for the refined realist this search is modified only by prudence, never by any notion of righteousness or justice. Idealists (poor term that it is) argue that human beings are creatures who seek meaning and that the realist position dismisses important aspects of what it means to be human. They do not deny the reality of human passion and desire, but human beings are not limited to their appetites and passions. They are not just flesh or matter. Human beings also are spirit and seek the Good. According to the idealist position, people must constantly ask themselves what it means to be human; in particular, what does it mean to be a person who believes in a divine order in a world that does not? Historically, this has been a difficult decision for those required to make it.

In *The Apology,* Socrates maintained that the just individual must choose between staying out of politics and being ruined by it. Eric Voegelin talks about the tension experienced by ancient Israel as it found that, although the Israel of the covenant could not survive without the protection of some political form, political forms led to deformation of the covenant:

> The promised land can be reached only by moving through history, but it cannot be conquered within history. The Kingdom of God lives in men who live in the world, but it is not of this world. (1956:114)

The Israel of the covenant was caught in the dilemma posed by C. S. Lewis. Theology teaches us about ends, while politics is about means. Is it possible to order the world of politics to just ends? Is it possible to integrate politics into life in the metaxy (the in-between world where God and humans meet) in such a way that it can be ordered to help human beings achieve the Good?

Augustine and Aquinas found the same problem as they sought to explain their understanding of human frailty and its relation to politics. Augustine argued that human beings are both flesh and spirit and that spirit is superior to flesh. Spirit is made manifest in the natural law, which can be understood through human reason, which reflects God's thought impressed upon the human soul. By understanding the natural law, human life can mirror God's governance of the world and differentiate the spheres of the kingdom of God and the kingdom of humans. Positive human law can only be a reflection of God's natural law. God's law would be used to judge human law, but was something different from it. This led Augustine to de-divinize politics by breaking up the ancient unity of politics and religion. However, he still recognized the tension and symbiosis between the City of God and the City of Man. There would be a distinction between politics and religion. The City of Man was built on *amor sui*—on glory, bloodshed, self-interest, and fraud. Yet despite its flaws, the City of Man also was supposed to provide a specific type of peace, order, and justice that would link the human and transcendent. And God would hold the City of Man accountable for the order it built. The fifth-century implications were an undermining of the divine right of kings. The modern implications, although certainly not envisioned by Augustine, or even later on by Aquinas, were the bifurcation of politics and faith and the appearance of the state as an end in-and-of-itself.

Any society or group that believes that understanding of transcendence is essential to the ordering of existence on earth must face the problem of integrating the City of God and the City of Man. How can religious symbolization provide a source of order in history without being corrupted by the exigencies of political life? That dilemma can be seen throughout the debates of the Christian Right on how much to accommodate to modern American life in order to win electoral power, how far to go in adapting to mainstream Republican politics, and how "different" to make their politics, their life-styles, and their schools. Just how far should the movement go toward looking at politics as "what we do when metaphysics fails" rather than as a means of effecting the joint participation of God and human beings in the metaxy? The Christian Right instinctively searches for some Good outside the physical reality of this world. At the same time, however, it is still looking for its place in American political life. Should it try to influence American politics from the inside, by becoming part of the Republican party's coalition, or should it act as prophet, standing on the outside of mainstream political life in obedience to scriptural warning, "Be ye not yoked together with unbelievers" (II Corinthians 6:14)?

In some ways, conservative Christians face the same dilemma as did Israel at the time of the conquest of Canaan and the anointing of Saul as king:

> It was this establishment of a kingdom which inevitably produced the conflict between the Israel that was a peculiar people under the kingship of God, and the Israel that had a king like other nations. (Voegelin 1956:142)

On the one hand, the Christian Right movement sees itself as the nation's only chance for salvation: "Only we can restore this nation. Only the people here today, and people like us, can turn this around . . . only Christian believers doing the work." Or as a Colorado Christian Coalition member put it: "We helped elect the candidates God wants in office" (quoted in Cooper 1995:89). Herein lies the root of conservative Christianity's argument with secular humanism. Lisa Langenbach argues that Concerned Women for America's ideology views secular humanism as:

an international religion which puts people before God and which has taken control of the major institutions of America. Humanism, in the eyes of the CWA, preaches that there is no one God, there are no moral absolutes, people need only please themselves. Secular humanism, then, leads to an abandonment of biblical law and biblical prescriptions. (Langenbach 1994:3)

The ideology espoused by Concerned Women for America understands the problems inherent in the realist position and seeks solutions. However, it also suffers from the problem shared by all ideologies. It is important to remember the difference between a philosophy and an ideology. To the Greeks, the philosopher was a lover of knowledge. The knowledge the philosopher loved was understanding of the Good. The philosopher viewed life as a constant search for the Good, but a search with no end because human reason would never fully understand the Good. An ideology, on the other hand, is a worldview—an integrated set of beliefs that explains the world and our place in it. As such it provides answers and tends to prohibit questions. Ideology is the province of the sophist, not the philosopher. In the case of the Christian Right the answer is that only a return to biblical concepts, as understood through a literal reading of the Bible, will remedy the problems endemic in American society. When conservative Christians set about influencing social and political life, it is from an initial position of radical change in accordance with known "truth." For example, when opening a Christian school they talk about "building" a new culture (Wagner 1990). Conservative Christians teach their children that they are a "separate people," a "people apart" from "the world."

Yet conservative Christians are not ever really a "people apart." They are part of an American political and social culture that is thoroughly embued with the ideals and beliefs of the modern project—with the idea that the modern commercial state exists to satisfy the needs and appetites of its citizens.[1] Hunter (1983, 1987) talks about some of the accommodations in his work. Indeed, the conservative Christian church is not as "separate" from the ways of the world as it could be. Marc Cooper describes a church service in Colorado Springs this way:

> Later that evening I returned to see Tomberlin conduct his new Saturday-night service, a convenience for those too busy to come to church on a Sunday. A light snow was falling, but the parking lot overflowed with Cherokees, Range Rovers, and vans. Inside the chapel 500 or more parishioners, most under 40, had taken their seats. I didn't see a single tie but rather lots of suede and leather, a whole array of Patagonia and Esprit, and more than a handful of MCI and Apple company sweatshirts. The chapel had no cross, the pews were as plush as movie seats, and the wood trim made the church seem more like a ski lodge. (1995:94)

Yes, conservative Christians view humans as creatures of passion and self-interest (just as did Hobbes and Locke). Yes, they see the family and church as working to help control human nature. But, as Locke told us over two hundred years ago, the "good" person is still the person who works hard and accumulates material possessions, and he or she should, therefore, be allowed to enjoy them. Thus, for many of the Christian Right, the social, political, and cultural accommodations to modernity they make are God's will. And they go to great lengths to discern God's will (Wagner 1990).

Research on Christian schools also supports the conclusion that, despite attempts at boundary maintenance, conservative Christians are embedded in the overall American culture, recognize that fact, and often are aware of the compromises they make (Wagner 1990). Like the conservative Christian Church, the Christian alternative school is not as alternative as it could be. Within the Christian schools, compromises are evident everywhere. This brand of fundamentalism was born in the USA and is in some ways overwhelmed by American popular culture. Inside the schools, American individualism, competition, and materialism coexist or compete with the gentle fruits of the spirit that the conservative Christians say they have as their goal (love, joy, peace, long suffering, gentleness, goodness, faith, meekness, temperance; see Galatians 5:22–23).

It may be more appropriate to view the Christian schools as a revitalization process rather than as an attempt to build a new culture. In Wallace's terms, a revitalization movement is "any conscious, organized effort by members of a society to construct a more satisfying culture" (1966:39). This appears to be close to the way the Christians themselves view their task. Using Wallace's terminology, the conservative Christians' model of an ideal society would be their "goal culture." The "existing culture," on the other hand, is seen as "inadequate or evil in certain respects" (ibid., 160). For the conservative Christians, the American way of life, and particularly "secular humanism," is the denigrated "existing culture." The Christian schools themselves are the "transfer culture," the crucible of change that connects the denigrated and the ideal. Inside the Christian schools the revitalization process—"the process by which cultural materials which have hitherto appeared to the members of a society as dissonant are analyzed and combined into a new structure" (ibid., 211)—is ongoing. Yet they will do their revitalizing within the framework of the modern project.

It should not be a surprise that conservative Christian educators create a school culture that borrows from the surrounding mainstream culture or that conservative Christians both condemn and actively participate in the world of the modern project. How successful would a more "alternative" alternative be? Research indicates that the success of a genuinely "alternative" alternative would be meager. Sahlins makes this point about new cultural forms, using the example of the fashion designer who "appears" to pluck ideas of out the air:

But the fashion expert does not make his collection out of whole cloth; he uses bits and pieces with an embedded significance from a previous existence to create an object that works, which is to say that sells—which is also to say that objectively synthesizes a relation between cultural categories, for in that lies its salability. (1976:217)

The Christian school must also "sell" its product. It must forge compromises that "objectively synthesize a relation between [competing] cultural categories." Christian school administrators voiced this necessity when they told one of these researchers, "you can't take it all away" from the students. Their schools, homes, and churches, they said are "not heaven," and compromises are made while "living on this earth."

In constructing these compromises, conservative Christians manifest a mode of thought discussed by Levi-Strauss (1966), who made a distinction between the methods of the engineer, who plans what materials and resources are needed for a project and sets about to acquire them, and the *bricoleur,* the handyman Jack-of-all-trades, who works with what is at hand. He applied the term to the building of cultural forms as well as to technological labors. Conservative Christians appear to work in the *bricoleur* mode, picking and choosing from what is available, and making alterations to popular cultural themes and artifacts, rather than using an entirely new pattern to fashion alternative cultural forms out of whole cloth. Thus, they create Christian alternatives, based on popular culture templates.

WHEN METAPHYSICS FAILS: THE CITY OF MAN

There are definite political implications in the attempt to create Christian alternatives based on popular culture templates. These are very evident in the 1994 Virginia Senate campaign. First, the race's outcome means that coalition-building within one of the existing major political parties, rather than forming a separate party, is not only possible, it is probably inevitable. According to one exit poll in Virginia, 37 percent identified themselves as born-again or evangelical Christians. In a second exit poll, 15 percent of those who voted identified themselves as White fundamentalists and 14 percent associated themselves with the Christian Right (Wilcox et al. 1995:16). This is a significant bloc, but it is not monolithic, at least not yet, and it is not enough to form its own party. What most political analysts maintain, and the election data support them, is that Republicans can win if they nominate mainstream conservatives, such as Governor George Allen and Attorney General Jim Gilmore, who support major aspects of the Christian Right's political agenda, but who lack the hard edge and personal liabilities of an Oliver North. Further, it will not be enough to appeal to Christian Coalition activists. Like Israel, political candidates must be both within and outside the "world." The problem, then of course, becomes steering the narrow course between co-optation and a gnostic belief that your group has all the correct answers because "of a direct connection to God" (Birnbaum 1995:34).

The second political implication relates directly to this need to build successful coalitions while steering that narrow course. Green argues that the strengths of the Christian Right are "zealous activists, sophisticated leaders, and dedicated voters" (1995:5). These strengths can be used either to build coalitions or to dominate them. And these strengths, he says, also suggest the limits of such groups' effectiveness. Oliver North's loss shows the perils of attempted domination within the American political party system.

In Virginia it is still possible to nominate candidates through party conventions. In 1994, Virginia Republicans chose to use the convention to nominate its candidates. Conventions favor the nomination of candidates who possess exactly the kind of backing Green describes—the support of dedicated, zealous activists willing to pay the convention fee and lobby hard for their candidate. The Christian Right produced that kind of backing for North at the Republican Convention and gained his nomination over Jim Miller, another social conservative, but one who had not courted the Christian Right. The activists won the battle, but at a great cost. The convention split the party and engendered a countermobilization on the part of Republican party centrists led by Senator John Warner. As often happens in party conventions, the group that dominated selection of the nominee was not representative of party adherents as a whole. That could make holding rank-and-file partisans to the ticket more difficult at polling time. In the case of the 1994 Virginia senatorial election, it did. The countermobilization is most evident in the split between rural and suburban voting. North could not hold well-educated, suburban, conservative, Christian voters who were moderate in their views and who sought incremental movement within the existing political framework rather than a total reworking of that framework. Although much attention has been given to the resource mobilization factors that have an impact on the growing place of the Christian Right in American society, we would argue that matters of cultural style cannot be ignored. Oliver North mobilized far more resources than his opponent. However, his cultural style did not garner votes in the Virginia suburbs essential to any candidate's success.

Thus, in order to overcome the difficulties caused by desertion of more moderate Republicans, North's supporters needed to be able to count on what Green contends is another of the strengths/weaknesses of such movements: an ability to mobilize the rank-and-file believers. North was unable to do this and this was due, in large measure, to a candidate-specific characteristic: questions about his personal moral integrity. In this instance, the

Christian Right failed to see the limits of its resources and of the political situation in Virginia. In so doing, it turned its political strengths into weaknesses.

Lisa Langenbach's work supports this contention. In her analysis of Pat Robertson's 1988 presidential campaign she found that:

> having the correct position on issues of importance is not enough to secure their constituent base. [Voters' decisions rest on] candidate specific factors, such as image, viability, leadership qualities, and party identification, and not with factors most commentators believed motivated Robertson's supporters: namely religious right issues. (1989:300–1)

Robertson was unable to expand his initial base beyond "charismatic and Pentecostal clergy," and "a narrow segment" of people characterized by "lower levels of education" and "social issue conservatism" (ibid., 301; see also Langenbach and Green 1992). This, in large measure, was Oliver North's problem as well. He carried rural areas by eight percentage points. However, although the suburbs also favored North, his margin was only 0.7% and his relatively poor showing there "sank his candidacy" (Sabato 1995:3). And all across Virginia, "upper-crust, reliably GOP precincts turned in disappointing margins for the flannel-shirted North" (ibid., 5). Robb held 90 percent of Democrats. North only held 75 percent of Republicans and those who deserted were predominantly suburban and well-educated (ibid.).

A May 1995 *Time* article on Ralph Reed and the Christian Coalition focused the issue well. Voters are looking for more morality in their politics. They are fiscally and socially more conservative than they were 25 or even 10 years ago. The Christian Right has sophisticated leaders, zealous activists, and a motivated rank-and-file. However, the American electorate is still less polarized than the political discourse of activists and pundits would suggest. Currently the Christian Right is debating its future. Should it compromise more or less? Should it adopt the "big gaudy umbrella" version of coalition politics that has traditionally been associated with American party politics? Should it listen to those of its leaders who urge participation in the system or its more ideologically pure leaders who urge dominance or separation? The 1994 Virginia Senate race suggests that political success for conservative Christian candidates, if that indeed is what interests the movement, is more likely to come from compromise with the world than from separation from it.

Students of American party politics have been talking about realignment for over twenty-five years.[2] In *The Emerging Republican Majority* (1970), Kevin Phillips predicted the collapse of Democratic hegemony and its replacement with Republicans attuned to Americans' concerns over social issues. Scammon and Wattenberg (1970) argued, ungrammatically, that

Americans were "unyoung, unpoor, and unblack," and that a Democratic leadership that continued to support those constituencies ultimately would destroy itself. Yet realignment in the traditional sense seemed to elude American political parties, and some researchers believed that America would see the disintegration of political parties as we knew them. Voting based on issues would replace voting based on party affiliation, they argued.

Twenty-five years later, political parties in America, though weaker, refuse to die. Issue-based voting has increased, but is not the sole determinate of voters' electoral decisions. Instead, candidate image has become a competing factor in American elections, matching the growth of issues as a determinant of voting choice (see DeClercq, Hurley, and Luttbeg 1976:9–33.). Candidate image relates to the personal characteristics of a candidate that voters find appealing or unappealing; it is unrelated to the candidate's policy views or political party affiliation (see Luttbeg and Gant 1995). We are still arguing about the same social issues—abortion, homosexuality, a woman's "place," welfare, race, and that combination of values connoted by the phrase "secular humanism." Realignment, in the traditional sense, seems no closer to occurring. Politics remains polarized, angry, and based on interest-group coalitions. The distrust of politics and politicians engendered by the Vietnam war and Watergate has not lessened.

At the same time, however, the American political scene is different, vastly different, than it was in 1970. One of the differences is the increasing reliance on candidate-centered politics. Related to this difference and in large measure both feeding it and benefiting from it is the evolution of the Christian Right from a cultural oddity to a driving force in American political life. The 1994 midterm elections are a testament to its current powerful influence. On paper it is still party politics. Republicans, not the Christian Coalition, gained fifty-two seats in the House of Representatives (giving them control of that body for the first time in forty years), nine seats in the Senate, and eleven governorships. In addition, every Republican incumbent was reelected (*Time*, November 21, 1994). But those new and incumbent Republican lawmakers owe a great deal to the Christian Right, and particularly to the Christian Coalition. As Green argues, "the real story of the Christian Right is the steady growth in size and sophistication of a modern political movement, which like other movements, has both strengths and weaknesses" (1995:5). The Christian Right is seeking a permanent and important role in American politics. The Republican party knows it owes this part of the electorate a debt and is willing to listen and pay. However, if political power is its goal, the Christian Right will probably have to participate in the political world it finds in order to have the maximum possible effect. The Christian Right is an increasingly powerful political force, but it might do well to remember the advice of Richard Nixon to Robert Dole. Nixon told Dole that to get the Republican nomination for president he would have to run as far as he could to the right because 40 percent of the nominators are there. Then, as soon as he was nominated, he would need to run as fast as he could to the center, because only 4 percent of the total electorate is located on the far right end of the political spectrum.

The 1994 Virginia Senate election supports the argument that to be successful in American politics the Christian Right will have to listen attentively to its civility/accommodation faction. The political career of another Virginia politician, Michael Farris, also will be a telling predictor of the place of hard-line conservative Christian politics in the Commonwealth. Farris was the attorney for the Concerned Women of America's challenge of school textbooks in Hawkins County, Tennessee. He began his political career with Jerry Falwell's Moral Majority and is an advocate of home schooling. Yet Farris ran a losing campaign for lieutenant governor in 1993 with religion "a centerpiece of his campaign" (*Roanoke Times and World News,* November 14, 1994). It will be interesting to see if he begins to modify his positions enough to gain suburban support. Even the Old Testament prophets who railed against the defections of the Kingdom of Judah from Yahweh ultimately found themselves making compromises in order to try to ensure the continued existence of a people who could be obedient to the God of the covenant:

> [Elijah] went down to the river with his successor. There, on the bank of the river, he took his mantle, rolled it up, and struck the waters. They divided as the Red Sea had done before Moses and Israel, so that the two could cross over on dry ground. That was the crossing into the last Desert and its freedom. "As they still went on and talked, behold, a chariot of fire and horses of fire separated the two of them. And Elijah went up by a whirlwind into heaven" (II Kings 2:11). Elisha saw it and cried out: "My father, my father! The chariot of Israel and its horsemen!" Then he took up the mantle that had fallen from Elijah, used it as Elijah had done to part the waters of the Jordan, and walked back into the world. (Voegelin 1956:351)

Walking back into the world means having to deal with those difficult questions about ends and means suggested by C. S. Lewis at the beginning of this chapter. It means the Christian Right will have to eschew easy answers and attempt to find a genuine way of meeting God in the political world. But why should contemporary Christians be exempt from the same sorts of hard choices that faced the prophets?

NOTES

1. American political culture has its roots in Machiavelli's break with medieval thought and creation of the core of modern political philosophy. Machiavelli is also

associated with the realist position in political thought. Machiavelli's legacy include the beliefs that: (1) the state is an artificial creation designed to meet the needs of the ruler (whether defined as leader or populace); (2) justice is a human artifice created to paper over the harsh realities of power politics; (3) no individual or state is willingly just; rather all are motivated by self-interest (defined in a variety of ways); and (4) human beings are organisms in an environment who seek satisfaction of basic needs and desires, rather than creatures who seek meaning in the world.

The classical liberals (Hobbes, Locke, Hume, Smith) accepted these basic premises and developed from them what C. B. MacPherson (1970) called "the possessive individual." This individual is an organism in an environment desperately seeking to satisfy his/her needs and desires. Citizens are understood as individuals and proprietors:

> the human essence is freedom from dependence on the will of others, and freedom is a function of possession. Society becomes a lot of free individuals related to each other as proprietors of their own capacities and of what they have acquired by their exercise. Society consists of relations of exchange among proprietors. (ibid., 56)

In such a society, there is no authoritative allocation of work or any authoritative provision of rewards for work accomplished. Rationality is defined in economic terms—in terms of the individual's ability to maximize his/her utilities and acquire possessions. The greater an individual's economic rationality, the greater his possession, and the greater his/her worth. The modern project as an idea is the political heir of Machiavellian and classical liberal thought as filtered through the Enlightenment's vision of science, reason, and the individual. It contends that using the methods of science we can unlock the power of nature and solve the problems of human existence. In politics this means that the role of the state is to satisfy the appetites of its citizens.

2.   Realignment is a profound shift in voter identification with the major political parties. It generally results in the reversal of majority and minority status for the Democratic and Republican parties. Researchers have identified four signs usually associated with realignment: (1) an increase in the number of independent voters; (2) success of third parties; (3) an increase in the number of voters who base their electoral choices on issue rather than political party; and (4) a decrease in respect for and confidence in traditional political parties. See Luttbeg and Gant (1995) for a fuller description of realignment.

REFERENCES

Barber, Benjamin. 1984. *Strong Democracy.* University of California Press.
Birnbaum, Jeffrey. 1995. "The Gospel According to Ralph." *Time,* May 15, pp. 28–35.
Bradley, Martin B., Norman M. Green, Jr., Dale Jones, Mac Lynn, and Lou McNeil. 1992. *Churches and Church Membership in the United States 1990.* Atlanta, GA: Glenmary Research Center.

Broder, David. 1995. "Christian Group Flexes Newfound Muscles." *Washington Post,* September 10.

Cooper, Marc. 1995. "God and Man in Colorado Springs." *Utne Reader,* May–June.

DeClercq, Eugene, Thomas Lane Hurley, and Norman R. Luttbeg. 1976. "Voting in American Presidential Elections: 1956–1972." Pp. 9–33 in *American Electoral Behavior: Change and Stability,* edited by Samuel A. Kirkpatrick. Beverly Hills, CA: Sage.

Edsall, Thomas B. 1995. "Robertson Urges Christian Activists to Take Over GOP State Parties." *Washington Post,* September 10.

Green, John C. 1995. "The Christian Right and the 1994 Elections: A View from the States." *PS: Political Science and Politics,* March.

Hobbes, Thomas. 1962. *Leviathan.* New York: Collier.

Hunter, James Davison. 1983. *American Evangelicalism: Conservative Religion and the Quandary of Modernity.* New Brunswick, NJ: Rutgers University Press.

———. 1987. *Evangelicalism: The Coming Generation.* Chicago: University of Chicago Press.

———. 1991. *Culture Wars: The Struggle to Define America.* New York: Basic Books.

Langenbach, Lisa. 1994. "Concerned Women of America and the Politics of the Christian Right." Paper presented to Society for the Scientific Study of Religion, Albuquerque, New Mexico, November.

———. 1989. "Evangelical Elites and Political Action: The Pat Robertson Presidential Candidacy." *Journal of Political and Military Sociology 17*(Winter):291–303.

Langenbach, Lisa, and John C. Green. 1992. "Hollow Core: Evangelical Clergy and the 1988 Robertson Campaign." *Polity 25*(Fall):147–58.

Levi-Strauss, Claude. 1966. *The Savage Mind.* Chicago: University of Chicago Press.

Lewis, C. S. 1970. *God in the Dock.* Grand Rapids, MI: Eerdmans.

Luttbeg, Norman, and Michael Gant. 1995. *American Electoral Behavior 1952–1992.* Itasca, IL: Peacock.

MacPherson, C. B. 1970. *The Political Theory of Possessive Individualism.* London: Oxford University Press.

Phillips, Kevin. 1970. *The Emerging Republican Majority.* Garden City, NY: Doubleday.

Sabato, Larry. 1995. "The 1994 Election in Virginia: The Senate Race from Hell." *University of Virginia Newsletter,* Weldon Cooper Center for Public Service, March.

Sahlins, Marshall. 1976. *Culture and Practical Reason.* Chicago: University of Chicago Press.

Scammon, Richard M., and Ben J. Wattenberg. 1970. *The Real Majority.* New York: Coward, McCann and Geoghegan.

Voegelin, Eric. 1956. *Israel and Revelation.* Baton Rouge: Louisiana State University Press.

Wagner, Melinda Bollar. 1990. *God's Schools: Choice and Compromise in American Society.* New Brunswick, NJ: Rutgers University Press.

———. 1997. "Generic Conservative Christianity: The Demise of Denominationalism in Christian Schools." *Journal for the Scientific Study of Religion 36*(1):13–24.

Wallace, Anthony F. C. 1966. *Religion: An Anthropological View.* New York: Random House.
Wilcox, Clyde, Mark J. Rozell, and J. Bradford Coker. 1995. "The Christian Right in the Old Dominion: Resurgent Republicans or Holy War?" *PS: Political Science and Politics,* March.

9

The Myth of Culture Wars:
The Case of American Protestantism

CHRISTIAN SMITH, with MICHAEL EMERSON, SALLY GALLAGHER, PAUL KENNEDY, and DAVID SIKKINK

Culture wars is a myth. The conventional wisdom that Americans are divided into two warring camps slugging it out over abortion, prayer in schools, and homosexuality is greatly exaggerated. Growing empirical evidence suggests it just is not true. In fact, most Americans are not very invested in culture wars issues. Nor have they taken up oppositional sides with warring "traditionalist" and "progressive" forces to wage their local and national battles. The vast majority of Americans are much more interested in whether their kids learn to read well, whether they can walk their streets safely at night, and whether the government can get the deficit under control than they are in protesting obscene art and gays marching in parades. The important issues for the mass of Americans, in other words, remain economic and social, not cultural-wars issues.

The actual culture wars that we do see on television—shrill fights over abortion, homosexuality, prayer in schools, obscenity in art, and so on—are being waged by a fairly small group of noisy, entrepreneurial activists at the extremes, whose interests are served by the impression that all of America has taken up arms to join their fight. And too many in the academy and the media have cooperated in fostering this perception. But it is a misperception. Most of America is not at war over culture. The Pat Buchanans and Kate Michaelmans of the airwaves have declared war, but very few Americans have shown up for the fight.

How do we know this? We know this because, when one listens more closely to the broad array of ordinary Americans than to the protests and press releases of militant activists, that is what one hears. A wide range of available quantitative and qualitative evidence from opinion polls and in-depth research interviews tells us that the majority of Americans are simply not very interested in culture wars.

Countless hours of media programming covering controversies surrounding Operation Rescue, Pat Robertson's presidential race, multiculturalism in schools, the Mapplethorpe exhibits, gay pride parades, vulgar "gangsta rap" lyrics, *The Last Temptation of Christ,* antiabortion shootings, and now Ralph Reed and the Christian Coalition would suggest that a national culture war is tearing America apart. One would think that most Americans are ever arming for battle, ever mobilizing for the next demonstration, blockade, hearing, protest, debate, and rally. Thankfully, that is not so. In fact, these books, articles, and broadcasts have together far overblown the story. This chapter is an attempt to help put matters back into perspective, focusing particularly on evidence of culture wars or lack thereof within the immense and important institution of American Protestantism.

WHAT'S BOTHERING AMERICA?

Before examining Protestantism, the first bit of evidence that should cause us to suspect the culture wars story are the answers that people give to questions about America's problems. Political scientists and pollsters who conduct surveys frequently ask the question, What do you think is the biggest problem facing America today? The results are instructive. Most people say things like the federal deficit, crime, unemployment, health care, poverty, and racism. Somewhere down the list you find a few people saying moral decline. People almost never mention abortion, multiculturalism, prayer in schools, secular humanism, the imposition of the Christian Right agenda, pornography, or homosexuality.

For example, a 1994 poll of 1,492 Americans (APOUSFP 1995) asked, "What do you feel are the two or three biggest problems facing the country today?" Forty-two percent of respondents—who were asked to name two or three problems—said crime was the biggest problem. Twenty percent said unemployment and low wages, 19 percent health care costs, 18 percent drug abuse, 15 percent poverty and homelessness, 12 percent poor education, 10 percent the economy, 9 percent bad government, and 9 percent the federal deficit. All answers regarding ethical problems in society, moral decline, the decline of religion, and pornography were combined into one "immorality" category, which garnered a mere 8 percent. Only 1 percent mentioned teenage pregnancy, and less than 0.5 percent mentioned abortion. Nobody said prayer in schools, secular humanism, threats to civil liberties, multiculturalism, or any of the other contentious and highly publicized culture wars issues.

Even when the question is asked differently, the results are the same. A 1995 Harris poll of 1,004 Americans (Harris 1995), for example, asked, "What do you think are the two most important issues for the government to address?" Twenty-two percent reported crime and violence, 18 percent the federal deficit, 16 percent health care, 14 percent welfare, 10 percent taxes, 10 percent education, 8 percent each for programs for the poor, the economy, and programs for the elderly, 7 percent unemployment, and 6 percent foreign policy issues. Only 4 percent mentioned morality and sex on television, 2 percent abortion, 2 percent the decline of family values, and 1 percent the decline of religion. Not an overwhelming interest in culture wars issues here.

Examples could be multiplied, but one final case should suffice. A 1989 Washington Post survey of 1,009 Americans (*Washington Post* 1989) asked, "When you think about the future of our country and the next generation, what things concern you the most?" Respondents were allowed to name two issues. Twenty-five percent said they were concerned about drugs. Fifteen percent said the threat of war, 14 percent the environment, 13 percent the economy, 12 percent crime and violence, 9 percent unemployment, and 9 percent education. Nine percent said they were concerned about moral decline, 2 percent ethics, 1 percent the lack of religion, and 1 percent abortion.

It is possible to salvage the culture wars story even in the face of these survey results. One could argue that people view crime and welfare, for example, as the results of a serious moral decline, which itself must be reversed through culture wars. One wonders, however, why, if moral decline were the perceived root cause of these problems, more people would not simply report moral decline as the biggest problem facing America. On the other hand, one might argue that, although survey respondents really do believe things like abortion and school prayer are the most important issues, either they think that is not what the survey researchers want to hear, or they are reluctant to state views they think are socially undesirable. However— aside from the fact that some respondents *did* think it okay to mention abortion and immorality—if this is so, it speaks volumes about people's convictions and militancy on these matters.

Although one would not want to base an entire case on these opinion data alone, it does tell us something. It tells us that the issues that really interest the vast majority of Americans are economic and social issues, not the much-ballyhooed culture wars issues. And though it is clear that some Americans *are* concerned about what might be thought of as culture wars issues, extrapolating their numbers from these kinds of polls shows that they represent no more than 4 or 5 percent of all Americans. Furthermore, we will argue below that many of those who truly are concerned about moral decline—in these polls the most frequently mentioned conceivable culture wars concern—are deeply ambivalent about what actually to *do* about moral decline. Few of them evince a crusading spirit ready to wage a cultural war to reverse this moral decline.

Ironically, some of the most outspoken culture wars activists are coming to this very realization, and are significantly altering their strategies and rhetoric simply to maintain their appeal with already sympathetic sectors of the American public. Take, for example, a 1993 article in *Policy Review* by Ralph Reed, the youthful but adroit leader of Pat Robertson's political organization the Christian Coalition, entitled "Casting a Wider Net: Religious Conservatives Move Beyond Abortion and Homosexuality." In it, Reed argues that conservative Christian activists need to recognize that the abortion and homosexuality issues simply do not animate most Americans, and that, therefore, "the most urgent challenge for pro-family conservatives is to develop a broader issue agenda." Reed notes that in 1992 election exit polls, only 12 percent of voters, and only *22 percent* of self-identified, born-again Evangelicals listed abortion as an important voting issue. Likewise, only 16 percent of all voters mentioned family values as an issue affecting their vote. He also cites a survey showing that, besides the economy, "the chief concern of voters who attend church four times a month was not abortion, pornography, or prayer in school, but cutting waste in government and reducing the deficit." Reed concludes, "There is growing evidence to suggest that evangelicals and their Roman Catholic allies are concerned about the same issues as the broader electorate, but with a pro-family twist. Their primary interest is not to legislate against the sins of others, but to protect the health, welfare, and financial security of their own families" (1993:32).

Survey data can be deceiving, however, for they can fail to reveal the cultural *meanings* that respondents attach to "issues." Just because many people are concerned about welfare, for example, does not mean that they share a common interpretation of what is wrong with welfare. A leftist structuralist might think the problem is that welfare is a cheap "payoff" to the poor to prevent them from realizing their true class interests and overthrowing the exploitative capitalist order. A conservative individualist, on the other hand, may think the problem is that welfare erodes individual responsibility and initiative and drains resources away from productive investments. Yet they both could easily end up on the same tally of people claiming that "welfare" is the biggest problem facing America.

To get at how people really make sense of their world, to really understand which issues concern them and why, one has to get out and actually converse with them, to sit down in their living rooms for a few hours and let them talk about themselves. Only then do we really begin to understand what animates people and why. This is what we have done. As the first phase of a collaborative, three-year study of American Evangelicals in the summer of 1995, we conducted 128 open-ended, in-depth interviews with a

random sample of churchgoing Protestants in Boston, Chicago, Minneapolis, Portland, Oregon, Birmingham, and Durham, North Carolina. Our
interviews lasted two hours each, and involved Protestants from every major
tradition and denomination, sampled in proportion to their actual numbers
in the American population. We surveyed the full spectrum of Protestantism,
from liberals to fundamentalists, from the marginally committed to the fervent believer, from Black Episcopalians to White Pentecostals. Admittedly, a
complete study of culture wars also needs to research Roman Catholics and
secularists. But if personal investment in culture wars is ever to be found,
according to conventional wisdom, it surely should be found within the
institution of Protestant Christianity, particularly among the most conservative and liberal Protestant Christians. That is where we looked.

METHODS

Churchgoing Protestants were our target population. Our strategy was to
capture the diversity of Protestantism, while achieving proportionate representation for relevant theological and denominational traditions. We attempted to represent the population heterogeneity first by stratifying the
sample by race, denominational tradition, and, where appropriate, presumed theological orientation of liberal versus conservative. This stratification yielded thirteen White categories and three African-American categories of Protestants.[1]

We then determined the number of Protestants in each category and
assigned denominations to categories using Melton (1992, 1993), Bradley et
al. (1992), Mead and Hill (1990), Murphy, Melton, and Ward (1993), and
Payne (1991).[2] Our 128 interviews were distributed evenly among four
researchers. The number of interviews in each category was based on the
proportion of the population in that category, calculated from the Melton
(1993) directory. However, as mentioned above, in order to adequately
account for small but distinct and historically significant denominational
traditions, a minimum of five interviews were assigned for each of the following categories: Anabaptist, Conservative Presbyterian/Reformed, Conservative Pietist/Methodist, Liberal Episcopal, Holiness, and Independent/
Non-denominational. To achieve this diversity, we partially relaxed the proportionality principle, and reduced the number of interviews from the largest
three denominational traditions, conservative White Baptist (from thirty-
seven to twenty-seven), conservative African-American Baptist (from
twenty-one to fifteen), and liberal Methodist/Pietist (from fourteen to ten).[3]

We conducted our interviews in Minneapolis, Minnesota; Chicago, Illi-

nois; Birmingham, Alabama; Durham, North Carolina; Essex County, Massachusetts (north of Boston); and Benton County, Oregon (south of Portland).
The interviews conducted in each area accounted for regional strongholds
of denominational traditions.[4] Sampling frames for each category at each
location were compiled using lists of local churches drawn from telephone
directories, and checked for relative comprehensiveness with Bradley et al.
(1992; contact the authors for a list of denominations by category). Churches
without telephones, or that declined to have their telephone number listed
in the telephone directory, were not included in our sample. This created an
inevitable sample bias against the poorest churches, separatist churches,
and house churches.[5]

We randomly selected individual churches from the lists, then contacted
church pastors to secure cooperation and complete lists of church members
and regular attenders. In order better to diversify at the level of individual
churches, the maximum number of respondents was limited to four per
church. We then systematically selected potential respondents and took a
second random sample for alternates. The list of sampled potential respondents was checked with the pastor to eliminate members completely unin-
volved in the church. In fact, none needed to be eliminated in this way. All
in all, we interviewed members or regular attenders from forty-four local
churches. None of the churches we contacted refused to participate. Of the
individuals randomly selected from the church lists, our response rate was
94 percent (128 interviewed of 139 selected).[6]

The sample also attempted to maintain a rough gender stratification.
General Social Survey (GSS) data show that the female/male ratio among
churchgoing Protestants is 60/40. Therefore, if a researcher was assigned an
odd number of interviews for a given category, the "extra" interview was
conducted with a randomly selected female. For example, if a random
sample from a church list yielded one female, one male, and one couple, a
female in the household was contacted for an interview. In fact, our interview subjects were precisely 60 percent female and 40 percent male.[7]

THE OBLIVIOUS AND DISDAINFUL

What we learned is that many churchgoing Protestants are deeply troubled by where they see America heading. They can articulate in heart-felt
and sometimes sophisticated terms the problems they see around them and
what they think the consequences will be. However, we also discovered—
much to our surprise, since we began our work believing the national culture wars story—that these concerns that trouble them so deeply are not
actually producing among them much of an interest in fighting culture wars.

We began by asking all of our 128 interviewees a series of open-ended questions about how their own sense of religious identity relates to other religious and secular groups, their experiences living as Christians in American society, and their perceptions of how American society is changing. After lengthy discussions on these questions, we then asked our interviewees to name the three specific issues or problems that they thought should be of greatest concern to Christians today. We continued by asking a variety of questions about Protestant cultural disestablishment and status decline, what should make Christians distinctive, Christian involvement in politics, the separation of church and state, and attitudes about materialism, the family, the media, morality, and cultural pluralism. If ever a study could detect Protestants' investment in culture wars, this was it.

In fact, we didn't detect much of it. To the contrary, through our in-depth interviews we made three interesting and mind-changing observations. First, more than a few interviewees, when probed, turned out to be unaware of the existence of culture wars. Second, more than a few others who knew about culture wars proved to have a strong distaste for them. Third, others who initially sounded like they might be good culture warriors turned out, in fact, either to interpret America's problems in a way or to hold certain beliefs that neutralized any serious involvement in culture wars. Almost all of the churchgoing Protestants we talked to, in other words, demonstrated a clear lack of either awareness of, enthusiasm for, or engagement in culture wars.

First, coming from university environments, we were startled by so many people's obliviousness to culture wars. Not uneducated people, but college-educated people. Young and old. Men and women. Many we interviewed, for example, were unaware of the existence of any important Christian political organizations. Many had either never heard of or knew very little about Jerry Falwell or the Moral Majority. Even fewer had heard of Ralph Reed or the Christian Coalition. Some confused the two. Others confused one or the other with an entirely unrelated person or organization. Many had not heard of Operation Rescue, and many more who had heard of it were not familiar with its goals and tactics. Only a minority of churchgoing Protestants we interviewed had ever heard the phrase "secular humanism," and almost nobody that had heard it could tell us what they thought it meant—especially in terms reflecting its widespread use by conservative Christian activists and writers. One conservative United Methodist man explained confidently, though mistakenly, that it referred to humanitarian efforts of good people to help the needy, like soup kitchens for the homeless. Furthermore, most interviewees confessed that they had either never heard of or did not really understand much about multiculturalism, school choice, tuition vouchers, New Age religion, or issues surrounding federal funding for the arts or alternative definitions of the family.

This observation confirms the growing suspicion among professional pollsters that most Americans do not know what the "Religious Right" is or stands for. Polls show that about 65 percent of Americans have never heard of the Religious Right. Of those that do, 29 percent think it has something to do with freedom of religion and 26 percent simply "don't know." Only 11 percent associate the Religious Right with political activism. For another 9 percent, political extremism comes to mind, and for 5 percent, school prayer.

This confusion only exacerbates the fact that many people do not even seem to know if they belong to the Religious Right or not. In a July 1994 CBS News/*New York Times* poll, 9 percent of Americans said they thought of themselves "as a member of the religious right movement." Two months later, 17 percent responded affirmatively to the same question. That same month, a Gallup poll using the identical question found that 11 percent of Americans identified with the Religious Right. Then Gallup polls in October showed 16 percent affirming, in November, 22 percent affirming, and in December, 14 percent affirming their membership in the Religious Right. Well, which is it? Nine percent or 22 percent?

Amazingly, of those in the December Gallup survey who said they belonged to the Religious Right movement, 30 percent said they were Democrats or leaned toward the Democratic party, 14 percent said they were political liberals, and 37 percent gave a positive approval rating of President Clinton (only 5 points below the national rating at the time). And in a March 1995 Gallup poll, 59 percent of the self-identified Religious Right thought that abortion should be legal in some circumstances, and 9 percent believed abortion should be legal in *all* circumstances. This is the Religious Right? It makes you wonder: maybe the "Religious Right" is more a product of activists' and academics' projections than anything out there in the real world.

Second, given the expectations that we took into the field about Christians' social and political involvements—developed by reading the salient academic and popular literature—we were equally startled by the distaste among many of our interviewees, who *were* aware of culture wars, for culture wars. Our interviews, for example, revealed an almost universal distrust of Christian leaders associated with television or politics. Everybody thought Billy Graham was a saint. But the only saint. A virtual consensus declared the Pat Robertsons, Oral Roberts, and Jerry Falwells of the world to be misguided at best, greedy and exploitative at worst. It was clear that the fallout from the Jim Bakker and Jimmy Swaggart televangelist scandals of the 1980s has not dissipated, but has tainted every other Christian television figure but Graham. As to Ralph Reed, because he seemed to many people to be "just old enough to attend the prom," many were willing to give him a chance. But most were quite pessimistic about his ability to remain clean, given the money and power at his disposal.

Another target of universal antipathy among the people we interviewed who had heard about it was Randall Terry's pro-life organization, Operation

Rescue. Not one of our interviewees spoke positively about him or it. Even the most committed pro-lifers were turned off by Operation Rescue's confrontation, shouting, and perceived negativity. Very many associated the shootings of abortion doctors and receptionists with Operation Rescue, and they wanted no part of it. They were not taking sides against Terry to fight him back, but just wanted to avoid that whole kind of struggle. Most thought that opposition to abortion should be expressed in loving, constructive ways, such as providing supportive counseling and generous financial support to pregnant teenagers, but that controversy and confrontation should be avoided.

Furthermore, more than a few of our interviewees thought that many specific culture wars issues were unimportant or foolish. Some, but certainly not all, thought that the fight for prayer in public schools, for example, was silly. Christian kids, they said, can already pray silently anytime they want. Anyway, everybody already prays before exams. What would a moment of silence gain anybody? And why make Jewish or nonreligious kids feel uncomfortable? Christians, these people asserted, should pay more attention to prayer in their homes and churches. Similarly, various of our interviewees expressed complete lack of interest in a variety of other culture wars issues. One forty-five-year-old Mennonite woman, for example, who called herself traditional and evangelical, confided, "Don't tell anyone I said this, but I really don't care about abortion. It's just not an issue for me. I think it's just as much a sin to bring a child into the world and not take care of him than it is to have an abortion. But I don't say that in public."

Finally, many interviewees voiced a complete lack of interest in "legislating morality," sexual or otherwise. Drawing on a tradition deeply rooted in American Protestantism, many maintained that individuals have to decide for themselves whether or not to obey God, and then live with the consequences. You can't force someone to act like a Christian. It has to come from a change of heart. If some people want to live in sin, as long as it is not really hurting someone else (and sometimes even if it is), there is not much you can do about it. Ultimately, each person will have to answer to God for his or her own life. Obviously, this kind of mentality does not lend itself to cultural crusading.

FAMILY AND EDUCATION ISSUES
AT THE GRASS ROOTS

Far more interesting and important, however, than the unaware, the uninterested, and the antagonistic that we interviewed (of which there will always be some in any group) are those who were aware of and apparently friendly toward culture wars issues. They are the ones who we need most to understand, who most matter for our purposes. Their stories deserve careful attention and analysis.

When we asked interviewees our open-ended questions about their Christian experience in and perceptions of the direction of American society, the vast majority of interviewees were united in voicing grave concerns about two issues: the breakdown of the American family and the decline in American education. Far and above every other concern, family and education emerged as the two areas where churchgoing Protestants believe ominous trends are hurting American society and impinging on their personal lives. And when we asked what specific issues or problems should most concern *Christians* today—a question virtually begging for culture wars answers—the results were congruent. Far and above the list of thirty-three different concerns, topping the list with 17 percent was concern over the state of the family. Eight percent said poverty and unemployment, 6 percent poor schools, and 6 percent mentioned crime and violence. (Only 7 percent said that abortion should be a primary concern of Christians today. Overall, more people were concerned about racism than prayer in schools, and government ineffectiveness than homosexuality or immorality in the media.)

On the surface, widespread troubles among Protestants about the state of the American family and educational system would seem to be a reservoir of emotional and cognitive fuel to inflame the culture wars. What better way to mobilize and deploy forces for and against prayer, multiculturalism, evolutionism, creationism, secular humanism, sex education, condom distribution, New Age curriculum, and homosexuals teaching in public schools than to tap into this deep-seated concern over the state of education? And what better way to call out the forces to fight for and against socially accepted homosexual marriages, abortion, feminism, inclusive definitions of the family, gays in the military, and the advocacy of sexual abstinence for teenagers than to connect those issues to the widespread troubles about the breakdown of the American family? The roots and resources for culture wars are widespread and deep. Or so it would seem.

In fact, they are not. Our interviewees' very real concerns about family and education did not appear to produce a strong investment or significant participation in culture wars. Indeed, overall, our interviews revealed a distinct lack of cultural or political militancy. The vast majority of people we talked with, including those more tuned in to culture wars issues, simply did not manifest a crusading spirit or tell stories of their engagement in culture wars battles. Why not? Why the disconnect?

A careful reading of interviewee's stories reveals two factors that counteract any serious involvement in culture wars. First, many of those who are deeply concerned about family and education interpret problems in these areas in such a way as to negate most culture wars impulses. Second, many others of those troubled by family and education who express an ideology and temperament seemingly well-suited to culture wars activism also embrace other beliefs that seem to effectively neutralize their engagement in culture wars.

When people reported to us that the breakdown of the American family was their primary concern, we asked them what they thought was causing this breakdown and what they thought should be done in response. With few exceptions, they did not claim that the family was under attack by liberal elites, secular humanism, feminism, the federal government, or an immoral mass media. Even when we fished about for such answers, we did not hear them often. Instead, we sometimes heard stories about irresponsible parents, the decline of community, and poverty. Mostly, however, we heard stories about economic pressures that are pulling families apart.

Some people concerned about the American family had no idea why it seemed to be coming apart. When we asked, they simply said, "I don't know." Most others, however, did have some idea. One explanation was irresponsible parents. One Black Baptist woman, for example, explained:

> A lot of parents fail to fulfill their responsibility. A lot of them. Lots of them are on drugs now, so they think it's okay for their kids. I think a lot of the problem falls back on the parents. If parents really did what they were supposed to do, then the children would be better than what they are.

Another explanation focused on the transience of modern life. One Pentecostal man, who works for American Airlines, observed:

> The family has been in decline for most of this century, with such tremendous changes in technology and lifestyles. American is so spread out now. We are no longer a family-oriented society. We move all over the place. And that changes attitudes and commitments.

Others blamed poverty for family breakdown. One Baptist man, in the middle of a long list of social ills, remarked, "There's the breakdown of the family, divorce. You know, the poverty, the cycle of poverty in the inner cities." A few attributed family breakdown to demonic spiritual forces. One United Methodist man, for example, declared:

> Satan is just taking over. He's more powerful than he ever was. I don't know what's responsible for it, unless it would be just Satan, completely. You see the breakdown in the family, high divorce rates, increase in unwed mothers, no respect for authority. All these things are growing. And the only thing I can say is responsible is the fact that Satan is just having his day.

However, far and away our interviewees' most common explanation for the breakdown of the American family was economic pressures. Over and over again, we heard people—conservative and liberal Protestants alike, those who listen to James Dobson on the radio, those with no love for feminism—claim that the main cause of family breakdown was the disintegrating demands of the changing U.S. economy. One Southern Baptist man, well-informed about culture wars, observed:

> The backbone of every country has got to be the family, but our family unit has broken down. The divorce rate is so high. And families are not raising their children with Christian ideals anymore. Parents are so involved in their careers that they are putting their children in daycare. They have to, in order to live in today's society, with the economy like it is, they just have to.

Some, such as this Black Baptist police officer, tended to blame our culture's materialism and overconsumption:

> We've spent a lot of time trying to get houses, cars, and we spend too little time raising our families. That's what's causing the breakdown of the American family. You know, everybody works. It takes two incomes basically to make it now. The husband and the wife. So everyone leaves home all the time, going to work, maybe on different shifts. The husband and wife rarely see each other, further breaking down the family. A lot of times we just over-extend ourselves, buying material things that we can't afford.

Many others, however, such as this Baptist man, believe both parents bringing home two paychecks is a basic necessity today:

> Look at kids of mothers who don't work and you can tell a difference in the way they're brought up. Still, mothers and fathers both have to work just to keep up, just to pay their bills and feed the kids. Fifteen years ago, both worked for a nice middle-class lifestyle. Now a days, it's a matter of survival.

A majority of the people we interviewed, then, were deeply concerned about family breakdown. But their analyses of the causes of that breakdown focused almost entirely on economic and social problems, not the intrusive values of secular humanism, feminism, or liberal elites.

We found the same kind of dynamic at work regarding education. As with the family, many of those deeply concerned about American education interpret what's wrong with it in a way that neutralizes their potential involvement in culture wars. People were not very concerned with multiculturalism, evolutionism, creationism, secular humanism, sex education, condom distribution, New Age curriculum, homosexuality, or prayer in public schools. Instead, they were concerned with children's physical safety in schools and the declining quality of basic education in reading, writing, and arithmetic. Listen to their grievances:

Education is the pits. I think it's terrible. Children are not being taught properly. And I don't mean manners and ethics. I'm just talking simple education. (Southern Baptist woman)

The problem is, kids go to schools and get beat up and are exposed to drugs and alcohol. (Assemblies of God man)

The real problem with this whole education system is that kids are not taught to think. (Presbyterian Church of America man)

What bothers me is the violence in schools today. Kids carry knives and guns to school, get in arguments, and get killed. (Southern Baptist woman)

Teachers have so much extra work to do now that the basics, reading, writing, and arithmetic, have gone out the window. (Christian and Missionary Alliance woman)

Public schools are in a very sad state. Violence in schools, kids carrying guns, illiteracy. (Southern Baptist man)

Schools have gotten away from their core business: teaching people to read, write, do math, learn facts, and how to analyze, understand scientific principles, that kind of thing. (Episcopalian woman)

The basic quality of education that children get is really what concerns me. And their safety worries me. (United Methodist woman)

But what did these people think were the *causes* of this educational breakdown? Again, it was bread-and-butter and not culture wars educational problems that people blamed. Very few faulted the spread of secular humanism, liberal influences, New Agers, or multiculturalists. Rather, they mentioned problems like underfunded schools; oversized classes; under-qualified, overworked, or uncommitted teachers; irresponsible parents; top-heavy educational administrations; teachers unions; and, for a few, busing and racial integration. The lack of discipline in the classroom was also a major concern. Over and over again, people claimed that teachers today— living in fear of lawsuit-happy parents—are not able to disciple unruly kids as they did in the old days.

Returning to their deepest concern, many of those we interviewed traced education's woes back to the breakdown of the family. The problem, they argued, is not so much with schools themselves, as with what society hands the schools to work with: kids who are not being properly parented. Again, interestingly, many we interviewed specifically indicted economic pressures that are pulling families apart as a main source of educational breakdown. One Christian and Missionary Alliance woman, for example, who works as a public school secretary, argued:

With the economic structure like it is, it's almost a necessity for both parents to work. Problem is, children come to school who are with dad four nights a week and mom three nights. They're pulled, they're loyalties are pulled. This little first-grader came in one day crying. And his teacher took him on her lap and asked what's the matter, and he says "Oh, I wish I could stay at one place all the time." That has a negative impact on a child.

Another man from a Holiness church remarked:

> Schools are a microcosm of society. Society's families have broken down, and schools have become a repository for watching children. With the hectic world of both parents working, schools are becoming expensive day-care centers. Teachers are now supposed to be therapists, baby-sitters, and playmates first, educators last. I really believe it's a mess.

We were amazed to hear many religious conservatives, in blaming economic pressures more than moral decline (or, rather, as a primary cause of moral decline), sounding as much or more like good liberals as the liberals we interviewed sounded.

But what about practical education policy? What kind of solutions did these people offer? Interestingly, precisely because of their recognized inability or lack of desire to achieve a Christian domination of the public schools, most respondents—including culturally aware conservatives—eschewed the crusading mentality of culture wars activists. Take, for example, this Southern Baptist man, who is very much tuned in to the anxieties and programs of conservative Christian political organizations. After hearing him lament in detail the declining quality of education, we asked whether he was concerned about morality in school. He responded:

> I am much more concerned about reading, writing, and arithmetic than moral issues. Morals should come out of the home. I don't really care about teachers teaching my kids morals. If they can teach them how to read and calculate and have good English and grammar, that's what I'm looking for from schools. I'm not looking for them to teach my kids ethics. I'll do that at home.

That sentiment was echoed nearly exactly by this man from a Christian and Missionary Alliance church, who is very tuned in to culture wars issues, but who has done very little to express his views politically:

> I would prefer that schools influence my children in a positive manner. But they've gone to the other extreme. Therefore, I would settle for them to be merely neutral. I don't care about school teaching about God. I'll do that. Schools should just stick with education—reading, writing, arithmetic. If they do that I'll be happy. I'll take care of the rest.

Similarly, for many (whether they could or could not control public schools), concerns such as the moral content of curriculum and textbooks and sex education are simply not burning issues. As one Black Baptist man put it, "Textbook battles and sex education? They're not on my agenda. No, not on my agenda."

But what about the one big education issue so dear to the hearts of so many Christian Right activists, prayer in schools? Was not that a question that concerned our ordinary Christians? A fair number of people, especially those *less* aware of culture wars, said that they would "prefer" a moment of silence or, sometimes, the Lord's Prayer in schools. They said, when asked, that it would "be nice" or that "this would be a good idea." But they typically did not raise the issue themselves, and were not terribly invested in it when we raised it. They certainly were not ready to take up arms for battle over it.

More interestingly, many of our conservative Christians either said they couldn't care less or were positively against fighting for prayer in public schools. The attitude of this Pentecostal man was typical of many others:

> Return prayer to schools? I'd just like to see prayer returned to Christian homes. Some are out there picketing. I say Christians should worry about their *own* righteousness and standing before God, and start living right themselves. They ought to worry about bring[ing] prayer back into their *own* homes and churches, their own lives. Let's start there before we start forcing prayer on others. No, I'm not for crusades for prayer in public schools.

THE PLURALISM-VERSUS-CHRISTENDOM DILEMMA

In talking with ordinary people, we observed another factor that appeared to neutralize culture warring among some who otherwise seem ideologically sympathetic to culture wars. That is a widespread commitment to certain theological and political beliefs that inhibit an all-out, bare-knuckled struggle to establish Christian values and morals over all Americans. It became clear in our interviews that very many Protestants are beset by a very deep and difficult quandary that we call the "pluralism-versus-Christendom" dilemma. In short, many Protestants think that Christian morality should be the primary authority for American culture and society, *and* simultaneously think that everyone should be free to live as they see fit, even if that means rejecting Christianity. Because they firmly believe both simultaneously, the logic of each restrains the tendencies of the other from being carried too far.

On the Christendom side, most churchgoing American Protestants have inherited (and more or less embrace) the theological notion that there is a transcendent God who establishes absolute and universal standards of morality for individuals and societies. They also tend to believe that obedience to God's ways ultimately produces abundant life, while the rejection of God's ways produces individual and social degeneration and, finally, death. Most American Protestants, too, are heirs of a faith that for centuries enjoyed the status of de facto religious establishment. This Christendom legacy—which mixes essential elements of Christian doctrine with aspects of the historical Protestant experience in America, particularly Puritanism—makes Protestants want *their* morality and standards to be normative for American society. Not only are these standards more familiar and comfortable to them, they are also assumed—even if only semiconsciously—to provide the only basis for the ongoing prosperity of American civilization. The Christendom impulse is illustrated in this exchange with a Baptist woman:

> Q: Would you support a law to recognize homosexual marriages?
> A: Well, no. The Christian laws shouldn't do that. I'm totally against gay mar-
>   riages and lesbians and them wanting to raise kids.
> Q: And if they say you're imposing your religious values and morals on them?
> A: Well, I'm just telling you what the Word of God says.
> Q: But if they said they don't believe in God or the Bible, then you would say?
> A: You can't change me, my beliefs.
> Q: So you're comfortable using laws to maintain Christian morals?
> A: Well, yes.

At the same time, the *very same* Protestants are committed to another belief that is fundamentally incompatible with the idea of Christendom: individual volunteerism. This belief reflects other age-old Christian doctrines colored not by Puritanism, but by the American Protestant experience of frontier revivalism, and by less religious aspects of American culture. Inherent in Protestant faith is the idea that each individual must ultimately decide for him- or herself to follow God or not; that truly meaningful moral actions cannot be forced, but must come voluntarily from the heart; and that Christians ultimately can't force people who do not want to be Christians to act as if they were. As one Pentecostal man said, "I am opposed to shoving anything down people's throats and I think God is too. He gives every person a right to choose. And we should also."

Furthermore, good old American individualism—which most Protestants, conservatives and liberals alike, have imbibed deeply—prescribes that individuals should not be coerced by social institutions, especially by the government, and particularly not on personal matters; that freedom to pursue individual happiness is a paramount good; that people shouldn't meddle too deeply in other people's business; and that government usually provides poor solutions to social and cultural problems. This belief in individual volunteerism naturally eschews the domineering spirit of Christendom, and instead accepts, if not embraces, social and cultural tolerance and pluralism. People should live how they choose to live, and be prepared to answer to God for their own choices. So, in the very same discussion, the very same Baptist woman also affirmed the individual volunteerism impulse:

Q: How do you feel about using laws to set social standards about family life or sexual morality?

A: Well, I don't think the law can do that because that's not the law's responsibility. The Bible says it's people's own responsibility, not the law's. I think that's what has America in trouble now: we try to make the law take care of everything. I don't agree with using laws for that kind of thing.

Q: You would rather have people live morally voluntarily, and not have the government trying to tell people how to live?

A: Yes, that's right.

Notice, it is not that some Protestants embrace Christendom and others embrace individual volunteerism. Most of the people we interviewed, just like this Baptist woman, fully embrace both, even if they are not aware of it in these precise terms. And being caught on the horns of this dilemma creates within them a powerful self-restraining ambivalence about Christian social and political activism. Their volunteeristic thinking evokes the concerns of Christendom—God's laws are not optional, but binding on all people and nations, for their own good. At the same time, however, mental steps toward Christendom automatically rouse the opposition of volunteerism—you shouldn't force people to live like Christians. In the end, neither gets very far.

Historically, this pluralism-versus-Christendom dilemma was fairly easily resolved by the fact that Protestantism, although officially disestablished, in fact for centuries dominated America's public discourse and its major institutions. By failing to see the degree to which theirs was an imposed domination, the Protestant establishment had its cake and ate it too: it enjoyed a "Christian America" that it believed was voluntarily chosen by the American people. But since the Protestant establishment has increasingly lost control of public discourse and major institutions since the turn of the twentieth century, the majority of Protestants who want to affirm both Christendom and individual volunteerism face an increasingly uncomfortable cognitive dissonance.

Most of the people we interviewed tried to resolve this dissonance by compartmentalizing both beliefs, strongly affirming them as separate commitments, and preventing each from having to face the full implications of the other. When we began to press people to decompartmentalize these conflicting convictions and choose one above the other, they fought long and hard to keep them in their separate compartments. When we persisted, sometimes people simply gave up and said, "I don't know how it fits together. I guess I'll have to think about it some more." But in the end, the ultimate practical consequence we saw in most of those we talked with was that any potential culture warring that Christendom tended to encourage was consistently reined in and subdued by the tolerance and pluralism inherent in individual volunteerism. Battling to Christianize America just didn't sit right.

CONCLUSION

Between those who are oblivious to culture wars, those disdainful of culture wars, those who interpret America's problems in a way that neutral-izes activism in culture wars, and those who hold beliefs about individual volunteerism that tend to counteract engagement in culture wars, there are not a lot of churchgoing Protestants left over to fight culture wars. And that helps to explain why even the Christian Coalition's relatively large number of member activists, impressive by standards of most social movements, still only amount to about *one-half of one percent* of the total population. Not quite a moral majority.

David Moore gives us another perspective in his April/May 1995 article in *The Public Perspective,* which uses survey data to identify the magnitude of the Religious Right. According to Moore, if you define the Religious Right as politically conservative independent or Republican Christians who say that religion is very important in their lives, who attend church services regularly, and who oppose abortion in all circumstances, then the Religious Right makes up only 4 percent of the American population, and only 9 percent of Republicans. Not exactly half of a nation torn in two.

In her award-winning 1986 book, *Cities on a Hill,* Frances FitzGerald (1986) described Jerry Falwell's Moral Majority as "a disciplined, charging army." That image lives on today, as conventional wisdom frames and frets about the Pat Robertsons, Ralph Reeds, Pat Buchanans, Randall Terrys, and James Dobsons of the world. We would like to suggest, however, that when you stop listening to these noisy, entrepreneurial elites for a moment, and begin listening to the great mass of ordinary Americans, particularly to those within the institution of American Protestantism, you don't hear the clamor of a disciplined charging army. You hear the struggles and worries of regular folks trying to get along in a world that seems to them increasingly danger-ous and dysfunctional. You hear people worried about their kids, about the economy, about their neighborhoods. You hear people often trying to follow God as best they know how. To most of these folks with these concerns, the brouhaha over culture wars is fairly distant and trivial.

Culture wars among some elites do exist. But the story that has been told about them has been quite overblown. Perhaps by putting matters back into perspective, the voices of ordinary Americans can help to refocus national attention on pressing issues: on matters of economic justice, fiscal responsibility, racial reconciliation, environmental stewardship, and support for the kind of stable, nurturing families that nearly all Americans so desperately desire.

NOTES

1.   For the White Protestants, we created a liberal and conservative category for the following denominational traditions: Baptist, Methodist/Pietist, Lutheran, and Presbyterian/Reformed. In our judgment, the predominantly conservative traditions of Holiness, Pentecostal, and Independent/Non-denominational did not warrant a separate liberal cell. The very small number of conservative Episcopalians were included in the conservative Presbyterian/Reformed group. For the African-American churches, we viewed Methodist, Baptist, and Pentecostal as sufficiently internally homogeneous in theological orientation to warrant one category for each tradition.

2.   We relied primarily on Melton's (1993) reported membership figures to determine the size of the denomination; we determined theological orientation from descriptive summaries of each denomination in Melton (1993), Mead and Hill (1990), Murphy, Melton, and Ward (1993), and Payne (1991). Bradley et al. (1992) provide an estimate of independent and nondenominational church membership.

3.   Since we were still conducting a large number of interviews from each of these three categories, we assumed that the marginal gain was higher if twenty interviews were reassigned from these three to the important, though numerically small denominational traditions. In the end, each of the six smaller traditions mentioned above gained two to three interviews on average, the three large categories lost a total of twenty interviews, and the rest of the denominational traditions were assigned interviews in proportion to their numbers.

4.   A disproportionate share of Lutherans was interviewed in Minneapolis, for example, and relatively more African-American Baptists were interviewed in Birmingham. The smaller categories, with only five allotted interviews each, were split among two researchers in order to assure geographical diversity and to keep the number of necessary church contacts from unreasonably proliferating.

5.   For the purpose of this research, however, this is an unavoidable and relatively insignificant bias, insofar as these churches would be expected to have little influence on the dominant character of Protestantism overall.

6.   While the sampling methodology worked efficiently for White Protestants, it became increasingly clear that a complete random sample of African-American Protestants would be difficult to obtain. Many pastors of African-American churches held second jobs, most churches did not have secretarial assistance, and many did not have an answering machine. Furthermore, in certain low-income neighborhoods we sampled, many African-American churches held a policy against distributing church membership lists because of threats from collection agencies, the IRS, etc.

Moreover, many randomly sampled African-American Protestants proved unwilling to do interviews with a researcher who called without a personal reference. After multiple unsuccessful call-backs and requests, it became apparent that in some cases the only reasonably effective means of obtaining interviews with African-American Protestants would be to work through existing social networks of African-American Protestants with which we did have prior contacts. In the sample of African-American Protestants, therefore, seven were sampled randomly and seventeen were not. However, with African Americans, we were able to achieve regional diversity (Chicago, Birmingham, Boston, and Durham), and to represent the three major traditions proportionate to their numbers in the population.

7. On other demographic variables, our interviewees were, on average, 47.6 years old (s.d. = 15.3) and had 15.6 years of education (s.d. = 2.4). Seventy-four percent were married, 12 percent never married, 7 percent divorced, 6 percent widowed, and 1 percent separated. Sixty-six percent were employed full-time, 11 percent part-time, and 23 percent did not work. Compared to churchgoing Protestants in the 1994 GSS, we find no age bias in our sample. However, our respondents are significantly more educated than the average churchgoing Protestant, more likely to be married, and more likely to be working full-time. Data on churchgoing Protestants in the 1994 GSS are as follows: mean age = 47.9 years old (s.d. = 17.4); mean years of education = 13.1 years (s.d. = 3.0); marital status = 54 percent married, 16 percent never married, 14 percent divorced, 12 percent widowed, and 4 percent separated; employment = 52 percent working full-time, 10 percent part-time, and 38 percent not working.

REFERENCES

APOUSFP. 1995. The American Public Opinion and U.S. Foreign Policy 1995 Poll. Sponsored by the Chicago Council on Foreign Relations. Conducted as personal-interviews, October 7–25.
Bradley, Martin B., Norman M. Green, Jr., Dale Jones, Mac Lynn, and Lou McNeil. 1992. *Churches and Church Membership in the United States 1990.* Atlanta, GA: Glenmary Research Center.
FitzGerald, Frances. 1986. *Cities on a Hill.* New York: Simon and Schuster.
Harris, Louis. 1995. Louis Harris and Associates telephone poll. Conducted June 8–11.
Mead, Frank, and Samuel Hill. 1990. *The Handbook of Denominations in the United States.* Nashville, TN: Abingdon.
Melton, J. Gordon. 1992. *Religious Bodies in the United States.* New York: Garland.
———. 1993. *Encyclopedia of American Religions.* Detroit: Gale.
Moore, David. 1995. "The 'Religious Right': Definition and Measurement." *Public Perspective* 6(3):35–38.
Murphy, Larry, J. Gordon Melton, and Gary Ward. 1993. *Encyclopedia of African-American Religions.* New York: Garland.
Payne, Wandell. 1991. *Directory of African-American Religious Bodies.* Washington, DC: Howard University Press.

Reed, Ralph. 1993. "Casting a Wider Net: Religious Conservatives Move Beyond Abortion and Homosexuality." *Policy Review* 65(Summer):31–35.

Washington Post. 1989. Washington Post telephone poll. Conducted May 12–16, by the I.C.R. Survey Research Group.

III

RECONCEPTUALIZING THE BATTLEGROUND
OF AMERICAN POLITICS

10

Lambs among the Lions:
America's Culture Wars in Cross-Cultural Perspective

N. J. DEMERATH III and KAREN S. STRAIGHT

A staple in modern popular fiction is the decline of the world as we know it into some form of bureaucratic, totalitarian, thoroughly invasive "new order." Sometimes the enemy is external, but often the seeds of destruction are internal weaknesses, conflicts, or failings that leave us susceptible to those with aspirations for power. And often, these very internal qualities make us passive in the midst of the process—passive until it is too late. For example, consider Margaret Atwood's *The Handmaid's Tale,* a nightmarish novel of a United States taken over by right-wing religious fanatics:

> It was after the catastrophe, when they shot the President and machine-gunned the Congress and the army declared a state of emergency. They blamed it on the Islamic fanatics, at the time. Keep calm, they said on television. Everything is under control. . . .
>   That was when they suspended the Constitution. They said it would be temporary. There wasn't even any rioting in the streets. People stayed home at night, watching television, looking for some direction. There wasn't even an enemy you could put your finger on. (1985:225)

Although fiction, not everyone reading the book thought it so farfetched. More directly to our concern here, Atwood's tale reflects in interesting ways an increasing concern over an American "culture war." Popular media political analysis carry ominous connotations of a looming pitched battle of a sort not seen in this country for almost a century and a half.

Some academics have participated in popularizing this concern. Just the titles alone of two recent books by James Davison Hunter, *Culture Wars* (1991) and the more mollifying *Before the Shooting Begins* (1994), point toward a bloody contest between liberals and conservatives, orthodox and progressive, modernists and fundamentalists. Further, the rhetoric suggests that Americans who have not yet chosen sides will have to soon. And some would say that this is no longer a war of mere words or government policy options, since the violence has already begun.

But we demur. Perhaps we are a tad naive (a charge we return to later), but what some pundits now see as cultural warfare, we see as cultural democracy at work. It is true that cultural discord over abortion, school prayer, family and gender roles, and racial and ethnic status have led to cultural hostilities, violence, and even murders—as recent events in Pensacola, Boston, and Oklahoma City attest. But while a minuscule minority has resorted to von Clausewitz's ultimate form of "politics," all of this falls short of what we would define as a true culture war, namely, *concerted violence over governmental legitimacy and control in the pursuit of non-economic interests.*

Let us clarify our intended meanings. We use "concerted violence" to mean a strategic use of collective force on a large scale. This stands in distinction to aberrant actions that are more individualized and sporadic; neither isolated murders of abortionists nor an almost universally condemned terrorist bombing (which even had many militia spokesmen running for rhetorical distance) qualifies. Further, our concern with "governmental legitimacy and control" is intended to distinguish conflicts where real power is at stake from other forms of violent confrontations, however tragic. Finally, we specify "noneconomic interests" to distinguish culture wars from what are thought to be more conventional forms of collective violence, those involving dimensions of class conflict. However, there are few "pure" forms of social conflict, as even class struggles require cultural constructions and frames of interpretation. More significantly, cultural conflicts can be greatly exacerbated by compounding structural inequalities, and may even require them in order to achieve "war" status. Because the risk of semantic inflation is, in this case, more than just an academic matter, we feel impelled to insist that if our definition of a culture war is accepted, the United States hardly qualifies. Recent research, much of it reported in this volume, makes that point *internally* on the basis of careful analysis of recent survey and ethnographic data.

But the argument in this chapter rests on more *external* evidence. Applying the phrase "culture war" to the United States makes a mockery of countries elsewhere around the world that fulfill the criteria all-too well. Nor are these countries hard to find. In the same issue of America's newspaper, *USA Today* [*sic*], two side-by-side front-page columns reported the 170 deaths in Oklahoma City and some 2000 bodies found in a mass grave in Rwanda. While not minimizing the human toll of Oklahoma City, only one of these examples represents mass, collective violence. For other examples, one need only turn to a recent United Nations report (U.N. Department of Economic and Social Development 1993) that lists some thirty-two ethnic and religious civil wars, each involving more than one thousand deaths in 1989–1990 alone. And Charles Tilly has reviewed a spate of literature on "state-incited violence" (including both state-sponsored and state-seeking violence) that would fairly describe the twentieth century as "the most virulently violent ten decades in human history" (1993:1; see also Sivard 1991; Gurr 1993).

As part of some current comparative research on religion, politics, and the state (e.g., Demerath 1994), the senior author has recently visited some fourteen countries around the globe, including a number for whom cultural warfare has become a way of life. Space constraints force us to set aside some obvious cases such as China, Egypt, Indonesia, and Turkey; moreover, the voluminous bibliographies for the cases we discuss here are postponed to a forthcoming book. Instead, this chapter contains three major parts. The first provides brief personal reports from the cultural trenches of Northern Ireland, Guatemala, Israel, and India. The second offers five conceptual distinctions that help to explain the difference between those countries where culture warfare is both deep-seated and routine, and countries, like our own, where such conflict is less common and less extreme. Third and finally, the chapter concludes with some broader comments on the culture war dispute in response to a recent critique of this and similar arguments by James Hunter.

NORTHERN IRELAND

Surely this is a country where religion is the prime political mover. Moreover, it is a country where one is said to be forced to take sides. And yet local knowledge does not always accord with those understandings. According to many informants, there are certainly small groups of religious zealots, especially clustered around centers such as Ian Paisley's Martyr's Memorial ("Presbyterian" [sic]) Church. But old-line theological differences have lost much of their salience after some three hundred years, and most people are now more "culturally" than "religiously" Protestant or Catholic. The current conflict is less exacerbated by class factors, since Catholics have begun to catch up with Protestants in economic terms. And the demographic realities are changing. At the time of partition in 1921, Catholics constituted roughly one-quarter of the Northern Irish population; they are now closing fast on the majority necessary for a vote to leave Great Britain for the somewhat reluctant embrace of the Irish Republic—and given the state of the Northern Irish economy, a dependent affiliation with one or the other would appear necessary.

The current changes are only partly and decliningly a matter of differential fertility. Many Protestants see the political writing on the wall and are leaving for England and the United States. Indeed, the Protestants remaining in Northern Ireland resemble the Catholics remaining in South Boston; both are losing victims of transformation, and in the time-honored tradition of rear-guard actions, have violence as one of their few remaining options. The fact that most of the recent deaths are Catholic rather than Protestant is a perverse harbinger of better times to come. In the past year, these signs have proved portentous and the early stages of negotiation augur well. By now most of the citizenry is weary of a war waged from the cultural margins. After all, if one extrapolates the numbers over the past twenty years, the "troubles" have cost more lives in Northern Ireland than did the Vietnam War in either England or the United States.

But there are no guarantees. The violent remnants may be on the margins, but they still have some ability to enflame what are Protestant-Catholic suspicions into what has historically been a violent mistrust. There is reason for hope, but the cultural tensions could too easily become cultural warfare once again.

GUATEMALA

Guatemala represents a country where the cultural and religious fault lines are more confused than in Ulster. A dramatic representation of those divisions was symbolized by the alabaster Virgin Mary looking down in stunning whiteness from her wall pedestal high above the dark-skinned women in their brightly woven *huipiles* who had come to attend a memorial mass in honor of a local agrarian reform counsellor killed by the military one year previously. Indeed, because of the military's killing of one priest and threats against others in the early 1980s, this Quiche parish had been formally closed for several years—the only one in the history of Christendom to experience this fate. The forces of traditional Catholicism, liberation theology, indigenous cultural pride, and evangelical Protestantism have kept Guatemala in cultural turmoil.

Estimates of the number of war deaths in Guatemala over the past twenty-five years range from 20,000 to 100,000, with uncounted others missing or in exile. Much of this conflict is undeniably economic as part of Latin America's continuing battle over land, agricultural control, and capitalist profiteering. But the struggle also has sharp cultural edges that reflect the ethnic, linguistic, and religious differences so deeply etched by Guatemala's 1992 Nobel laureate, Rigoberta Menchu (1983). Religion in Guatemala is no longer a single Catholic monolith but rather a series of conflicting movements often at each others' throats as well as competing for souls.

Although the Catholic Church was officially disestablished in 1871, it took more than one hundred years to mount an effective challenge to its place at the head of the state table. The challenge finally came from two contenders. First, in Guatemala as throughout Latin America, various forms of evangelical Protestantism are surging, both among the affluent and the working class. Second, again in keeping with other countries, there is also a resurgence of traditional Mayan religion, culture, and identity. This is especially strong among the *indigenos* in the rural countryside and mountains to the north, including members of the antigovernment guerilla movement still active there.

All of this has produced kaleidoscopic changes. The guerilla movement now has a traditionalist cultural agenda to complement its radical thrusts on behalf of economic rights, gender equity, and relief from political terror. Since General Rios Montt's regime of the early 1970s, the government and the military have become increasingly Protestant, including Latin America's first elected Protestant chief of state, Jorge Serrano, in 1990. Meanwhile, Guatemala's Catholic Church—led by archreactionary archbishops until late in the 1980s—has begun to follow some of its local priests to the left. Recently its criticism of the government and its human rights abuses have come to resemble the liberation theology that began in Brazil thirty years ago. And many small-town Catholic parishes in Guatemala have become surprisingly syncretic as their services reflect both Mayan and pentecostal Protestant elements, including a greater role for women.

In Guatemala, too, there may be good news in the recently negotiated peace accords between the government and the guerilla movement. On the other hand, if the country does not explode, it may implode largely because of the cultural fissures that give new meaning to its frequently devastating earthquakes.

ISRAEL

Israel's culture conflicts have been accorded even more American media time than our own, and many of us have seen the situation unfold on television from the highs of Camp David to the lows of Hamas, Hebron, and the assassination of Yitzhak Rabin. Recent events have been guardedly encouraging. Despite the efforts of obstructionist groups on both sides, the Israeli-Palestinian talks have not been canceled, and Israel's borders with Egypt and Jordan, if not yet Syria, appear more secure.

But in addition to the obvious culture war of long standing, there are several less obvious culture battles only now developing. Complicating the attempts by Israel and the Palestinians to settle their respective borders are the internal conflicts that keep any of the many sides some distance from a sense of unity. These will not only continue to pit Jew against Muslim, but Jew against Jew and Muslim against Muslim, as Israel begins again to shape itself as a state. Having postponed a formal constitution in 1948, Israel has operated in the interim with a half-dozen "Basic Laws" on important issues. But as circumstances change, so may the laws themselves.

In all of this, religion is deceptive. Among Muslims, the continuing dispute between Hamas and the PLO represents an internal power struggle that is only partly a function of their relative religious zealousness. And to say that Israel is a Zionist state is not necessarily to say that it is a Jewish state. Many members of the most passionately pro-Zionist movement—the Gush Emunim—are themselves secular. On the other hand, the most fervently and ultra-orthodox Jewish group—the Haredim of the Mia Sharim—oppose the very notion of the Israeli state that supports their educational and family system. These groups themselves are often perceived as hypocritical in their efforts to avoid military duty and other forms of state service.

Since the proportions of the Haredim and Israeli Arabs are roughly the same at 18 percent, it is sometimes difficult to know which group will be a greater instigator of cultural warfare in the future. Insofar as Israel proclaims its civil religion to be Jewish, it faces obvious problems from within the growing Muslim ranks; to the extent that it opts for a more secular self-conception, as many would like, it would face a wholly different opposition. It might even be preferable to engage in battles on both fronts at once, since at least a tricornered conflict would head off the escalation of a fully polarized war.

INDIA

As a last instance of cultural warfare, the South Asian subcontinent qualifies as a cautionary capstone. Cultural war has a tragic history, marked most grotesquely, perhaps, by the partitioning of India and Pakistan in 1947; estimates of the dead from that episode alone range from 250,000 to 500,000.

However, for some thirty years following independence, India was generally successful in avoiding the culture wars threatened by its uneasy pluralism. In large part, this was due to a constitution modeled much after our own and a system of government inevitably British. But beginning in the early

1980s, the secularity of Indian politics and statecraft began to give way. As too many political moths got too close to the religious flames—and vice versa—official religious neutrality was caught up in surging communal strife. But even here, the cultural warfare is not a simple two-sided affair. Violence can be found in the conflict over Kashmir between Hindus and Muslims (India and Pakistan), in the Sikh mobilization within the Punjab, among Tamil nationalists in southeastern India, and in many other troubled areas of an increasingly troubled nation.

As a case in point, consider the recent episode involving contested sacred land claimed both by Hindus and by Muslims in the north central city of Ayodyah. Here the very site that a Muslim mosque has occupied for some four hundred years is also revered by Hindus as the putative birthplace of the mythical godlike figure, Rama. The competing claims are not new, and actual legal disputes date back to the 1860s. The mosque was actually closed for years as a way of forestalling the dispute and quelling the violence associated with it. Meanwhile, the most recent round of conflict had an obscure beginning almost twenty years ago in a single crumbling marriage when an old and wealthy Muslim man divorced his long-time wife according to accepted Islamic practice, a practice that had also been accepted by the Indian courts and constitution in 1950. Surprisingly, however, the wife protested. Shah Bono defied her shabby treatment at the hands of Muslim personal law poorly administered, and she finally appealed all the way to the Indian Supreme Court in pursuit of full justice as an Indian citizen rather than a Muslim woman. In 1985, the Court declared in her favor. But in 1986 in response to enormous pressure from orthodox Muslim mullahs and imams, Prime Minister Rajiv Gandhi secured a reversal of the "Shah Bono" court decision from Parliament.

This evidence of Islamic power enraged the Hindu Right. Further, the government allowed a reopening of the controversial Muslim mosque at the alleged birthplace of Rama at Ayodyah. It was here that tensions so escalated over the succeeding five years that in December 1992 at an Ayodyah rally of the Hindu nationalist BJP party, thousands broke away and razed the mosque entirely. Yet another round of violence ensued, especially across the north of India and most particularly in Bombay. Once again Hindus and Muslims were locked in combat; in this instance the initiators were primarily associated with Hindutva and a rampaging Hindu Right, while the victims were disproportionately Muslims.

Even this seemingly straightforward culture war has more dimensions than first meet the eye. In the public views of a number of prominent Indian intellectuals these days, the true culprit in this communal violence is the intellectual legacy represented by Western social science and the attendant political theory that requires a secular state (e.g., Nandy 1990). The argument goes this way: India would never have secularized except under the influence of men like Gandhi, Ambedkar, and Nehru—all of whom were originally influenced by Western scholars and political figures who were themselves largely secular. Once the Indian state became secular, it really became both antireligious and anti-Hindu. Hence the only way for Hinduism to survive was by taking extreme action, represented by the increasingly militant nationalism. Often related to this diagnosis is the prescription that, since India is 85 percent Hindu, an officially Hindu government is not only well deserved but the only way to end the culture war now raging. How this solution will pacify militant Islamists is not easy to see, and there is much skepticism among many Indians over this entire line of reasoning. Hindu secularization has abundant internal as well as external causes, and the ironic truth may be that a government that is truly secular may be the only salvation of a culture that is truly but pluralistically religious.

FIVE PERTINENT DISTINCTIONS

Embedded in the four cases presented here are a number of reasons why many other countries have full-fledged culture wars, but the United States does not. These reasons pivot around five critical distinctions.

1. Civil Religion vs. the Religion of the Civil

The concept of civil religion has generally been articulated by sociologists as something of a nationally binding religious common denominator; at least that was the seminal articulation by Robert Bellah (1967). The theory assumes a relatively homogeneous society, or at least a manageable pluralism, in which a shared commitment emerges from an underlying consensus. However, recent accounts doubt that whatever civil religion may have integrated America culturally in the past may not have been the product of spontaneous, emergent consensus (Demerath and Williams 1985); and recent political changes and realignments have now produced two conflicting civil religions (cf. Wuthnow 1988; Hunter 1991). One might wonder if the phrase "two civil religions" is an oxymoron—if national unity is a prime criterion of civil religion itself. Certainly we agree that this country is increasingly in trouble if it depends upon religious consensus for its cohesion. This is not just because of disputes between orthodox and progressive Christians, but also the growing diversity of Jewish, Muslim, Hindu, and secular voices.

And yet compared to most other countries, our religious discord remains generally civil and involves very little serious effort to overturn the constitutionally embedded political system. Also, if our civil religion(s) emerge from the bottom up, many other countries have theirs imposed from the top down by those who have recently achieved power and are eager to solidify it. The latter is an often cynical use of religion to apply a sacred veneer to a profane reality. It is more likely to begin culture wars than to end them.

One should not be beguiled by a too literal interpretation of the phrase "civil religion." In relatively stable societies like the United States, it is not that religion is necessarily civil but rather that the civil has a way of becoming religious. That was not Bellah's point, but it was most assuredly Durkheim's ([1912] 1915). What strikes many an American about this country whenever they leave it is the extent to which our most basic common culture exists neither prior to nor independent of our system of governance; instead it derives from it and is largely coterminous with it. Such quintessential American values as democracy, freedom, individualism, and equality are all grounded in the Constitution and other sacred political documents and institutions. Indeed, in many everyday conversations about politics, some people will criticize an issue with the phrase "That's unconstitutional" in much the same way their nineteenth-century forebears might have said "That's unscriptural." The legitimacy of our governance system stands virtually without question and without active threat—militia activism in Montana and Texas notwithstanding. Of course, incumbent officeholders of the moment may be swiftly discredited and replaced, but apathy, not revolution, is our dominant political challenge.

In many other countries, by contrast, governance is an intrusion that is often at odds with the host culture and is constantly scrambling for legitimacy. This offers not only an incentive to culture wars, but an opportunity for them to succeed. And to the extent that imposed governments and ruling elites overplay their ties to religion and other cultural forms in the search for legitimacy, this sets an inviting precedent for outside religious and cultural movements to do the same in pursuing power for themselves.

2. Nationalism vs. Tribalism

One major structural constraint to cultural conflict has been the nation-state itself. For more than two-hundred years—and especially within the twentieth century—the nation-state has been the organizing reality of international politics. The United States is one of the very few "new" nations to prosper in its own terms. Each of the four cases described earlier provides a counterinstance, since each is a created nation in which the state is unable to sustain itself easily. Northern Ireland, Guatemala, Israel, and India are all products of *realpolitik* in which structural straitjackets have been imposed upon diverse and conflicting cultural subjects. While this secured order in the short run, it only postponed longer-term cultural struggles. Indeed such struggles were often exacerbated by forced political confinement under a shared national banner.

Further examples around the globe are conspicuously—often tragically—abundant. In the West they include not only the former Yugoslavia and the USSR but "devolution" movements in Canada's Quebec, Britain's Wales and Scotland, and France's Brittany and the Basque region. Examples elsewhere stretch from Liberia and Rwanda to Iraq, Burma, Sri Lanka, and Indonesia. Benedict Anderson (1983), Rogers Brubaker (1992), and Liah Greenfeld (1992) have all written penetrating accounts of the syndrome in different settings.

The common term for culturally based movements that have either state domination or political autonomy as their goal is "nationalism," but it is only half-accurate. These are national movements insofar as they seek for themselves a distinctive national political identity. On the other hand, they are also "tribal" movements insofar as they are shucking off the unity of a nation-state designed specifically to defuse ethnic differences rather than inflame them. Today we see far more tribalism than nationalism, and it is tribalism that is especially responsible for culture wars.

Of course, cultural identities of all sorts deserve respect, and culture becomes a more salient source of identity as structural entities and arrangements break down. But it is difficult to imagine a world in which every cultural group becomes its own nation. The problem of sophisticated statecraft is to construct and maintain nations without merely cobbling them together insensitively. Successful nations can accommodate cultural differences, but this is far more likely to occur when it results from mutual interests and structural interdependence rather than from political subordination and forced assimilation. When faced with cultural diversity, successful nation-states in this century have been secular states, not only with respect to religion but all other sacred cultural matters (cf. Demerath 1991). This is certainly a major key to the United States's success as the oldest constitutional democracy and federated nation-state still standing. Our First Amendment guarantees free exercise and prevents undue state entanglements for religion, and by implication extends this attitude to other forms of cultural identity as well. True nationhood flourishes best when no power-seeking or power-wielding group can use cultural dominance as a controlling weapon.

This returns us to the constraints represented by a nation-state. Without them, power can become both more absolute in the short run and less stable over the longer haul. Cultural movements are more inclined to pursue power directly and even illicitly when the rules of the political game are made up as the game proceeds. Under these conditions, ends truly justify means, and it is often tempting to eschew conventional politics in favor of a down-and-dirty grab for power. This, of course, is a prime source of culture warfare.

In fact, a major issue in many countries concerns the advisability of observing the democratic procedures stipulated by the constitution of the moment. Over the past thirty years in Brazil, Indonesia, Pakistan, and most recently Algeria, elites have sent in the military and suspended elections when a culturally insurgent movement seemed poised to win. Western and Western-influenced liberals are understandably affronted by such cases; after all, free contests are the essence of democracy, and canceling elections is a betrayal of the system itself. And yet the question can become more complex. Sometimes the issue is not just one of following electoral rules but also about following the rules of governance itself. Thus, the Algerian ruling party canceled elections largely because of its concern that a winning Islamic movement would suspend the government as a whole to follow the example of the Iranian Republic under the Ayatollah Khomeini. Of course, the oligarchic elite in charge was hardly democratic in its own right, and some might reply, "Better the devil you *don't* know than the devil you do." Still, it is clear that democratic shibboleths can be applied at several different levels with sometimes conflicting results.

3. Stacked vs. Cross-Cutting Grievances and Identities

One possible reason to doubt the American culture wars thesis is the argument that culture itself lacks the power required to provoke and sustain such combat. This hard-core "structuralist" perspective is still in vogue in some circles, but not here. As Demerath and Williams have argued, "cultural power" can be a great reservoir of movement passion, resolve, resources, and tactical advantages—at least under certain conditions. While culture and structure are always interconnected in everyday life, culture is often a critical source for political movements of all sorts.

Cultural claims become exponentially more compelling when they are arithmetically aggregated. This is the obverse of American pluralism, where cross-cutting divisions of class, race, region, and religion prevent any one cleavage from serving as a single axis of polarization. From the standpoint of conflict alone—not always the only or most morally defensible standpoint—situations are less disrupted when, for example, the lower classes comprise both Irish and Italians, Whites and Blacks, Protestants and Catholics, and urban and rural residents. All of these differences prevent any one from serving as a single basis of coalescence.

While the United States has some experience with stacked grievances among, say, our religious Right, this is actually declining with the current increase in the Right's internal diversity, at least in part a result of its growth. This development makes it both easier and more difficult for cultural movements. For example, the pro-life movement no longer has to mobilize along dominantly Catholic lines, and it no longer can. By contrast, large-scale cultural divisions between aggregated cultural camps are more likely elsewhere. Stacked class grievances, political disenfranchisement, and cultural defensiveness have long been true of Northern Ireland's Catholics, Guatemala's *indigenos,* Israel's Palestinians, and India's Muslims. A spark in one area can lead to spreading flames. The result is not always a "pure" culture war. However, cultural identities not only form important issues in their own right—they often provide critical symbolic fuel and moral weaponry for use with other causes. And of all cultural identities, religion can be the most urgent and intense (cf. Juergensmeyer 1992).

4. Fundamentalisms vs. Fundamentalists

A word that crops up frequently in matters of politics and religion is one we have so far avoided. Concern over "fundamentalism," as the perceived motive for the recent global resurgence of politicized religion, has produced a growth industry among scholars of religion (e.g., Marty and Appleby 1993). Virtually defined to death, it has been given so many meanings that it now means all too little. Originally coined some eighty years ago to refer to a group of California Protestants seeking dispensations for the Armageddon ahead and investing their faith in biblical inerrancy (Ammerman 1987, 1990), it has too often become synonymous with religious extremism or traditionalism of any form in whatever setting. This has not advanced conceptual understanding, of either fundamentalism or other forms of politicized religion. Some scholars have eschewed the term altogether (e.g., Juergensmeyer 1992).

Of course, there is no question that many fundamentalist religious movements have mobilized for public activism. Many such movements are responding to the secularization represented by modernity and what they perceive as a decline of religion's voice at both the public and private levels. The mobilization of these movements is enhanced when their religious commitments are reinforced by other cultural bonds, or by the process of conflict itself. When religious movements find themselves in conflict with each other, the escalation of action and rhetoric can lead to violence. This can happen whether the contest is for state power, or over sacred texts, sacred pedigrees, or—most strikingly—sacred space. Contested sacramental land is a major source of religious violence, as evidenced at Ayodyah in India, or Jerusalem and Hebron in Israel. While this factor applies to Native

Americans within the United States, it is mercifully absent in our other religious conflicts.

But contrary to prevailing perceptions, not all who march under the banner of religious extremism are deeply or principally religious. Some find religious movements either supportive or intoxicating even without believing deeply, though that may come later. Others are downright cynical in using movements for personal gain. For many participants, there is a deep and abiding commitment but to a basically secular agenda for which the sacred movement provides legitimacy and cover. This is especially likely in countries where outright political opposition is illegal. In such settings, so-called culture wars may be less religious and more conventionally political than they appear. Fundamentalism is a not infrequent proxy for movements opposed to regime corruption, Western imperialism, and a whole series of other forms of exploitation and predation. It can also be a surrogate for movements that would replace one form of oppression with another.

Certainly the United States is not immune to fundamentalism in any of its myriad forms. These forms may be Protestant-based biblical inerrancy and dispensationalism, broader religious extremism, or indeed a cultural extremism that may have little to do with religion itself, for example, fundamentalist nationalism, racial separatism, gender androgyny, or class loyalty. Yet the latter forms are more in the minority here than in many other countries, and they tend to have a shifting base and agenda. As noted earlier, one's attitude on abortion is no longer a fail-safe litmus test of one's religious affiliation. The pro-life movement has lost much of its distinctively religious flavor to become a more secular moral movement that cross-cuts various religious denominations.

One hears a great deal these days about the New Christian Right on the move in local politics and within the Republican party. However, there are ample reasons to be skeptical about its chances of becoming a prime contender for national political dominance (cf. Bruce 1994). For one thing, traditional American fundamentalists remain split between the Democrats and Republicans, and there is an important ceiling effect that applies to extreme religious movements generally within either party. While religion can be effective in mobilizing a minority, the very tactics and appeals used to this end tend to alienate more than they attract. As in the time-honored American tradition of primary versus general election politics, a rush to the flanks often militates against a successful retreat to the middle. As the Pat Robertson campaign of 1988 illustrated, once the Religious Right reached a certain level, this in itself sounded the alarm that prevented it from going further. America is not fertile soil for a mass religious movement. Its basic affluence and its pluralism interact with both a social structure and a culture of individual and collective, political and economic, opportunity to militate against the sort of stacked grievances already discussed.

5. Church/State Entanglement vs. Separation

As a fifth and final distinction to help explain the difference between cultural discord and actual cultural warfare, we offer one that may seem all too American. Insofar as we have a single bit of advice for those who would curb religiously based political violence, we are embarrassed to confess that it involves the United States's own "separation of church and state." Certainly one mark of provincialism is prescribing one's own medicine for other peoples' illnesses. However, we maintain that our putative separation is misunderstood at home almost as much as abroad, and is less a matter for self-congratulation than it is a source of cautious optimism.

One reason for this misunderstanding is the paradox that is at the core of the separation. While many assume that a secular state necessarily leads to a secular society, the reality is very often the reverse. The United States has a separation of church and state; it is simultaneously among the most religious nations in the world. While this seems to be a contradiction, it is not. In fact, each condition is contingent upon the other, as Demerath and Williams (1992) have demonstrated. The country can endorse religion's separation from the state precisely because religion is free to function elsewhere in the national experience; conversely, it is precisely because religion flowers so luxuriantly in the society at large that separation is needed to protect the state and governance process from it. Put more pithily, having rich religious traditions, we need church-state separation; having church-state separation, we need other gardens for cultivating religion and can well afford them. Northern Ireland, Israel, Guatemala, and India are only a few of a host of societies that stand to benefit from a similar combination.

Finally, the point reaches beyond religion to culture more broadly. In its 1965 *Seeger* and 1970 *Welsh* decisions, the U.S. Supreme Court extended conscientious objector status to persons who were avowedly not religious but held beliefs that occupied "in the life of that individual a 'place parallel to that filled by God' in traditional religious persons." In some sense, this radical allowance was precedent shattering, and it represented a potential expansion of the notion of religion that had no theoretical limit. It is not surprising that the Court soon dropped it as a judicial hot potato and has seldom referred to it since. But it does suggest that there is a thin line between formal religion and other sacred cultural tenets, convictions, and associations. If it is sensible to observe a distinction between government and religion, why not mark a similar gap between government and culture in its wider sense?

At first blush, this may seem like extending the sublime to the ridiculous. A government without culture suggests a nation without a soul. However, our separationism applies only to the state, not to society at large or even to politics. While mixing religion and politics can be both volatile and violent, it can also animate and energize. Certainly the idea is not to expunge either religion or culture from the individual consciences of state officeholders but rather to avoid particularistic and hegemonic "entanglements" between the state apparatus and specific cultural groups, whether these are defined in terms of religion, class, race, ethnicity, gender, or any other potentially invidious reference point. This is not the time to explore the issues of culture/state separation in detail, but neither is the idea dismissable out of hand.

A CONCLUSION AND A RESPONSE
TO A CRITIQUE

Does America host cultural tensions, culture battles, and cultural violence? The answer is most assuredly yes. Are its cultural wounds now deeper, more frequent, and more threatening than in the past? Not likely, since our history is as littered with examples as our current landscape. But is America engaged in the kind of culture wars that have become so tragically apparent elsewhere? Clearly not. And yet this is not an all-or-nothing concept, contrary to its treatment here. Just as the United States has experienced some of its features, it would be a mistake to portray countries like Northern Ireland, Guatemala, Israel, and India as fully obsessed war zones. The degree of cultural warfare is an important variable for every society, and one that alerts to us to a range of cultural dynamics that, for the sake of analytic honesty, cannot be ignored.

Meanwhile, a centrist consensus is not the only alternative to culture war. A more plausible case can be made for the United States as a fractured pluralism without even the dubious structure of a dichotomy. And yet it is not just cynical to suggest that in some ways the particular conceptual model of what politics is like at any given moment is in fact the model that best suits the dominant elites of that moment. Thus it is quite possible that those most interested in promoting "cultural war" as an analysis may also be among the "culture warmongers."

There are few better ways to summarize a paper than to explain its title. In this case, we had three connotations for our reference to "Lambs Among the Lions." First, it refers to the relatively lamblike United States in contrast to those specified countries that resemble warring lions. Second, it suggests the danger of introducing any religious (and cultural) lamb into the den of political lions—though there are also instances that justify the reverse argument. Third, we have begun to feel a bit lambish ourselves in the company of other culture war analysts who are both more lionlike and more lionized.

But we have had our shot at the purveyors of a U.S. culture war through-out this chapter; we should note that one has fired back. As part of a collection of essays entitled *The American Culture Wars: Current Contests and Future Prospects* (Nolan 1996), James Hunter has offered his "Reflec-tions on the Culture Wars Hypothesis," in which he responds to a number of his critics and criticisms, not least those herein. In fact, Hunter was present when this chapter was originally presented by the senior author as a set of remarks at the American Sociological Association meetings in 1994. Nancy Ammerman, Hunter, and Demerath had been commissioned to exchange views on culture wars as the "entertainment" portion of a dinner meeting of the Sociological Research Association. While Hunter's response recalls the event as his "lecture," with us as "respondents," he may have every right to misremember, since, as he notes, "only thirty-six hours" later, he was in "the White House for a breakfast meeting with President Clinton and Vice-President Gore" (1996:244).

It is probably fair to say that Hunter was not pleased with Demerath's response. While Hunter's recent reflections mention Demerath's name only in the footnotes, there is little doubt at whom such phrases as "intellectually facile" and "more than a tad naive" are directed. Of course, Demerath has been more than a little guilty on both counts, but perhaps not necessarily in this context.

For one thing, there is a good deal of agreement between the two posi-tions. Both Hunter and Demerath agree that culture is an important and long overlooked dimension of social conflict today. Both concur on the potential importance of religion within the cultural domain. Both now concede that cultural conflict is more often the product of movement leaders and institu-tionalized rhetoric than of militantly polarized cultural preferences within populations at large. Finally, both even acknowledge that the extent of culture conflict is an important variable that is usefully compared between societies.

However, there are clearly abiding disagreements, too. Basically these involve the two key terms at issue in the contentious phrase, "culture" and "war." In what follows, we consider each in turn.

"Culture": In What Form and by Whose Criterion?

As much as we concur with Hunter over the importance of culture and cultural conflict, there remain significant differences between us concerning the very nature of culture itself. Hunter is not alone in promoting culture's recent comeback against more structural theories of order and disorder; other recent work includes Samuel Huntington (1996) on the "clash of civilizations" and Mark Juergensmeyer (1992) on the "new cold war" between religious nationalism and secular states. But if what subverted culture before in sociological analysis is not to do it again, we must beware of overstating its claims and ignoring its critical interactions with structural factors themselves. As an example, both Hunter and Huntington tend to portray conflict as involving whole cultural blocs or civilizations pitted against each other. In fact, some of the most intense conflict occurs within rather than between such camps, and it often amounts to either a struggle for control over the camps or the deployment of cultural symbols as means to more structural ends—whether these involve, class, gender, race, ethnicity, or political nationalism—as our earlier remarks on "fundamentalism" illustrate.

In all of this, there are some important distinctions between culture as ends versus means, embedded versus enacted, mass versus elite, and broader gestalt versus single issues. Hunter is certainly aware of these issues, but in each case, his analysis seems to want to have it both ways. His conception of culture conflict really comes closer to the second options in each of these (admittedly overstated) dichotomies. This makes it all the more puzzling when he insists on identifying his argument with the first and more Durkheimian options. In fact, he admonishes his critics for failing to see the Durkheimian genius behind his argument—and then proceeds to restate what is, in our view, anything but a Durkheimian position. This concerns "citizens . . . separated from our own speech":

> [T]he nub of the problem: the form by which the dynamics of faith and culture get played out most sharply is not the accumulated subjective attitudes of independent citizens but rather the competing moral visions in public culture that have evolved and crystallized over the past several decades—the institutions and elites that produce them and the structures of rhetoric by which they are framed and articulated [and] become a "reality sui generis." (Hunter 1996:248)

This hardly seems like the culture Durkheim found emerging from the social connections and profound sense of the sacred among societal members in *The Elementary Forms of the Religious Life* ([1912] 1915); nor does it sound like the culture that gave coherence, boundaries, and legitimation to social formations in *The Division of Labor in Society* ([1893] 1933), or the culture that integrated and regulated individual lives in *Suicide* ([1897] 1951; and about which, incidently, Durkheim could infer from aggregate statistics). For what it is worth, we tend to agree with Hunter's politically sensitive and movement-based conception of culture conflict, and we find Durkheim's notion of culture too static and amorphous. But when Hunter flails us with a mere Durkheimian phrase ("reality sui generis") rather than an accurate Durkheimian premise, we are reminded once again of the use of cultural symbols as a gloss on political strategies.

In fact, Hunter sometimes seems to scoff at Americans (and American culture) as a whole for *not* being more polarized. This is his response to studies finding public opinion clustered in the moderate middle on most divisive issues:

> It may be that there is a "center" to American public opinion but if there is, it is statistical in nature and therefore contentless—it has no coherence or teleology as a system of moral public reasoning. (1996:247)

While there is always the possibility of a clumsily constructed statistical middle that misrepresents the views of any given individual, that is not at issue. Hunter seems to feel that a moderate position on any issue is the intrinsic intellectual equivalent of a "don't know." Again, one can imagine a valid point within limits, but the limits seem exceeded here. One could just as easily argue that extreme positions on any issue are motivated less by knowledge and conviction than by political interests and association. In any event, Hunter goes on to indicate that the attitudes of the American public are almost immaterial to the real and inevitable war that will ensnare them regardless of their culture:

> [H]owever individuals or organizations align themselves on particular issues, they become subservient to, and if unwilling, must struggle against, the dominating and virtually irresistible categories and logic of the opposing visions and rhetoric of the culture war. (ibid., 251)

Somehow this smacks more of a political jeremiad than a sociological investigation.

War, Wars, and Democratic Discourse

Regardless of how "cultural" the new conflict may be, to what extent is it a "war?" Actually Hunter is ambiguous on whether the operative term should be war or war*s*. Nor is the difference trivial. Just as we saw earlier that more than one civil religion may be no civil religion at all, so may more than one war be no real war at all. To recall still another of our earlier arguments, multiple "wars" are like cross-cutting grievances that prevent any one from becoming stacked and all-engulfing.

References to war are problematic in other ways. Hunter rejects the definition of "culture wars" used at the beginning of this chapter because:

> it is intellectually facile not to see the disturbing parallels of social forms of conflict in different national settings. It is even more facile not to acknowledge the continua upon which conflict exists, as opposed to forcing conflict into either/or categories. (ibid., 249)

Of course, he is right to insist that countries range along continua of social and cultural relations—even social and cultural conflict. On the other hand, he is wrong to insist that war itself must form the continuum as opposed to occupying only one point along it. Perhaps an analogy will help. While temperature ranges along a continuum, it would be folly to confuse the boiling and freezing points by arguing that they themselves are free-floating variables.

But what seems to particularly peeve Hunter is our notion that, when compared to other countries, America's culture conflicts are better conceptualized as "democracy in action," or "normal discourse," as Michele Dillon (1996) in fact characterizes the abortion debate in the same collection. It is here that Hunter scolds us for being:

> more than a tad naive—their naiveté born of distance from what they have observed only from afar; a distance or a (blindness) [*sic*] to the consequences to the lives of real communities and real people for [*sic*] whom these conflicts touch. Such distance is, unfortunately, an occupational hazard in the academy. (1996:250)

But this too is perplexing. All of us are now American academics, Hunter included. But at least Professor Dillon comes from Ireland and has done considerable cross-cultural research, while Demerath has made it a point to seek out comparative conflict in some fourteen other societies. Perhaps they should have joined Hunter in remaining in the United States to benefit from the private insights of President Clinton and Vice-President Gore. Come to think of it, if this is Professor Hunter's subtle way of extending an invitation to another White House breakfast, Demerath will have to check his calendar.

Finally, Hunter's political pessimism seems to get the better of his sociological inquiry. After (rightly) acknowledging the possibility that American "culture conflict has the potential to revitalize democratic institutions and ideals," he concludes his essay on a far darker note:

> The question, it would seem, is whether democracy was ever intended to mediate conflicts as rudimentary as these. If it wasn't, then sociological theory will have the challenge of clarifying the cultural and historical contingencies upon which substantive democratic political orders are based. Historical sociology will have the challenge of recounting how, in America, it came to an end. (ibid., 254)

And so we have the prospect of democracy at an end. Of course, this would not be the first sociologist adrift in the singular present with no historical anchor. But perhaps our differences are not really a matter of scholarship. There is no question that this is a topic in which one's values and interests are implicated, and it may be simply that our glass is half-full while Hunter's is half-empty. If so, it seems disturbingly likely that he would refuse a refill.

While the notion of an American cultural war may be overwrought and overblown, it does alert us to some distinctive aspects of American society, some important comparisons with other societies, and some critical features of culture more generally. Our purpose in this chapter was to, in a sense, raise the bar on what can be legitimately called a culture war. We did so, not with the legendary academic intention of creating yet another distinction without a difference, but rather to argue that this is a case in which the differences matter—both for intellectual accuracy and for democratic politics.

ACKNOWLEDGMENTS

This is a revised and significantly expanded version of a talk first given at the American Sociological Association meetings in Los Angeles in 1994, then a paper delivered at Messiah College, Grantham, Pennsylvania, June 2, 1995, as part of a conference concerning, "Are There Two Parties Today: American Protestantism Since 1960." The original version of the paper appears in the proceedings of that conference, *Re-Forming the Center* (Jacobsen and Trollinger forthcoming).

REFERENCES

Ammerman, Nancy Tatom. 1987. *Bible Believers: Fundamentalists in the Modern World*. New Brunswick, NJ: Rutgers University Press.
———. 1990. *Baptist Battles*. New Brunswick, NJ: Rutgers University Press.
Anderson, Benedict. 1983. *Imagined Communities*. London: Routledge, Chapman and Hall.
Atwood, Margaret. 1985. *The Handmaid's Tale*. New York: Fawcett Crest.
Bellah, Robert N. 1967. "Civil Religion in America." *Daedalus* 96:1–21.
Brubaker, Rogers. 1992. *Citizenship and Nationalism in France and Germany*. Cambridge, MA: Harvard University Press.
Bruce, Steve. 1994. "The Inevitable Failure of the New Christian Right." *Sociology of Religion* 55:223–41.
Demerath, N. J. III. 1991. "Religious Capital and Capital Religions: Cross-Cultural and Non-Legal Factors in the Separation of Church and State." *Daedalus* 120:21–40.
———. 1994. "The Moth and the Flame, Religion and Politics in Comparative Blur." *Sociology of Religion* 55:105–17.
Demerath, N. J. III, and Rhys H. Williams. 1985. "Civil Religion in an Uncivil

Society." *Annals of the American Academy of Political and Social Sciences* 480:154–66.

———. 1992. *A Bridging of Faiths: Religion and Politics in a New England City.* Princeton, NJ: Princeton University Press.

Dillon, Michele. 1996. "The American Abortion Debate: Culture War or Normal Discourse." Pp. 115–32 in *The American Culture Wars: Current Contests and Future Prospects,* edited by James Nolan. Charlottesville: University Press of Virginia.

Durkheim, Emile. [1893] 1933. *The Division of Labor in Society.* New York: Free Press.

———. [1897] 1951. *Suicide.* New York: Free Press.

———. [1912] 1915. *The Elementary Forms of the Religious Life.* New York: Free Press.

Greenfeld, Liah. 1992. *Nationalism: Five Roads to Modernity.* Cambridge, MA: Harvard University Press.

Gurr, Ted Robert. 1993. *Minorities At Risk: A Global View of Ethnopolitical Conflicts.* Washington, DC: U.S. Institute of Peace.

Hunter, James Davison. 1991. *Culture Wars: The Struggle to Define America.* New York: Basic Books.

———. 1994. *Before The Shooting Begins: Searching for Democracy in America's Culture War.* New York: Free Press.

———. 1996. "Reflection on the Culture Wars Hypothesis." Pp. 243–56 in *The American Culture Wars: Current Contests and Future Prospects,* edited by James L. Nolan. Charlottesville: University Press of Virginia.

Huntington, Samuel P. 1996. *The Clash of Civilizations and the Remaking of World Order.* New York: Simon and Schuster.

Jacobsen, Doug, and William Vance Trollinger, Jr., eds. Forthcoming. *Re-Forming the Center.* Grand Rapids, MI: Eerdmans.

Juergensmeyer, Mark. 1992. *The New Cold War? Religious Nationalism Confronts the Secular State.* Berkeley: University of California Press.

Marty, Martin E., and R. Scott Appleby, eds. 1993. *Fundamentalisms and the State.* Chicago: University of Chicago Press.

Menchu, Rigoberta. 1983. *I, Rigoberta Menchu.* London: Verso.

Nandy, Ashish. 1990. "The Politics of Secularism and the Recovery of Religious Tolerance." In *Mirrors of Violence,* edited by Veena Das. Delhi: Oxford University Press.

Nolan, James L., Jr., ed. 1996. *The American Culture Wars: Current Contests and Future Prospects.* Charlottesville: University Press of Virginia.

Sivard, Ruth Leger. 1991. *World Military and Social Expenditures, 1991.* Washington, DC: World Priorities.

Tilly, Charles. 1993. "State-Incited Violence, 1900–1999." Working Paper Series, No. 177. New School for Social Research, New York City.

U.N. Department of Economic and Social Development. 1993. *Report on the World Situation.* New York: United Nations.

Wuthnow, Robert. 1988. *The Restructuring of American Religion: Society and Faith Since World War II.* Princeton, NJ: Princeton University Press.

11

Religion, Ideology, and Electoral Politics*

GERALD M. PLATT and RHYS H. WILLIAMS

The relations between religion and American politics have been remarked upon. From Alexis de Tocqueville to Talcott Parsons, Seymour Martin Lipset, and Robert Bellah, scholars and social critics have observed the influences of colonial religious beliefs on political ideologies and policies in America. Recently, Everett Carll Ladd (1987), using what he admittedly refers to as the broad brush strokes of survey data, commented upon and documented this relationship.

Ladd notes, consistent with the observations of both Max Weber and contemporary political scientists, that in general secularization correlates positively with industrialization: that is, the greater a society's degree of industrialization, the greater its secularization and the lesser its religiosity. Among modern nations, American society constitutes a paradox in this association: Walter Dean Burnham's article in T. Ferguson and J. Roger's *The Hidden Election* (1981) makes this point clearly. By many different survey measures of religiosity, Americans are intensely religious—particularly when compared to the populations of other Western industrial nations. From this analysis Ladd concludes:

> It is to the considerable embarrassment of contemporary social science that it has not built upon, but rather regressed from the stark brilliance of Tocqueville's insight into the relationship of religion and modernity in colonial New England. He saw that "the Americans have succeeded in incorporating to some extent one with the other and combining admirably" two distinct elements. (1987:64)

The second important point Ladd wishes to convey is consistent with one Lipset impressed upon social scientists in *The First New Nation* (1963). The ideological or value content of American religious heritage is imprinted

*First published in 1988; reprinted with only minor editing.

upon American politics. Accordingly, Ladd suggests, American religious doctrine has emphasized individualism, equality, and freedom in the political sphere. These, Ladd informs us, have been lasting values for three centuries.

In the broadest sense our study complements Ladd's thesis; but it is also critical of his perspective. His use of survey data, and his less visible commitment to a Durkheimian sociology that posits a one-to-one determinism between religious beliefs and political values, are the elements about which we are most critical.

We too suggest the significance of the religiosity in American politics and political culture. We also suggest that when we consider the practice of politics, this religiousness is not monolithic. While Americans may share the same religious cultural values, they are simultaneously engaged in interpreting those values in terms of their own interests. At this level of the application of American values, very different politics present themselves. These politics have enormous consequences for the lives of American citizens across important lines of differentiation such as social class, ethnicity, race, and gender. It is at this level that the religious values influencing American politics must be analyzed if we are to address their practical consequences.

This article provides a case study attempting just that. We examine and illustrate the ways in which American religious beliefs have expressed themselves in concrete political terms in recent years. The conceptual key to our approach is the openness of the interpretation of cultural and religious values. Thus, we ask about the real political expressions of religious beliefs. There are, and have been, more and less radical and conservative political incorporations of colonial religious doctrine. These historical variations in interpretation have created a unique American Left and Right political spectrum.

We begin by developing ideal types of the American Left and Right, insofar as these political persuasions exist in American society. We portray the Left and Right in ideological and policy terms with regard to economic and political interests but also with regard to cultural and social issues. In these descriptions we highlight the infrequently recognized commitments of the Left and the Right to both individualistic and collectivistic values and policies. We then describe the religious origins of the Left and Right ideologies and policies as well as the structural sources for their varying interpretations of our colonial religious heritage. In this interpretive process, material interests and experiences of the waves of immigrants to North America play significant roles. Using speeches from the 1984 Democratic and Republican conventions we illustrate the religious themes in their political rhetoric. We conclude by suggesting social scientists are too wed to a Durkheimian model of religious influences on the American political idiom, missing the importance of the interpretive spectrum. Even a cursory look at the 1988 presidential primaries indicates this interpretive process is still very much alive.

AMERICAN LEFT AND RIGHT

It is difficult to describe American Left and Right politics in all their complex realities. Because both sides contain a paradox that we find uniquely American, these formulations are all the more troublesome. We present these positions as ideal-typical ideological and policy preferences in order to characterize the American political spectrum.

A locus classicus of contemporary American political Right ideology resides in its liberal bourgeois doctrine of individual freedom; that is, the canons of personal liberty, freedom of speech, thought, faith, action, the right to the ownership of private property, and to make contracts. By contrast, a doctrinal center for the American political Left is collective interests—a concern for the rights of all societal citizens and the establishment of an equitable and just society.

As an outgrowth of these doctrinal differences there are policy differences between the Left and the Right. For example, the Right advocates policies of aggrandizing rational acquisitiveness, utilitarian self-interest, traditional forms of individualism and liberty, entrepreneurialism, upward mobility, and equality of opportunity. These are formalized in terms of political and economic policies associated with the development and perpetuation of bourgeois capitalism.

By contrast the Left is oriented to a Lockean conception of citizenship. This conception emphasizes viable access to societal resources for all citizens. The implementation of this conception in Western societies has evolved historically from access to monies, through access to power, to access to social esteem. Thus, the American Left has been the champion of the inclusion process in the economy, the polity, and social status. The Left favors the disenfranchised and excluded segments of society by advocating policies instituting universal suffrage, minimum wages, unemployment insurance, social supports, retirement insurance, medical plans, and universal education. The Left is oriented to the full inclusion of the working classes, ethnic groups, women, and minorities. All of these are directed to achieving a minimum standard of living, an equality of circumstances, inclusion, and justice for all members of society.

These ideological and policy positions have resulted in characterizations of the political Right and Left as oriented to the privileges and interests of individuals and collectives, respectively. That is, the Right has been seen as primarily oriented to individual self-interests, typical liberal bourgeois values, while the Left is primarily oriented to interests of the collective, contemporarily associated with the values of socialist doctrine.

This reductionist conception of the American Left and Right is the result of a focus upon what political-economic analysts consider most fundamental—policies regarding the allocation of scarce resources such as money, power, and esteem. These are the traditional variables of analysis for this approach, but political economists also focus upon resource allocation and attendant policies because they are the most visible and calculable, and thus offer certainty of interpretation. In fact, analyses based on these variables are for the most part correct in their portrayal of the American Right as individualistically oriented concerning the individual's rights and access to economic and political resources, and the Left as collectivistically oriented in their desire for access to these resources for the underclasses and the disinherited.

These analyses fall short because there is another less visible and less calculable dimension involved in American political positions. On this less visible dimension the Right and Left reverse orientations; the Right is collectivistic and the Left individualistic. Thus both the Left and the Right advocate doctrine and policy that is alternately collectivist and individualist.

With regard to the cultural values surrounding personal morality, the Left and the Right reverse positions; on these dimensions the American Left is individualistic and the Right is collectivistic in doctrine and policy. With regard to cultural values and morality, the Left insists upon the rights of individual freedom, the pursuit of individual self-interest, and the maximization of self. This is reminiscent of liberal bourgeois ideals regarding the private acquisition of scarce resources. Conversely, the political Right advocates doctrine and policies about cultural values and morality which preserve and elevate collective interests. Serving the common good and the collective well-being of the community is expressed in a manner similar to the high moral-mindedness often found in Left-socialist communities.

On the Left, this individualism is expressed especially in the advocacy of policies emphasizing the private control over one's emotions, decisions, forms of expression, choices, and self; it has been termed an "expressive individualism." Concretely, this involves the desire for policies such as the unobstructed right to abortion, the liberalization of drug use laws, private selection of life-styles and sexual preferences. The collectivistic moral orientation of the Right is couched in terms of the community's welfare and its survival. The survival and health of the moral community is given primacy over the desires or preferences of individuals. Thus, the policies of the American Right regarding personal morality, in contrast to its concern for individualism in economics and politics, are those of antiabortion, the illegality of drug use, strict control of deviant behavior including varying life-

and sexual styles, and emphasis upon the virtues and sanctity of traditional institutions such as the family, education, and church.

The total picture of the American political Right joins entrepreneurial capitalists to religious fundamentalists. The boundaries of the Left include welfare liberals in conjunction with expressive individualists. In class terms the Right links business owners and executives; professionals; white-collar, skilled, and unskilled labor; farmers; and antifeminists of all classes together. The Left joins together intellectuals, professionals, skilled and unskilled labor, minorities, and feminists of all classes. Thus, social class, at best, minimally distinguishes these ideological positions and alliances. Where else may we look to find a fundamental coherence in these patterns?

The recognition of these dual commitments to individualism and collectivism for both the Left and Right begins to highlight the peculiarity of American politics and to explain its contradictions and paradoxes. Since the publication of Robert Bellah's "Civil Religion in America" (1967) and his *The Broken Covenant* (1975), it is well understood that the American religious heritage has advocated the simultaneous commitment to collective and individual interests. Any understanding of the peculiarity of the American political spectrum must begin by recognizing this fact: the American Left and Right have common origins in the American religious tradition. It was Puritan culture that emphasized individualism in relation to a covenant with God, church, and community.

RELIGIOUS HERITAGE AND CONTEMPORARY POLITICS

The Puritan Covenant of God, church, and community was a complex idea. It was a community of individually called saints, morally equal but entitled to exclude the nonelect—yet morally bound to reform and eventually convert all human institutions. The church and the state were separated and distinct, and yet both were charged with defending and enforcing moral and religious doctrine. Although God was inscrutable and immutable, His community had both the right and duty to bring political actions into line with moral ideals—perfection was impossible but progress was mandated. Individual persons had a direct relationship to God and individual rights granted by God alone, but they were subject always to the understanding and moral consensus of the gathered elect. These theological, moral, and political themes, filtered through the experiences of settling a frontier society with waves of immigrants, are still vibrant in contemporary American political thought. Although these themes are often in competition, they are ever-present and a consistent source for varying interpretations.

The analogy between America's religious heritage and its contemporary political culture is clear. What is more difficult to explain are the influences that have shaped the Left and Right versions of that cultural heritage.

Protestant beliefs, filtered through ethnic and religious cultures, and the experiences and interests of immigrants to the New World, shaped the Left and Right ideologies in the United States. Older immigrants—the British, Scottish, and Welsh—came closest to the culture of the Protestant ethic. These peoples manipulated colonial society successfully in their interests, resulting in entrepreneurial advantages. According to E. Digby Baltzell in *Puritan Boston and Quaker Philadelphia* (1979) and Michael Hughey in *Civil Religion and Moral Order* (1983), they were the predecessors of modern capitalists, evolving from small-scale early nineteenth-century businessmen and industrialists to the late nineteenth-century captains of industry.

Older immigrants to the southern United States were of the same ethnic and religious stock as those of the North; however, their experiences and interests in the New World were of a very different character. An economy based in agriculture and slavery separates the southern from the northern experience; but, more importantly, the older immigrants of the South suffered the social and personal defeat of the Civil War. Defeat in the war destroyed antebellum society at every level and, coupled with the geographic and cultural isolation of Reconstruction, engendered in southern Whites a sense of cultural separation, economic and personal failure, and loss. One response to this was a turn to religious fundamentalism. The split between the northern and southern Protestant churches, the latter supporting slavery, buttressed the sense of difference and loss among southerners. This resulted in a defensive, status quo attitude underwritten by religious fundamentalism, which is still very much alive today in the South.

Southern religious conservatives, joined by dogmatic segments of late nineteenth- and early twentieth-century "new immigrant" Catholic urban working classes, such as the Irish, Poles, and Italians, combined with the somewhat politically and geographically isolated western Protestants, constitute the mainstream of the current American conservative movement. Theirs is a conservatism which emphasizes a utilitarian, often aggressive, independent, and yet mythical frontier-type individualism that serves the entrepreneurial interests of one segment, and an obedience to religious doctrine that honors the ideological leanings of other segments. The resulting attitude among the political leadership is much like that of the saintly elite of the Puritan community, who were shepherds to their flocks, charged with providing communal support for the poor even if the latter were held in abhorrence and suspicion. Such commitment to community was a sign of the unseeable, internal covenant with God. Thus the American Right combines a self-interested individualism with a dogmatic conception of doing good works by providing, if hesitantly, begrudgingly, and patronizingly, for the less fortunate of the community.

The American Left finds its origins in similar integrations between Protestant beliefs and contemporary cultures and experiences. In this segment of the spectrum, immigrants from the late nineteenth century to the time of the Great Depression—such as commonwealth Catholics and the deracinated European ghetto Jews—especially played a significant role. The covenant emphasis for these groups is with the community, rather than God and the church. This form of covenant appears highly secularized. Communal support for it is consistent with the ideological orientations of liberal Catholic theology and secular doctrine; recent bishops' letters chastising capitalism and urging support for the poor are only the most recent in a series initiated as early as the 1930s. This form of covenant is also consistent with the experience of the *shtetl* Jews in Europe and America, where segregation enhanced existing communal ties.

Liberal Catholics and ghetto Jews were oriented to utilitarianism; however, significant for them, as for no other previous immigrant groups up until World War II, was the need for the enforcement of individual freedom and diversity. Catholics in the United States found it in their interest to support such values as religious tolerance. Protestantism was the establishment in America, pluralism not always as observed as it was esteemed. Jews supported liberal conceptions of civil liberties not only for religious freedom, but also for tolerance for variant life-styles grounded in religious observances. Liberal Catholics and Jews thus became the bulwark populations supporting expressive individualism.

Our analysis carries us through the middle of the twentieth-century because the American Left and Right ideological patterns were set for this century by that date. The conservatism of the postwar Eisenhower period, or the anticommunism of the McCarthy era, the liberalism of the Kennedy and Johnson administrations, and the right-wing, religious conservatism of the Reagan presidency have not fundamentally altered these ideological stances, although they have been fine-tuned to the issues and foci of pertinent events, as has been done in the 1988 presidential primary campaigns in Iowa, New Hampshire, and the South.

Recent waves of immigrants from Asian and Hispanic nations have not yet altered these ideological perspectives. Voting patterns indicate that Hispanic Americans, with the notable exception of Cubans, have generally adopted the Left ideological positions. Asian Americans, pre–World War II Japanese and Chinese, and postwar Koreans, Vietnamese, and Cambodians are more difficult to interpret in these terms. This may be due to the blend of Asian and American cultures; also the material conditions faced in the United States do not easily suggest a single ideological direction for the many different groups often placed in this ethnic rubric of Asian Americans.

In all of this analysis we are not advocating an assimilation thesis. Rather, immigrant groups have conjoined their own cultures and material interests with the colonial American heritage shaping the positions that define American Left and Right political ideologies. These have been uniquely American blendings, but there is no ethnic homogenization. The ideological rightness and leftness, to use those awkward terms, reside in the way these ideologies have reflected and interpreted bourgeois capitalist and Marxist doctrine respectively, but not in the support of particular class interests.

However halting this analysis, the significance of the interpretive process in the relation of religious heritage to politics is important to recognize. There are fundamental similarities between the American political Left and the Right, the two political wings reflecting each other, each committed to ideologies of collectivism and individualism; but there are significant differences involving their idiosyncratic interpretations of the same religious doctrine.

THE CAMPAIGNS AND BEYOND

Right and Left collectivist and individualist ideologies were nowhere better evidenced than in the political rhetoric of the 1984 presidential campaign. Analyses of the so-called New Right in the 1984 presidential campaign, in contrast to the hysteria of 1980, indicate it was not monolithic. A distinction among factions sometimes referred to as "social conservatives" and "laissez-faire conservatives" (or "evangelicals" and "yuppies") was often present, centering around different issues and varying social characteristics of adherents. Common political symbols, particularly anticommunism and, to a lesser extent, antiabortion, combined with the personal charisma of Ronald Reagan to keep an inherently shaky coalition together.

These trends fit nicely with our own analysis of the ideological themes and strains in the American political Right. What has been less recognized is that similar strains, with the themes reversed, also characterize the American Left. To illustrate both the divergences and overlap between the Left and Right, we draw on speeches made at the 1984 Republican and Democratic national conventions. These are public statements that do not necessarily reflect underlying political reality; yet they are interesting and relevant because they represent the parties' attempts to distinguish themselves from each other while simultaneously reaching out to the same religious heritage of American politics. Much obeisance is paid in these speeches to common American values and themes such as "equal opportunity," "liberty," and "faith."

Yet there is a decided difference in tone, terminology, and ideological emphasis between the two parties. The focus of most of the texts is on economic records, policies, and rationales; the contrasting individualist and collectivist themes are most easily seen in that realm. This difference is most commonly analyzed. Nonetheless, what references there are to moral-cultural issues do reveal the differing assumptions the Left and Right affirm.

Ronald Reagan illustrates clearly the individualist themes the American Right has inherited from classical bourgeois liberalism, utilitarianism, and Protestant individualism. His deference to individual economic rights and opportunities was often coupled with an attack on left-type collectivist sentiment:

> Their government sees people only as members of groups. Ours serves all the people of America as individuals. . . . We don't lump people by groups or special interests. We believe in the uniqueness of each individual. [The choice is] not left or right, but up or down: down through statism . . . less individual liberty . . . or . . . up to the ultimate in individual freedom consistent with an orderly society.

Katherine Davalos Ortega, a Republican and the Treasurer of the United States, echoed both these sentiments and images: "not because I am a woman, not because I am Hispanic. . . . But because I am an American. [Democrats are the] party of narrow special interests . . . not freedom and individual opportunity." Thus, Reagan and Ortega coupled images of individuals competing in a society of open opportunity with those of a moral community, but the latter is also distinct from the constituted government. Ortega illustrated this nicely when she continued in her address to the convention: "America stands for freedom, for opportunity, for the right of every individual to fulfill his or her potential as members of the family of God, not creatures of an almighty government." Such mention of the moral and religious imagery was frequently made in connection with issues from the so-called social agenda of the New Right. Reagan, in deriding the economic policies of the Democrats, stated:

> If our opponents were as vigorous in supporting our voluntary prayer amendment as they are in raising taxes, maybe we could get the Lord back in our schoolrooms and get the drugs and violence out. Teen-age drug use, out-of-wedlock births and crime increased. . . . Government became a drug.

Reagan rarely used the term *fairness* in his convention address; but he did so while deriding the Democrats and calling for tuition tax credits for "parochial or other independent schools." It was Reagan who connected the current Republican program directly with America's Puritan heritage: "We proclaimed a dream of an America that would be 'a shining city on a hill.'"

The Republicans' image of individual liberty within an orderly society rests on the respective visions of classical economics and a common moral/religious value system; note, for example, that Reagan used the Christian notion of "the Lord" rather than a less sectarian concept. The community they conjure up is not the contractual society of bourgeois liberalism— although they borrow liberalism's minimal, "night-watchman" state—but a nation of individuals held together by shared values. Most strikingly, the language of liberty, opportunity, and achievement, and discussion of economic issues and policies, including national defense, dominated the oratory.

The speeches at the 1984 Democratic convention stressed fairness and inclusion. America as "family" dominated references to economic policy, with those that are comfortable providing for those that are not. Individual civil rights were consistently emphasized also, particularly for the disenfranchised. Tolerance for minorities was coupled with inclusion into the political and economic community. In part, the emphasis on family and values was a tactical maneuver: the Democrats were waving the flag and using Horatio Alger imagery in a calculated attempt to recapture some moral high ground from the Republicans. But Walter Mondale had also faced a stiff challenge from Jesse Jackson and the party's left wing; no move to the center could forsake the inclusionary images of American society that have dominated Democratic economic and political policies from Franklin D. Roosevelt to Martin Luther King. Family themes were rampant, but they expanded beyond the New Right's image of the conjugal family with traditional values and the roles of working husband and housewife.

Walter Mondale consistently attacked the Republicans for their lack of fairness and their bias toward the upper class: "[W]hat we have today is a government of the rich, by the rich, and for the rich. . . . Mr. Reagan believes the genius of America is in the boardrooms and exclusive country clubs." The Reagan administration, he charged, had broken faith with those who voted for it: "[H]e promised that you'd be better off. And today, the rich are better off. But working Americans are worse off; and the middle class is standing on a trap door."

Mondale's answer was fairness and compassion. His attack was not against the rich per se, but against an administration that unjustly favors them: "When he raises taxes, it won't be done fairly." Geraldine Ferraro repeated that theme; her call was not for a fundamental redistribution of wealth, or strict economic equality, but for rules that allowed all Americans to share in the nation's wealth:

The promise [of America] is that the rules are fair. . . . [But] the rules are rigged . . . the share of taxes paid by individuals is going up, while the share paid by large corporations is getting smaller . . . it isn't right that women should get paid fifty-nine cents on the dollar.

The rules of a decent society, she countered, allow for the inclusion, or at least potential inclusion, of all. Drawing on liberalism's standards of formal or procedural equality, Ferraro sounded much like the other party when she claimed that the Democrats "place no limits on achievement . . . [but] move forward to open the doors of opportunity" through the Voting Rights Act and Equal Rights Amendment. It is the inclusion principle itself which distinguishes the parties: "What separates the two parties in this election campaign is whether we use the gift of life—for others or only ourselves."

Gary Hart explicitly tied together the Democrats' allegiances to an inclusive economy with centrist American notions of opportunity and mobility: "Compassion is based on justice. Justice requires resources. Resources flow from opportunity. . . . [We have] a passion for justice and a program for opportunity." But community and commonweal are still paramount:

> [O]ur Government continues to replace the words "Give me your tired, your poor, your huddled masses yearning to breathe free" with "What's in it for me, tighten your belts and show us your identification card. . . . " [But] I see an America . . . where greed, self-interest and division are conquered by idealism, the common good and the national interest.

Mario Cuomo and Jesse Jackson most clearly delineated the concept of commonwealth versus the bourgeois liberal society of self-interested, contractual individuals. Cuomo was explicit: after refuting Reagan's "shining city on a hill" with a "tale of two cities" ("the lucky and the left-out, the royalty and the rabble") he claimed that Democrats "believe that we can make it all the way with the whole family intact . . . constantly reaching out to extend and enlarge that family." He was unusually blunt: "To succeed we will have to surrender small parts of our individual interests." He spoke of democracy as shared sacrifice as well as opportunity, as "obligation to each other" as well as individual rights. Yet, Cuomo also engaged in public debate with Cardinals O'Connor and Law over the government's proper stance toward abortion; he argued that religious liberty and moral pluralism necessitated a legal situation that guaranteed individual choice, even for those individuals who found it morally repugnant.

Jesse Jackson, an ordained minister whose 1984 campaign relied on the rhythmic cadences and organizational support of Black Protestantism, directly connected America's religious and political missions:

> We are called to a perfect mission . . . to feed the hungry, to clothe the naked, to house the homeless, to teach the illiterate, to provide jobs for the jobless . . .

there is the call of conscience, redemption, expansion, healing and unity. . . .
[O]ur nation is a rainbow . . . all precious in God's sight . . . [and we] measure
greatness by how we treat the least of these.

Jackson quoted from Ecclesiastes; Cuomo called for government modeled
on St. Francis of Assisi, rather than the Republicans' Social Darwinism.

The Democrats were clear in their preference for the health of the economic community, understood inclusively, over the property rights and interests of individuals; but their coalition was diverse and often at odds. The
best example was an angry, taunting confrontation between union members,
marching in an AFL-CIO demonstration supporting the Democratic candidates, and a lesbian/gay rights march, also in support of the Democratic
party. The potential tensions between groups prompted many calls for tolerance of minorities, dissenters, and others on the margins of American social
life. "As we expand our family to include new members," said Jackson, "all
of us must be tolerant and understanding." Jackson called America a "quilt"
made up of many patches, not a seamless, uniform blanket; Cuomo referred
to "the mosaic that is America." Mondale criticized: "the drowsy harmony of
the Republican Party. They quelch [sic] debate; we welcome it. They deny
differences; we bridge them. They are uniform; we are united." Ferraro
added; "We are going to restore those values—love, caring, partnership—
by including, and not excluding, those whose beliefs are different from our
own. Because our own faith is strong, we will fight to preserve the freedom
of faith for others." Mario Cuomo claimed the Democrats were proud of
their diversity—"we don't have to manufacture it"—and defended their
commitment to expressive individualism by asking: "What kind of [Su-
preme] Court and country will be fashioned by the man who believes in
having government mandate people's religion and morality?"

Jesse Jackson illustrated most clearly that Republicans and Democrats
emphasize the collective good over individualism in different realms of
social life: "Mr. Reagan is trying to substitute flags and prayer cloths for food
and clothing and education, health care and housing. Mr. Reagan will ask us
to pray . . . but we must watch false prophesy. . . . The requirement for
rebuilding America is justice." For the Democrats, the commonweal is cen-
tered around economics and political rights; for Ronald Reagan's Republicans, the moral community is focused on social and symbolic issues such as
personal morality, prayers in public schools, and civic religiosity.

The issue that offers the clearest difference in this regard is abortion. No
speakers at either convention spoke about it, but the relevant planks from
each party's platform tell the story. The Democrats had a section labeled
"Reproductive Freedom," which read in part: "[We] oppose government
interference in the reproductive decisions of Americans, especially [when it]
denies poor Americans their right to privacy . . . we recognize . . . that a

woman has a right to choose whether and when to have a child." The Republicans, on the other hand, affirmed that "the unborn child has a fundamental individual right to life which cannot be infringed upon. . . . [We therefore] support a human life amendment [which would define human life as beginning with conception]." The Republicans also opposed the use of public revenues for abortion and vowed to eliminate funding for organizations that advocate or support abortion. They called specifically for the appointment of federal judges who are opposed to abortion. The role of the government, as representative of the moral community, is thus very different from the one it would play in each party's economic policies.

Both parties fell all over themselves in support of a strong national defense; but even here there was a varied emphasis: Republicans wanted to stand up to the Soviet Union and preserve our liberties (only Barry Goldwater spoke at any length in terms of doing one's duty to the nation); Democrats called for a strong defense as a tool for pursuing the nation's mission. For example, former president Jimmy Carter proclaimed: "Ours is the only country on earth with the strength, the moral commitment, the influence and the economic independence to be chief spokesman for those who suffer from oppression or torture or murder."

The 1984 conventions offer convenient, coherent, and delimited focuses to illustrate our analysis. In the spring of 1988, campaigns for the presidency were heating up, again illustrating themes similar to those encountered four years earlier at the Republican and Democratic conventions. Indeed, 1988 has offered a neat symmetry with two ordained ministers, Jesse Jackson and Pat Robertson (who resigned his ordination shortly before he became an official candidate) initially occupying the figurative poles on the Left-Right continuum. Pat Robertson's "social agenda" is well known and fairly typical of the so-called Religious Right. He describes himself as "pro-family," meaning the earlier twentieth-century, white middle-class ideal of the nuclear family in which dad worked and mom stayed home with the kids. For Robertson the problems facing America are those of obedience and respect for the moral community; the solutions are restraints on personal expressions, expressions he considers license.

Robertson has simultaneously played to the business side of Right ideology by shucking his identity as a "televangelist" in favor of calling himself a "religious broadcasting executive." The "Lord's work" and Armageddon imagery have been replaced by market share and balanced budget talk. He pledges fidelity to low taxes and supply-side economics, policies that dominate current conservative laissez-faire approaches.

Jesse Jackson, on the other hand, focuses his concerns on community and collective needs for economic and political inclusion. He reaches out to disenfranchised minorities, unemployed industrial workers, striking workers in New England, coal miners in Appalachia, textile workers in the South, and ailing farmers with the message of inclusion into America's bounty. His well-designed metaphor, reflecting his supporters more accurately in 1988 than in 1984, is the "rainbow coalition." Jackson also continues, against advisers' counsel, to speak candidly for gay and lesbian rights. For Jackson, the right of personal diversity is one protected by the Constitution and insured by government.

We observe in 1988, as well as in 1984, that for all the centrist tendencies of both the American Left and Right, their converse assumptions about the respective importance of the community and the individual are very much apparent and significant for political practices. America's religious heritage, informed by its Puritan past, links individualism to covenants with God, church, and community. The American Right has drawn on that heritage, advocating a utilitarian individualism regarding economics and politics while simultaneously emphasizing the covenant with God and church concerning moral and cultural issues. Conversely, the political Left has drawn upon that same heritage to create an opposing stance—that is, an expressive individualism regarding moral/cultural issues and a vision of a just covenant community in economic and political realms.

There is considerable self-interest in both the Left and Right's versions of individualism and covenant, although both have described as "correct" their interpretation of the American Puritan heritage and the intentions of the Constitution's framers. Less important for us is the veracity of the arguments about continuity.

Our focus is upon the continuing duality of these orientations. Even more significant is recognizing the openness of American cultural heritage to different interpretations by diverse populations currently resulting in polar political orientations. Of late much has been made of the failure to emphasize the common good and thus of the abandonment of the American communal tradition. Recent books, among these *Habits of the Heart* (1985) by Robert Bellah et al., have decried the contemporary emphasis on individualism, both utilitarian and expressive.

The solutions in that volume appear to us as ad hoc combinations of criticisms derived from circumscribed analyses of both the Left and Right's versions of the American tradition. The call for more community immediately raises a question: Whose conception of community? Because the authors proceed with a partially analyzed conception of community as a religious-political theme in American culture, they cannot provide a straightforward answer to that question. Rather, they have posed a subrosa, somewhat ambiguous formulation favoring the liberal-left conception of collectivity; their hope is that political and economic inclusion would not overly constrain personal freedoms. They submit this suggestion for repair of society as one they have inferred from their interviews with citizens. We find it to be a prejudicial assumption, unexamined for its consequences for personal freedoms and for the traditionalist conception of a moral community.

It is no surprise that feminists find *Habits of the Heart* insufferable, assuming the book advocates the right-wing conception of community that mitigates against their commitment to expressive individualism. Bourgeois individualists rage against that volume because of its implications for Left covenant commitments to the redistribution of middle-class wealth in favor of the underclasses. Once again, roots in a shared cultural heritage produce opposing interpretations of the body politic.

We have offered a more systematic framework for the analysis of the themes of individualism and collectivity in American religious culture and political ideology. The question that now has to be raised in light of this framework is: At what costs for society, and for those committed to each of the ideologies/political positions, is one position extended over the other? The structure of the current discourses is such that there is no easy solution; even uneasy compromises are difficult, given the mirrorlike contrast in the positions. One pole, as a set of ideological and policy preferences, can be chosen only at the expense of the interests and sensibilities of those committed to the other tradition. A third alternative ideology is needed but is not forthcoming.

The United States faces several political and social dilemmas that do not yield themselves to uncritical, programmatic responses. For example, American society over the last twenty years has neglected its underclasses, and this is a tragedy. There are also negative consequences to uncritical acceptance of either of the versions of the American political ideologies. The problems of drug abuse among the young, and across a broad spectrum of social classes, is significant for the health of the society. To date, no simple-minded doctrinal solutions, either of suppression or permissiveness, have been successful. Similarly, the spread of AIDS represents a potential disaster which cannot be resolved by moral repression or unrestrained individual choice. The oppression of personal freedoms is harmful, but so too is injury to a traditional moral community. Collective orientations can be positive when they involve the redistribution of wealth, but they can also be repressive when they involve the suppression of expressive personal freedoms.

This is not a call to balance among Right and Left versions of the American political spectrum. Rather, we wish to call attention to the cultural and political interests served by each of the orientations and the implications of policies that emphasize one direction over another.

REFERENCES

Baltzell, E. Digby. 1979. *Puritan Boston and Quaker Philadelphia*. New York: Free Press.
Bellah, Robert N. 1967. "Civil Religion in America." *Daedalus* 96:1–20.

Bellah, Robert N. 1975. *The Broken Covenant.* New York: Seabury.

Bellah, Robert N., Richard Madsen, William Sullivan, Ann Swidler, and Steven Tip-
    ton. 1985. *Habits of the Heart.* Berkeley: University of California Press.

Burnham, Walter Dean. 1981. "The 1980 Earthquake: Realignment, Reaction, or
    What?" Pp. 98–140 in *The Hidden Election,* edited by Thomas Ferguson and
    Joel Rogers. New York: Pantheon.

Hughey. Michael W. 1983. *Civil Religion and Moral Order.* Westport, CT:
    Greenwood.

Ladd, Everett Carll. 1987. "Secular and Religious America." *Society 24* (3):63–68.

Lipset, Seymour Martin. 1963. *The First New Nation: The U.S. in Historical and
    Comparative Perspective.* New York: Basic Books.

12

Dimensions of Cultural Tension among the American Public

DANIEL V. A. OLSON

In *Culture Wars* (1991) Hunter extends and dramatizes a claim first made by Wuthnow (1988). The claim is that in America, religious, political, and cultural tensions are becoming increasingly aligned along a single liberal-conservative dimension. Religious, political, and cultural conservatives are coming to share a common cluster of values and beliefs that stand in opposition to a cluster of values and beliefs that are increasingly shared by religious, political, and cultural liberals. According to Hunter, these liberal-conservative tensions are especially problematic since they are rooted in two different views of moral authority, a situation that makes compromise difficult, if not immoral. "The end to which these hostilities tend," he writes, "is the domination of one cultural and moral ethos over all others" (1991:50).

Responding to early reviewers of *Culture Wars* who rightly pointed out that Americans are not as polarized as the book implies, the preface to Hunter's *Before the Shooting Begins* notes that the culture war is more a battle between moral visions than it is a war between persons. The culture war, he claims, "cannot be explained in terms of ordinary people's attitudes about public issues," but he goes on to note that "these moral visions are often enough reflected (imperfectly) in the world views of individuals" (1994:viiff.).

The goal of this chapter is to examine whether this "battle between moral visions" has left its traces (albeit "imperfectly") in the attitudes of ordinary people toward public issues. If there is to be a culture "war," it must involve the public as well as elites. There must be soldiers as well as generals. Without soldiers, generals can only engage in duels, not war.

In particular the goal of this chapter is to ask whether cultural tensions as reflected in public opinion are well described by a single liberal-conservative dimension. If the one-dimensional, bipolar, liberal-conservative tension that Hunter sees in the discourse of elites has any relevance beyond the elites themselves, then it should leave its traces in the opinions of average Americans, too. If Hunter is right about the one-dimensional structure of these tensions, then knowing a person's views on one or two liberal-conservative issues should enable one to make a good prediction about the person's views on other liberal-conservative issues.

This is an important issue. Cultural warfare depends on the ability of the soldiers to identify clearly which side they are on. Further, they must not switch sides with each new issue "battle." Those who are conservative on one issue should be conservative on other issues as well. When there is more than one dimension to cultural conflicts, people are exposed to important cross-pressures, cross-pressures that make them less willing to engage in an all out "us versus them" culture war.

I find that among the public there is a good deal of alignment on many of the religious, political, and cultural issues identified by Hunter (and earlier by Wuthnow 1988). But instead of a single liberal-conservative dimension, the issues identified by Hunter actually form two separate types of liberalism-conservatism that are unrelated in the minds of most Americans. Knowing someone's views toward the Bible will help you guess their views toward abortion, but it helps little in predicting their political party affiliation, for whom they voted for president, or their views toward welfare spending.

I begin by proposing a two-dimensional model of political division based on suggestions made long ago by Lipset (1981), and similar models used more recently by Maddox and Lilie (1984) and Fleishman (1988). Second, I use General Social Survey (GSS) data and a new graphical technique to examine the fit of the two-dimensional model with the values, opinions, religious, and demographic characteristics of the general public. I conclude by arguing that the two-dimensional structure of public opinions may actually constrain the positions taken by political and cultural elites. The unwillingness of the general public to align along a single liberal-conservative dimension defined by elites puts a brake on the type of runaway one-dimensional polarization that Hunter sees in the discourse of elites. The two-dimensional structure of public opinion may act as a preventative to culture war.

A TWO-DIMENSIONAL MODEL

In their book *Beyond Liberal and Conservative* (1984), Maddox and Lilie argue that scholars as well as the media have labored for too long under the

Table 1 American Political-Cultural Positions

		Regulation of Lifestyle, Sexuality, Sex Roles, and Free Speech (Personal-Moral Issues)	
		Oppose (Individualistic) "Liberal"	Favor (Communitarian) "Conservative"
Regulation of Economic and Social Behavior (Economic-Justice Issues)	Favor (Communitarian) "Liberal"	Left	Bicommunitarian
	Oppose (Individualistic) "Conservative"	Libertarian	Right

false impression that political differences vary along a single liberal-conservative dimension. Drawing on their work, I suggest that there are two separate types of liberalism and conservatism: economic-justice and personal-moral. Moreover, these two types of liberalism-conservatism are not themselves related (aligned) among the general public. Many people are conservative on one set of issues and liberal on the other. Table 1 shows these two dimensions and their cross-classification.

The first type of liberalism-conservatism concerns *personal-moral* issues, the extent to which people feel restrictions should be placed on personal behavior, especially life-style, sexuality, sex roles, and free speech. Personal-moral liberals (in the left-hand column of Table 1) favor greater personal freedoms because they believe that no government or church has the authority to determine what is best for an individual to think and do concerning such issues. It is an individualistic orientation having much in common with "expressive individualism" as described by Bellah, Madsen, Sullivan, Swidler, and Tipton in *Habits of the Heart* (1985). The goal of this orientation is greater individual self-actualization, discovery, and self-expression.

In contrast, personal-moral conservatives (in the right-hand column of Table 1) take a more communitarian orientation toward personal behavior, life-style, sexuality, sex roles, and free speech. They hold that it is vital for the common good of society to uphold certain standards in these areas, and thus society has a right to regulate certain individual behaviors and beliefs. Without such standards, they argue, increased "moral decay," dishonesty, corruption, sexual immorality, and irresponsibility in child rearing will result, threatening society and possibly leading to the nation's "downfall."

Thus there need to be restrictions on ideas and behaviors thought to have a corrupting influence. The goal of this orientation is greater righteousness[1] in cultural values and personal/interpersonal behavior. It is this concern for "righteousness" that explains why attitudes toward free speech also vary along this dimension. For personal-moral conservatives, unregulated free speech threatens to undermine the shared moral standards that help maintain social solidarity.

The second type of liberalism and conservatism deals with *economic-justice* issues. On this dimension people disagree concerning how much the government should restrict and regulate social, especially economic, behavior in order to bring about greater equality of wealth, power, and social esteem. Economic-justice liberals (in the top row of Table 1) favor affirmative action, economic regulation, and redistribution of wealth to aid the poor and the oppressed. It is a communitarian orientation in that it justifies the regulation of individual behavior for the sake of the common good. Economic-justice liberals argue that such controls are necessary to limit the inequality and injustice that hurt all members of society by fostering suspicion, hate, and violence. The goal of this orientation is equity, which is variously interpreted as equality, progress toward equality, or at least equality of opportunity.

In contrast, economic-justice conservatives (in the bottom row of Table 1) defend the right of individuals to pursue their economic self-interests in a marketplace free of government intervention. They argue that government regulations, taxation, and affirmative action stifle initiative and limit the prosperity that might otherwise accrue to rich and poor alike. It is an individualistic orientation having much in common with "utilitarian individualism" as described by Bellah et al. in *Habits of the Heart* (1985). The goal of this orientation is maximum economic utility, wealth, and happiness for the greatest number of individuals.

With regard to each issue dimension, there is an individualistic and a communitarian pole. People either oppose or favor (to varying degrees) regulation of the behaviors relevant to that dimension. Those who favor regulation argue that it is for the common good of society. Those who oppose it argue that society has no authority to regulate such behaviors. Thus, for example, personal-moral liberals oppose the regulation of behavior related to life-style, sexuality, sex roles, and free speech while personal-moral conservatives favor certain restrictions on these behaviors. Table 1 identifies the individualistic and communitarian ends of each dimension and shows what *liberal* and *conservative* mean with regard to each set of issues. Note that the term *liberal* is associated with *opposing* the regulation of personal-moral behavior but is associated with *favoring* regulation of economic-justice behavior. Similarly, the term *conservative* is commonly associated with *opposing* regulation of economic-justice behavior but also with *favoring* regulation of personal-moral behavior. This explains why many political commentators have attacked the inconsistency of both liberals and conservatives with regard to support for government "interference" in various types of behavior.

Table 1 cross-classifies these two forms of liberalism-conservatism to create a fourfold table that more adequately maps current political and cultural positions. Each of the four cells represents a combined position on the two types of liberalism-conservatism. Those in the upper left-hand cell are part of the *Left*: they are liberals in both personal-moral matters (opposing regulation) and economic-justice matters (favoring regulation). In contrast persons in the lower right-hand cell are part of the *Right*: they are conservatives in both personal-moral matters (favoring regulation) and economic-justice matters (opposing regulation).

If there were fundamentally only one liberal-conservative dimension in American politics, these two cells (left and right) would be sufficient to map the major differences between people and policies. However, Table 1 shows two other positions. *Libertarians* in the lower left-hand cell are liberals on personal-moral matters but conservatives on economic-justice matters. They consistently oppose the regulation of both types of behavior. *Bicommunitarians*[2] are found in the upper right-hand cell and are personal-moral conservatives but liberal on economic-justice matters. They are *bi*communitarians because they consistently favor the regulation of *both* types of behavior for the overall good of the society.

Of course, I am not the first to recognize these two sets of issues in American politics (e.g., Lipset 1981). Political commentators frequently refer to these different issue domains, but often assume that the two types of liberalism-conservatism go together, that people who are conservative on one set of issues are usually conservative on the other issues, too. However, Maddox and Lilie review national surveys of opinion and voting behavior going back to the 1950s and 1960s and conclude that there are actually more bicommunitarian and libertarian voters than there are persons in the Left and the Right. They further suggest that the preoccupation of the two major political parties with the concerns of the Left and the Right ignores the interests of libertarians and bicommunitarians and leads to the kinds of voter frustrations that make third-party candidacies common. Other survey research (e.g., Fleishman 1988; Olson and Carroll 1992) and cultural analyses (Platt and Williams 1988) confirm the statistical and conceptual independence of these two dimensions among the general public. Among the general public one cannot predict how liberal or conservative a person will be on economic-justice issues based on knowing their position on personal-moral issues.

Individualism and communitarianism receive relatively little attention in Hunter's analysis. This is because he sees the two communitarian orientations (as defined here) as standing at opposite ends of a single conservative-liberal dimension. This leaves no room for individualism. In contrast, a two-dimensional model makes it easier to see that many cultural conflicts are related to tensions between individualism and concern for the common good, a theme emphasized by many other cultural commentators, especially Bellah et al. (1985).

TWO DIMENSIONS OR ONE?

Conceptually the two-dimensional scheme fits together quite nicely, but does it fit with the views of the American public? Much of the analysis presented here is an extension of an earlier analysis (Olson and Carroll 1992). In that analysis Jackson Carroll and I identified thirty-one items used in the 1988 GSS that appear to measure values and beliefs identified by Wuthnow (1988) in his descriptions of conservatives and liberals. [See Olson and Carroll (1992) for a full description of these items.] We used the 1988 GSS since this version of the survey includes a special set of questions relating to religion.

We found that many of these items are strongly correlated with one another in a manner consistent with Wuthnow's, and later Hunter's (1991), descriptions. Yet, many pairs of these items were not correlated at all. Contrary to a one-dimensional model of cultural and political value alignment, we found that the items could be grouped into two subsets or factors[3] such that the items in each subset were quite highly correlated with other items in the same subset but not very correlated with items in the other subset.

The first subset of items we identified corresponds fairly well with the personal-moral dimension. It includes items dealing with sexuality (premarital, extramarital, homosexual, and teen sex), abortion (under a variety of circumstances), women's roles, and civil liberties–free speech (whether people with certain viewpoints should be allowed to speak in the respondent's community).

The second subset corresponds quite closely with the economic-justice dimension and includes views on federal programs designed to equalize income inequalities, help the poor, the sick, and minorities, and items related to defense spending, government spending on welfare, the environment, education, foreign aid, big cities, and assistance to Blacks. Of these items, those dealing with defense spending, the environment, education, and certain racial issues fit the least well (both empirically and theoretically) with the others in this group. Thus in the analysis presented below I use an economic-justice scale that differs somewhat from those described in Olson and Carroll (1992). Specifically, it does not include items related to defense spending, the environment, education, and certain racial issues. I consider these issues separately.

Because the items within each subset have fairly high intercorrelations, I combined the items in each subset to form a scale, a single score for each respondent representing their average views on all the items in the subset. Cronbach's alpha for the first scale, the economic-justice dimension, is .7311. Cronbach's alpha for the second scale, the personal-moral dimension, is .8599.[4]

In Hunter's analysis the issues represented by the two scales stand in opposition to one another, suggesting that the two scales should have a strong negative correlation. In fact, the two scales used here have almost no correlation (Pearson's $r = -.059$, $R^2 = .004$). Less than half of one percent of the variation in people's attitudes toward personal-moral issues is associated with variation in their views toward economic-justice issues. This is consistent with Maddox and Lilie (1984), who claim that the dimensions are essentially independent, and with Fleishman (1988), who used LISREL to perform confirmatory factor analysis on a nearly identical set of GSS items and found essentially the same two statistically independent dimensions. Fleishman concludes that a two-dimensional model fits the attitude variation of the American public quite well and much better than a one-dimensional model.

Figure 1 shows a scatterplot of respondents' views on the two scales created from these two sets of items. Both scales have been standardized. The horizontal axis measures respondent's views on the personal-moral issue domain. I have labeled this axis to show that scores higher than zero reflect viewpoints that are more consistent with personal-moral conservatism while scores less than zero reflect personal-moral liberalism. The vertical axis measures respondent's views on economic-justice issues. Scores higher than zero reflect economic-justice liberalism while scores of less than zero reflect economic-justice conservatism. For both cases, positive scores indicate more communitarian positions.

Consistent with Table 1, I divide the plot into four regions to represent the four combinations of viewpoints they identify. Each of the dots simultaneously represents one of the 1481 GSS respondent's views on both scales. Thus, for example, people plotted in the lower right corner are part of the Right. Respondents plotted in the upper right region are bicommunitarians, and so on. The scatterplot also shows an almost flat regression line sloping slightly down and to the right. This line represents the best fit of a straight line to the 1481 points plotted on the scatterplot. It is nearly flat because of the virtual lack of relationship between the two scales.

Two important conclusions emerge from Figure 1. First, the public does not appear polarized into two warring groups of Left and Right. The center is

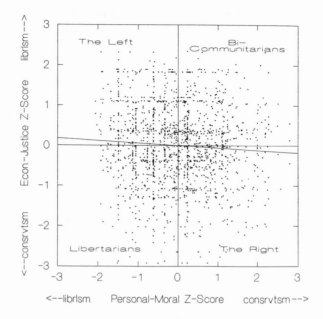

Figure 1. Scatterplot of respondents' views on the personal-moral issue domain are shown on the horizontal axis. The vertical axis measures respondent's views on economic-justice issues.

the most densely populated region of the scatterplot. Second, respondents' views on the two sets of issues are not related to one another. If they were, most people would be plotted in the upper-left or lower right, they would either be part of the Left or the Right. However, consistent with a two-dimensional model, about equal percentages of the respondents fall into each of the four regions (libertarian 25 percent, bicommunitarian, 24 percent, the Right 24 percent, and the Left 27 percent).

The failure of the two scales to be aligned is not due to their being based on poor-quality items that do not belong together. Nor does it reflect an inability of people in the general public to connect related issues in their minds, as Converse (1964) might suggest. The items used in each scale are strongly correlated with other items within the same scale, even among the general public.

This analysis suggests that Hunter is correct in terms of the themes he identifies as forming important clusters of related viewpoints. The difference is that, at least among the public, these themes do not sit at opposite ends of a single conservative-liberal issue dimension. They form two separate, unrelated, issue dimensions.

THE PUBLIC: UNDERLYING DIFFERENCES

Hunter (1991) and Wuthnow before him (1988) warn that cultural tensions could become especially intense since they are now aligned with important religious, educational, and political differences. But even if they are correct, Figure 1 suggests that there is more than one dimension with which these differences may be aligned. If so, then it becomes especially important to see how religious, educational, and political differences are associated with these two dimensions. Figures 2 and 3 examine the linkages between these issues and the two dimensions described above.

Figure 2 is based on Figure 1. The two axes are, like Figure 1, based on personal-moral and the economic-justice scales (though they are numbered somewhat differently). Figure 2 also shows the boundaries of the four regions. The main difference is that, in order to reduce clutter Figure 2 does not show the dots representing each respondent in the scatterplot. Instead, Figure 2 shows arrows drawn from the center of the figure pointing in the directions in which the values of other variables increase most rapidly among the survey respondents.

I determined the directions and lengths of these arrows using multiple regression. Each arrow is drawn from the center of the scatterplot to a point representing the two standardized regression betas from a regression having the following form: dependent variable = constant + (beta1 * score on personal-moral scale) + (beta2 * score on economic-justice scale). The horizontal and vertical axes of Figure 2 have been renumbered to correspond to these standardized betas.

Thus for example, the arrow labeled Education corresponds to a GSS variable asking respondents how many years of formal education they have received. When education is regressed on the personal-moral and the economic-justice scales, the standardized beta for the personal-moral scale is −.386, while the standardized beta for the economic-justice scale is −.015. Thus, the arrow for education is drawn from the center of the plot at (0, 0) to the point (−.386, −.015). Regressions of this type and their corresponding standardized betas show how strongly and in what way the dependent variable (in this case, education) is related, in a linear relationship, to respondents' locations on the two-dimensional scatterplot of personal-moral and economic-justice issues shown in Figure 1.[5] The arrows quickly sum up visually long lists of numerical results.

One can gain a better understanding of this and other figures in this paper if one imagines that it is a map of a large field on which all the GSS respondents are standing (in the positions indicated by the dots in Figure 1). Imagine further that one is standing at the center of this field, the position from which the arrows originate and the position which represents average

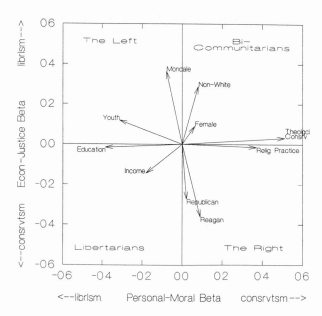

Figure 2. The two axes are based on personal-moral and the economic-justice scales. Arrows drawn from the center of the figure point in the directions in which the values of other variables increase most rapidly among the survey respondents.

views on both personal-moral and economic-justice issues. Now imagine that one would like to find those respondents with the most years of formal education. In which direction should one begin walking across the field to most quickly find respondents with more years of formal education?

The arrow labeled "Education" can be viewed as the compass course one should follow to best accomplish this task. If one began to walk outward along this line one would encounter and pass many respondents standing in the locations shown by the dots in Figure 1. If one were to ask these respondents how many years of formal education they had received one would find that the average number of years increases the farther one progresses in the direction of the line.

If instead of following the line in the direction of the arrow toward the left side of the figure, one were to make an about-face and march in the opposite direction away from the center toward the right, the respondents one would encounter would, on average, have fewer and fewer years of formal education.

Suppose once again that one is progressing outward along the line labeled Education. If at any point along this line one were to make a ninety-degree turn to the left or right and start walking in a direction perpendicular to the line, the average number of years of formal education among the respondents would encounter would stay about the same.

The line labeled Education can thus be viewed as the direction one should take from the center of the figure if one wants the average number of years of formal education of the respondents one passes to increase at the fastest rate possible.

The length of the arrows is also significant. The longer arrows represent stronger patterns (higher R^2) among the respondents, whereas the shorter arrows represent weaker patterns. Going back to the analogy, if one were to walk outward along one of the longer arrows, say the arrow labeled Theolgcl. Consrv., average support for items used in the conservative theology scale (described below) would increase quite rapidly and the respondents one would encounter as one approached the outer edge of the field (near the right side of Figure 2) would hold positions that are very different from the leaders near the center or the opposite side of the field (on the left side of Figure 2).

If instead, one walked away from the center in the direction of one of the shorter arrows, say the arrow labeled Relig. Practice, one would find that respondent's scores on a religious participation scale (also described below) would increase at a slower rate. Also one would find that even though the respondents near the edge of the field (on the right side of Figure 2) generally had higher rates of religious participation than those at the center or the opposite side of the field, the differences would not be as marked as the differences among views on conservative theology.

Figure 2 shows the patterns for several demographic, political, and religious variables. The arrow labeled Youth is based on respondents' ages (in all cases older than eighteen). The arrow indicates that younger respondents are more likely to be members of the Left, in the upper left region of the figure, while older respondents are more likely to be members of the Right, in the opposite, lower-right region of the figure. Non-White respondents, principally African Americans, are more likely to be bicommunitarians, conservatives on personal-moral issues but liberal on economic-justice issues. Women are slightly more likely to be bicommunitarians, while men are slightly more likely to be libertarians.

The arrow labeled Income is based on annual family income. Income and education often go together. Both appear to be associated with personal-moral liberalism, but people with more income are also more likely to be influenced by economic-justice conservatism (an orientation that places a high value on private property).

Two of the arrows in Figure 2 reflect aspects of respondents' religiosity. The arrow labeled Relig. Practice is based on several items asking how often respondents say they attend religious services, pray, and read the Bible. The arrow labeled Theolgcl. Consrv. is based on nine items from the 1988 GSS that ask about a respondent's interpretation of the Bible (literal vs. other), whether their faith is free of doubts, whether those who violate God's rules must be punished, and whether, when making important life decisions, the Bible and the teachings of one's church or synagogue are important factors in reaching a decision [see Olson and Carroll (1992) for details]. The arrows for both these scales point in a nearly horizontal direction toward the right side of Figure 2.

One nice feature of the items used in the theological conservatism scale is that they correspond fairly closely with Hunter's description of orthodox versus progressive orientations toward (in this case) religious truth. The horizontal orientation of this scale suggests that the primary underlying division identified in Hunter's analysis is almost entirely aligned with the horizontal, personal-moral, dimension and has virtually no relationship to the vertical, economic-justice dimension. Such a result is consistent with Steve Hart's (1992) analysis in which he argues that theological conservatism has no clear relationship to cultural conflicts over social justice issues. In terms of the two-dimensional model employed in this chapter, religious conservatives are just as likely to be bicommunitarians as part of the Right. To the extent that religious conservatism plays a role in cultural conflicts, most of the tension it generates appears to be in a "horizontal" direction, that is, along the personal-moral issue dimension.

Students of New Christian Right organizations often point out that the target audience of these groups is the most religiously active sector of the American public and is thus a rich potential resource if this religious activism can be converted into political activism. The direction of the religious participation arrow, and its alignment with the conservative theology arrow, is consistent with such analyses.

In the "horizontal" tension between personal-moral conservatism and personal-moral liberalism, the most visible opponents of theological conservatives appear to be those with more education and (to some degree) income. Differences along this dimension have been noted by others (Maddox and Lilie 1984; Hargrove 1986; Schmalzbauer 1993) who describe it as a "new" class division. Whereas the old class division was "vertical" between the wealthy, who are conservative on economic-justice issues, and the less wealthy, who support economic-justice liberalism, the new class divisions are horizontal between the more educated elites, who support personal-moral liberalism, and the less educated (on average) theological conservatives (regardless of denomination), who tend toward personal-moral conservatism.

In his book *Why Americans Hate Politics*, Dionne (1991) cites Maddox and Lilie's argument that many Americans are frustrated with the political process in part because their views differ along two separate dimensions, but only two major political parties are available to represent their diverse positions. Thus each party must build fairly complex coalitions among people with quite different points of view or, failing that, the parties are simply unable to represent the views of many Americans.

Figure 2 shows an arrow labeled Republican, which points in a downward direction. This is based on responses to a single item that asks people whether they usually think of themselves as a Republican, a Democrat, an Independent, or something else. The item is coded with Strong Democrat as a 1, Strong Republican as a 6, Independent as a 3, and intermediate responses (e.g., "Independent, close to Democrat") for other points in between. Very few choose Other Party.

The downward arrow in Figure 2 indicates that self-identified Republicans are more likely to be in the lower portion of the figure and Democrats in the upper portions. In 1988, self-identified Republicans were almost equally likely to be libertarians as members of the Right. Republicans appear united on economic-justice issues, but they differ on personal-moral issues, a point that became painfully obvious to many party regulars at the 1992 Republican National Convention, where personal-moral conservatives took control of the party platform. Whereas religious differences appear to animate the horizontal, personal-moral dimension, political party differences appear to animate the vertical, economic-justice dimension. Put another way, taking the American public as a whole, religious belief has almost no association with political party affiliation (correlation = .0103).

Figure 2 also shows an arrow labeled Reagan. This shows (for those who said they voted in 1984) the direction in which one is most likely to find people who voted for Reagan. For the sake of convenience I also show the arrow representing the direction in which one is most likely to find people who voted for Mondale. Like the Republican arrow, the orientation of the Reagan arrow is largely downward, suggesting that economic-justice issues played a much greater role in the 1984 election than did personal-moral issues. However, the arrow points slightly more to the Right and slightly away from the libertarian cell. This tilt confirms the effectiveness of Reagan's appeal to personal-moral conservatives (even if he did not enact much of their legislation once in office). The so-called Reagan Democrats located in the bicommunitarian cell played a critical role.[6]

A similar analysis using 1993 GSS data, not shown here, shows that an analogous arrow for the 1992 Clinton vote is almost identical to the Mondale arrow shown here. However, the arrow for the Bush vote points even more to the right than does the Reagan arrow in Figure 2. While this may reflect an increase in religious Right voters for Bush, it may also be due to the loss of many Republican voters in the libertarian region who voted for Perot. An arrow representing the Perot vote points toward the Libertarian cell, a group of mostly Republican voters Bush should have been able to rely on but could not.

DENOMINATIONAL IDENTITY

While Figure 2 shows the influence of theological viewpoints, it reveals little concerning religious affiliation and how this might be connected to these two dimensions. Hunter (1991) reiterates a claim made by Wuthnow that liberal-conservative divisions now supersede denominational divisions in terms of their importance for influencing political and cultural values. Differences between denominations have declined in relevance as the division between progressives and orthodox increasingly dominates not only public debates, but divisions within denominations.

Figure 3 is based on a set of questions that begin by asking respondents, "What is your religious preference? Is it Protestant, Catholic, Jewish, some other religion, or no religion?" Respondents who answer Protestant or Jewish are asked to further specify what denomination. I classified the Protestant respondents based on whether they identified with a liberal or an evangelical Protestant denomination. I further subdivided Evangelicals into White and Black Evangelicals based on the respondent's ethnic background [see Olson and Carroll (1992) for details].

Figure 3 shows the directions in which one is most likely to find people from various types of religious backgrounds. As with Figure 2, the longer arrows represent stronger patterns. White Evangelicals are more likely to be part of the Right, in the lower-right part of the figure, but Black Evangelicals are more likely to be bicommunitarians. Many African Americans combine personal-moral conservatism with economic-justice liberalism. The liberal Protestants (mostly laypeople) in the GSS tend to be more common in the libertarian region combining personal-moral liberalism with economic-justice conservatism.

Affiliates of non-Christian groups, principally Jews, are more likely to fit in the Left region of our map, in the upper-left, combining economic-justice liberalism with personal-moral liberalism. The same is true of those who said they their preference was "no religion." Figure 3 includes no arrow for Catholics since Catholics are internally very diverse and are equally likely to be found in all four regions. Thus with the exception of Catholics, each of the four cells is the most likely region to find members of at least one of the major religious groupings in America.

Figure 3 suggests that even if they have declined in importance, denomi-

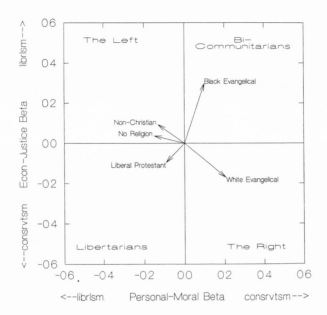

Figure 3. Directions in which one is most likely to find people from various types of religious backgrounds.

national differences are still strongly linked to attitudinal differences among the public. While Figure 2 shows that theological belief is primarily aligned with the horizontal, personal-moral dimension, Figure 3 shows that denominational identity has a more complex relationship to the two types of liberalism-conservatism. Contrary to Hunter, not all forms of religiously based division cut the same way nor is belief the only aspect of religion that continues to make a difference in attitudes toward public issues.

RACE AND OTHER NATIONAL DEBATES

While the personal-moral and economic-justice scales include items reflecting many issues of national debate, several important issues are only partly included in the two scales or not included at all. The most important of these is race. In their key works on cultural and religious division, neither Wuthnow (1988) nor Hunter (1991) focuses much attention on race. Yet, the riots following the Rodney King beating suggest that racial tensions have more potential to divide the country than does abortion. How are racial issues related to the two scales described above?

I identified eleven items in the 1988 GSS dealing with race. Two of these items (HELPBLK and NATRACE) ask whether or not the federal government should give assistance to minorities. Because these two items correlate especially well with the other items in the economic-justice scale, I included them in the scale itself.

The arrows in Figure 4 are based on regressions similar to the arrow diagrams in earlier figures and show (in the lower right region), for each of the remaining nine race items, the directions in which one is most likely to find respondents who support racial differences and oppose efforts to equalize racial differences. The betas for most of these items are stronger for the economic-justice dimension[7] than the personal-moral dimension. These include views on busing, support for open housing laws, whether or not respondents believe that economic differences between Whites and Blacks are due to discrimination, differences in educational opportunities, and differences in motivation and willpower. Three of the race items have about equal associations with both dimensions. These items ask whether residential segregation is acceptable, whether the respondent would vote for a Black presidential candidate, and whether respondents view economic differences between Whites and Blacks as being due to inborn differences in ability to learn. One item correlates most strongly with the personal moral dimension and asks about the respondent's view of legally banning interracial marriage.

The most important result from the pattern of these arrows is that if race is a separate, third dimension in public attitudes [as some, for example, Knoke (1979), have suggested], it is not an independent dimension. The length of these arrows suggests the strength of association between the racial items and the two issue dimensions.

The differing directions of the arrows suggests that racial issues are linked, in a complex way, to both the economic-justice and the personal-moral dimensions. Consistent with the description of the economic-justice dimension above as dealing with issues of equity, most of the items are more strongly linked to the economic-justice dimension. But some are also linked to the personal-moral dimension, especially views on interracial marriage.

Figure 4 shows four arrows in the upper-left quadrant. These represent four issues of national debate that also do not neatly fit, either theoretically or empirically, in the personal-moral or the economic-justice scales. The issue closest to the economic-justice dimension is represented by the arrow labeled Foreign Aid. It is based on two items that reflect support for federal spending on foreign aid. The arrow labeled Decrease Arms Spending shows the direction in which one is most likely to find respondents who feel that

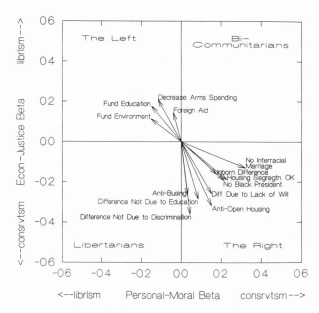

Figure 4. Arrows are based on regressions similar to the arrow diagrams in earlier figures and show the directions in which one is most likely to find respondents who support racial differences and oppose efforts to equalize racial differences.

arms spending should be reduced. The Fund Education arrow reflects support for increasing federal funding to education, and the Fund Environment arrow reflects support for increased federal funding for environmental protection.

While many issues of national debate are clearly associated with either the personal-moral or the economic dimension, Figure 4 shows that some issues are related to both, especially the economic-justice dimension.

PUBLIC OPINION RESTRAINTS
ON ELITE POLARIZATION

The above analyses imply that there are at least two important dimensions underlying cultural tensions among the public. But Hunter's main evidence for the existence of a culture war comes not from the public but from the polarized discourse of culture elites. Does public opinion really matter? The logic of Hunter's argument implies that public opinion will tend to be shaped by and follow elite opinion. If the elites are quite polarized, then it is only a matter of time before public opinion becomes quite polarized as well. But this may not be the whole story.

First of all, the greater polarization of elites may be nothing new. A long research tradition beginning with Converse (1964) and continuing with others (e.g., McClosky 1964; Knight 1985; Jennings 1992) suggests that elites have attitudes and beliefs that are much more highly organized than those of the general public. The classic explanation of this phenomenon is that elites, as opposed to the "masses," are better informed and are forced to justify their positions and their opposition to competing positions more frequently. This causes them to think through the various implications of their beliefs more carefully and construct a more consistent, and thus more defensible, system of beliefs. The implication is that elites and more educated persons see the "true" connections between ideas that others, who spend less time thinking about their beliefs, can safely ignore.

While plausible, it is equally plausible to assume that issue alignment arises among elites because they are under greater pressure than the public to conflate and merge issues that are conceptually separate. This can happen for a variety of reasons. Perhaps the most important is the need for coalition building in majority-rule voting systems. In order to achieve a majority coalition, leaders are pressured to take positions on a broad package of issues that may have no intrinsic relationship but come to be associated in leaders' decisions in order to avoid losing the votes of other coalition members on other issues. Thus a Republican legislator who wants to convince others to vote conservatively on tax cuts may find in exchange that he or she is expected to vote conservatively on legislation dealing with abortion and sexual morality. By merging several issue domains into a single package, political parties can mostly satisfy a broad constituency across a range of issues and gain the majority that is necessary to get elected and enact legislation.

In short, the greater issue alignment of elites may well reflect the social processes and organizations to which elites are exposed more than it reflects their greater intelligence, education, and knowledge of the underlying logical connections among issues. While a lower level of issue constraint among the general public undoubtedly reflects, as Converse suggested, a good deal of simple ignorance concerning political issues, it may also reflect the public's lower exposure to the social pressures of coalition building. This could actually free public attitudes to follow patterns of organization more consistent with the logic of the issues. This is important because it suggests that the structure of public attitudes may be more reflective of the "true" linkages among issues than the one-dimensional, liberal-conservative structure exhibited by politicians.

This opens the possibility that instead of passively following elite opinion, public opinion may act back upon and reshape elite opinion. More specifically, the two-dimensional structure of public opinion may act to retard the tendency toward issue alignment among elites.

How might this happen? Leaders depend on followers for resources and votes and can only lead where followers are willing to go. This is certainly the case for legislators and their constituents. While legislators may serve their own interests and the interests of pressure groups or wealthy donors, abundant research[8] suggests that the roll call votes of legislators (and thus public policy) are heavily influenced by legislators' perceived views of voter opinions (Stokes and Miller 1962; Erikson et al. 1991:278ff.) especially as the time for reelection approaches (Thomas 1985). Politicians and leaders of religious and special interest groups cannot stray too far or for too long from their supporters' agenda, at least not in public, visible ways. They are tethered, perhaps on a long leash, to public opinion.

Politicians, cultural elites, and special interest groups may align along a single dimension running from the left to the right, but if they do, they risk frustrating libertarians, bicommunitarians, and others whose views are not well represented in a bipolar, two-party cultural or political system. By withholding support, switching support, or supporting alternative or even "third party" candidates and policies, these frustrated segments of public can act to retard the tendency toward all-out, bipolar, winner-take-all, cultural conflict that Hunter sees as the nearly inevitable outcome of discourse among elites. In order to get their support, elites must moderate their discourse to take the views of these frustrated groups into account.

Thus, when the Democratic party turned solidly toward the agenda of the Left during and following the 1972 presidential campaign (Dionne 1991) bicommunitarian Democrats began to defect to the Republican party. In order to win back the support of these "Reagan Democrats" many successful Democratic candidates such as Clinton have had to move toward more moderate and even sometimes conservative views on personal-moral issues. A similar pattern of adjustment, readjustment, and balancing of interests goes on in the Republican party. The Christian Coalition draws its support from among personal-moral conservatives and is appreciated for the new-found financial and organizational resources it brings to the party. However, some blame Bush's 1992 loss partly on the high visibility of personal-moral conservatives at the 1992 convention and a resulting desertion of Republicans in the libertarian cell to Perot and Clinton. Worried about again losing personal-moral liberals, Republicans tried to keep the Christian Coalition in the background during the 1996 campaign.

Hunter emphasizes the especially divisive role of special interest groups like Right to Life, People for the American Way, the Eagle Forum, and the American Civil Liberties Union. Such groups are not constrained by the need to win elections and thus they can grow organizationally while appealing only to a small, committed, subgroup of the public. Though such groups can do much to inflame debate (as Hunter documents), if they wish to enact policy, they must still press their claims through the legislative and judicial systems, where they can rarely be successful in enacting long-lasting policy changes without moderating their positions to take into account the complex, cross-cutting variety of public opinion. In short, the two-dimensional structure of public opinion could well prevent a one-dimensional culture war.

CONCLUSION

This somewhat more complex view of cultural division suggests that rather than being pulled toward opposite ends of a single liberal-conservative dimension, the public is exposed to important cross-pressures, cross-pressures that may cause them to switch sides on different issue debates. Moreover, the cross-pressures present among the public may also constrain the tendency of elites to align along a single liberal-conservative dimension. If so, severe "us" versus "them" cultural conflicts, the type warned of by Hunter in his book *Before the Shooting Begins* (1994), seem less likely.

My analysis suggests that more caution may be needed in making predictions of cultural warfare. This is partly because predictions of an impending culture war may help to bring about a culture war in much the same way that rumors of an impending bank failure help to create a real bank failure. Instead of listening, learning, and working out our disagreements together, we become suspicious, antagonistic, and divisive. By arming ourselves for war we make war more likely.

NOTES

1. Within personal-moral conservatism righteousness is usually thought of as behavior and belief that is consistent with some collectively held external standard most often based on an interpretation of religious scriptures and/or tradition, or some standard that is thought to be "natural" or self-evident.

2. Admittedly, *bicommunitarian* is an awkward label, but it avoids some of the misunderstandings involved in the term *populist*, the term used by Maddox and Lilie.

3. We used factor analysis to identify the subsets of items.

4.   Because of space limitations I do not include the details of scale construction here, but they are available upon request. Briefly, the scales are nearly identical to those described in Olson and Carroll (1992) except that the economic-justice scale used in this chapter does not include the following GSS items that were part of the "Peace and Justice" scale in Olson and Carroll: NATARMS and NATARMSY, NATENVIR and NATENVIY, NATEDUC and NATEDUCY, NATAID and NATAIDY.

5.   In regressions of the form, dependent variable = constant + (beta1 * score on personal-moral scale) + (beta2 * score on economic-justice scale), the regression betas define the best regression plane for predicting the values of the dependent variable from the personal-moral and the economic-justice scales. The arrows in Figure 2 are drawn in the direction of the "steepest" climb up the regression plane. This is a direction perpendicular to the line formed by the intersection of the regression plane and the "flat" plane where the dependent variable = 0. Simple algebra shows that the slope (direction) of this perpendicular line is formed by the ratio of the beta for the y-variable (in this case the economic-justice scale) divided by the x-variable (the personal-moral scale). This is the same direction as that formed by a line originating at (0,0) and running to the point defined by the two standardized regression betas as is done in Figure 2.

6.   Among those in the bicommunitarian cell who say they voted, 54 percent voted for Reagan versus 43 percent for Mondale. Even though the Reagan vote among bicommunitarians is less than among all respondents (63 percent), it is significant that Reagan won a majority among people who, on average, self-identify as Democrats (56 percent Democrats to 30 percent Republicans in 1988). Only among the Left did Mondale voters outnumber Reagan voters (54 to 44 percent).

7.   The moderately high correlation of these items with the economic-justice dimension persists even when the two race-related items (HELPBLK and HELPRACE) are removed from the economic-justice scale.

8.   Jacobs and Shapiro (1994) review research on the relationship between public opinion and policymaking in democratic society.

REFERENCES

Bellah, Robert N., Richard Madsen, William M. Sullivan, Ann Swidler, and Steven M. Tipton. 1985. *Habits of the Heart: Individualism and Commitment in American Life.* Berkeley: University of California Press.

Converse, Philip E. 1964. "The Nature of Belief Systems in Mass Publics." Pp. 206–61 in *Ideology and Discontent,* edited by David E. Apter. New York: Free Press.

Dionne, E. J., Jr. 1991. *Why Americans Hate Politics.* New York: Simon & Schuster.

Erikson, Robert S., Norman R. Luttbeg, and Kent L. Tedin. 1991. *American Public Opinion,* 4th ed. New York: Macmillan.

Fleishman, John A. 1988. "Attitude Organization in the General Public: Evidence for a Bidimensional Structure." *Social Forces* 67:159–84.

Hargrove, Barbara. 1986. *The Emerging New Class: Implications for Church and Society.* New York: Free Press.

Hart, Stephen. 1992. *What Does the Lord Require? How American Christians Think about Economic Justice.* New York: Oxford University Press.

Hunter, James Davison. 1991. *Culture Wars: The Struggle to Define America.* New York: Basic Books.

————. 1994. *Before the Shooting Begins: Searching for Democracy in America's Culture War.* New York: Free Press.

Jacobs, Lawrence R., and Robert Y. Shapiro. 1994. "Studying Substantive Democracy." *PS: Political Science and Politics 27:*9–17.

Jennings, Kent M. 1992. "Ideological Thinking among Mass Publics and Political Elites." *Public Opinion Quarterly 56:*419–41.

Knight, Kathleen. 1985. "Ideology in the 1980 Election: Political Sophistication Matters." *Journal of Politics 47:*828–53.

Knoke, David. 1979. "Stratification and the Dimensions of the American Political Orientations." *American Journal of Political Science 23:*772–91.

Lipset, Seymour Martin. 1981. *Political Man.* New York: Free Press.

McClosky, Herbert. 1964. "Consensus and Ideology in American Politics." *American Political Science Review 58:*361–82.

Maddox, William S., and Stuart A. Lilie. 1984. *Beyond Liberal and Conservative: Reassessing the Political Spectrum.* Washington, DC: Cato Institute.

Olson, Daniel V. A., and Jackson W. Carroll. 1992. "Religiously Based Politics: Religious Elites and the Public." *Social Forces 70*(3):765–86.

Platt, Gerald M., and Rhys H. Williams. 1988. "Religion, Ideology, and Electoral Politics." *Society 25*(5):38–45.

Schmalzbauer, John. 1993. "Evangelicals in the New Class: Class versus Subcultural Predictors of Ideology." *Journal for the Scientific Study of Religion 32*(4):330–43.

Stokes, Donald E., and Warren E. Miller. 1962. "Party Government and the Saliency of Congress." *Public Opinion Quarterly 26:*531–46.

Thomas, Martin. 1985. "Electoral Proximity and Senatorial Roll Call Voting." *American Journal of Political Science 29:*96–111.

Wuthnow, Robert. 1988. *The Restructuring of American Religion: Society and Faith Since World War II.* Princeton, NJ: Princeton University Press.

13

Culture Wars(?):
Remapping the Battleground

FRED KNISS

Ever since the publication of James Davison Hunter's *Culture Wars* (1991), the idea that America is in the midst of a fierce "culture war" has been part of our public discourse. The rhetoric of recent presidential campaigns has amplified the idea in the popular consciousness. However, it may be that the evocative character of the culture wars metaphor and its ready acceptance by the public has led to a too-easy acceptance of the notion by social scientists.

This essay takes a critical look at the common wisdom that a culture war is under way. I argue that the picture of two diametrically opposed parties is too simplistic, drawn from artless unidimensional conceptions of the issues at stake. It exaggerates the level of conflict in society and ignores the presence and impact of groups that do not fit the model. Recent studies based on survey and polling data (e.g., DiMaggio, Evans, and Bryson 1996; Davis and Robinson 1996) have shown that, at the level of the general populace, polarization is difficult to identify. The public does not seem to be divided into warring camps as the culture war metaphor might suggest.

However, defenders of the culture wars thesis might respond that at the level of groups and ideologies, such polarization is real. They point to the public discourse dominated by the cultural elite as evidence for a cultural war. Even if the general public is "all over the map," the political and social groups that count in public life are polarized and have coalesced into two warring camps.

It is this latter form of the culture wars thesis that I want to critique in this essay. That is, even at the level of groups and ideologies, the bipolar culture war model is misleading. In its place, I propose a multidimensional model that is only slightly more complex; but adding one additional dimension produces a more effective mapping of the "moral order," the terrain upon which cultural conflicts are fought. Such a map includes groups who do not fit the usual bipolar conceptions of conflict, providing some fresh insights on old questions as well as suggesting some new questions. I illustrate this by application to a case study of cultural conflict among American Mennonites.

CONCEPTUALIZING THE CULTURE WAR

A number of political observers and social scientists have suggested that post-1950s America has seen a cultural and/or religious polarization that has increased the level of conflict in our public and private lives. Various ways of explaining this divide have been put forward, but most share a unidimensional, bipolar conception of the conflict. For example, attempts at explaining the decline of liberal Protestant denominations have posited cultural polarization between "locals" and "cosmopolitans" (Roof 1978) or between "traditional Christianity" and "scientific humanism" (Hoge and Roozen 1979). Such stark conceptualizations have significant rhetorical payoffs, but at the cost of analytical rigor and subtlety.

Wuthnow (1988), in a somewhat more sophisticated treatment, suggests that American religion has been restructured into liberal and conservative camps, a divide that increasingly occurs within denominations rather than between them. The effect is that the general level of social conflict is raised. Increased conflict occurs within denominations around liberal/conservative issues, but the restructuring also leads to polarization in the larger culture. This occurs as individuals experience an attenuation of denominational loyalty, transferring their commitment to "parachurch" and other special interest groups that are part of the liberal or conservative nexus and cross cut denominational organization.

Wuthnow refers primarily to religious liberalism and conservatism, but he views these two camps as also sharing liberal or conservative views on moral, social, and political issues. The ideological affinity within the two parties across issue domains contributes to the macrosocial polarization. Others concur with Wuthnow's claim of a widening "great divide" in American religion, but debate whether this divide occurs primarily within or between denominations (cf. Roof and McKinney 1987; McKinney and Olson 1991).

But it is Hunter (1991, 1994) who has explored the recent polarization in American culture most generally and before a larger public audience. He views the situation more apocalyptically than other analysts and has helped to bring the notion of a culture war into the American public consciousness.

Like others, Hunter sees Americans divided into two opposing camps, "orthodox" and "progressive." The key distinction he draws between the two camps is the issue of cultural or moral authority. The orthodox party adheres to "an external, definable, and transcendent authority" while the progressive party follows "the prevailing assumptions of contemporary life" (Hunter 1991:44–45). Hunter analyzes this polarization across a range of cultural fields and suggests that it poses a threat to the democratic order. Hirschman (1991), writing from further left on the political spectrum, makes a similar argument about the recent polarization of public discourse, referring to the sides as "reactionary" and "progressive." However, unlike the other analysts noted here, he views the current polarization as a normal part of the cycle of public political discourse and concerns himself more with the form of the debate than with its content.

A second related set of bipolar distinctions is found in the venerable literature on the tension between individual and community. Bellah, in much of his writing (alone and with colleagues), has dealt with the polarization between "utilitarian individualism" and "civic republicanism" (e.g., Bellah 1975; Bellah and Hammond 1980; Bellah, Madsen, Sullivan, Swidler, and Tipton 1985). This parallels Marty's (1970) notion of a split between "private" and "public" religion that has framed a number of sociological and historical studies of American religion since then.[1] Harold Bloom's recent (1992) controversial characterization of American religion as essentially gnostic is a current example of the ongoing life of this debate.

What all of these scholars share is a bipolar conception of the conflict in American culture/religion. This conceptual logic has at least two key problems. The first and most important is that it assumes that all or nearly all individuals and groups (or at least those who matter in the public discourse) fall into one of two camps. Occasionally there are passing references to the fact that, of course, there are many groups who do not fit the picture and many individuals who fall somewhere between or outside the poles, but these references are seldom more than passing (e.g., Hunter 1991:105). Groups that do not fit the proposed bipolar conception are left outside the explanatory model. Methodologically, this makes it difficult to disconfirm hypotheses and, substantively, it leads to a rather static picture of American culture.

The static, unilinear character of bipolar conceptions raises the second problem with these models. They do not easily lend themselves to generating explanations of historical change in the form or content of cultural conflict. Most of the treatments speculate about ways that polarization could or should be reduced, but these tend to be "jeremiadic" perorations rather than the applications or predictions that a more sophisticated model might produce.

In the following section, I propose a multidimensional conception of the cultural battleground that addresses these problems. It takes into account the polarization around the policy issues noted by Wuthnow and others, the authority issue noted by Hunter, and the individual/community tension noted by Bellah and others. By proposing a two-dimensional rather than a one-dimensional map, I make space for groups and individuals who lie outside the mainstream discourse and enable the generation of more sophisticated explanations and hypotheses about the dynamic process of cultural conflicts.

MAPPING THE MORAL ORDER

Here I propose four paradigms that may be used to characterize different positions within the mainstream American ideology or "moral order," to use Wuthnow's (1987) term. This is an attempt to specify more concretely key constituent elements of the American moral order. Wuthnow, of course, is not the only observer to posit the existence of an overarching ideological system within which religious and political movements pursue various interests. A similar conception is present in the work of those mentioned earlier. But in addition to the problems of unidimensionality noted above, most analysts have been rather vague about exactly what makes up the moral order.

I address this problem by proposing a slightly more complex two-dimensional heuristic scheme. Adding another dimension makes it possible to propose a kind of "ideological map" of the moral order. Such a map still permits the analysis of a dominant or mainstream ideological spectrum, but also permits inclusion of various peripheral positions and, thus, analysis of the relationship between the periphery and the mainstream. That is, the various configurations of these paradigms will influence ideological conflict both within peripheral ideologies and between them and the mainstream.

The two dimensions represent two central issues in any moral order. The first is the locus of moral authority and the second is what constitutes the moral project. The first issue is concerned with the fundamental basis for ethical, aesthetic, or epistemological standards (i.e., the nature of good, beauty, and truth). The second issue addresses the question of where moral action or influence should be targeted. That is, if good, beauty, and truth are to be enhanced, what needs to be changed? There is something of a parallel here to Weber's distinction between *wertrational* and *zweckrational* (Weber 1978). That is, the issue of moral authority is concerned with the grounds for defining or evaluating ultimate ends, while the question of the moral project is concerned with means to those ends. The former provides the foundation for central values. The latter provides the foundation for particular policies.

The poles on each dimension represent the tension between the individual and the collective that most analysts of American political culture have noted. On the first dimension, the locus of moral authority may reside in the individual's reason or experience or it may reside in the collective tradition. On the second dimension, the moral project may be the maximization of individual utility or it may be the maximization of the public good. While I am provisionally presenting these two dimensions as dichotomies forming distinct ideal types, the later discussion will indicate that I really view them as spectra along which a wide variety of ideas may occur. The two dimensions are crosscutting and interact in complex ways.[2]

With respect to the first issue (locus of moral authority), the paradigm of modernism holds that the fundamental authority for defining ultimate values (good, beauty, and truth) is grounded in an individual's reason as applied to and filtered through individual experience. Reason is located in particular individuals in particular times and places. Thus, there is a denial of any traditional transcendent absolute authority. Authority is always subject to rational criticism and legitimation. Ethics are situational, in that determining the good requires the application of reason to particular circumstances. Since modern society is based upon reason in the form of scientific technologies and rational forms of social organization, modernists are optimistic about progress and tend to be open to change. Further, insofar as rationality is basic to human nature, human nature is basically "good." There is within modernism, therefore, an inherent trust in human beings, resulting in an emphasis upon individual freedom and civil liberties. The expressive individualism of recent decades noted (and often decried) by many of the scholars discussed above is a product of modernism as a fundamental paradigm.

Within religion, modernism has been the focus of much conflict during the past century. Modernism legitimized rational criticism of ecclesiastical and biblical authority. Religious modernism holds that (1) religious ideas should be consciously adapted to modern culture; (2) God is immanent in and revealed through human cultural development; and (3) human society is progressively moving toward the realization of the Kingdom of God (Hutchison 1982). Religious conservatives have, of course, opposed this view as an attack on "fundamentals" and a challenge to traditional authority (Marsden 1980).

Traditionalism, in contrast to modernism, holds that the definition of ultimate values is grounded in the moral authority of the collective tradition. Rather than focusing on the free individual actor, emphasis is placed upon individuals as members of a collectivity, a social group defined by its relation to some higher authority. Authority transcends any particularities of person, place, or time. It is absolute and not open to criticism. The patriarchal nuclear family, as the smallest, most basic collectivity under a common authority is particularly valued. Practices that are seen to threaten it (e.g., promiscuity, homosexuality, or abortion) are opposed with special tenacity. In religion, this takes the form of obedience to ecclesiastical and scriptural authority. Ethics are not situational, but absolute. Individual actions are expected to contribute to the social good. Traditionalism stresses submission to the collectivity and restraint upon individual appetites. Respect for transcendent authority is paralleled by a respect for transcendent values. The goal of change, then, is not progress toward perfection, but recovery of traditional values. Modern culture is not seen as progress so much as a fall from paradise.

On the second dimension (locus of the moral project), the paradigm of libertarianism, like modernism, asserts the primacy of the individual. It holds that the primary moral project is the maximization of individual utility, that is, it applies individualism to questions of economic and political relationships. The ideal economic system is the free market, where free individuals acting in their own rational self-interest compete for resources. Economic growth is encouraged as a way of making more goods and services available to everyone. Growth in these terms requires unrestrained individual striving and minimal regulation by the state. Networks formed by the individual pursuit of self-interest in a free market are the bases of the social bond. Hence, only a minimal state is required—one whose function is protection of individual rights but is not concerned with the provision of social services or regulation of the economy.[3] The religious counterpart to libertarianism holds that the primary moral project is the individual's salvation and moral improvement.

As libertarianism is to modernism, so communalism is to traditionalism. That is, communalism takes the principle of individual submission to the collective good and applies it to questions of economic and political organization rather than questions of ultimate value. The moral project is the collective good rather than individual utility. A regulated market is valued over an unregulated free market. Egalitarianism is valued over limitless self-interested striving. The state is expected to promote these values by enforcing the redistribution of resources (entitlement programs are an example of public policy based upon the paradigm of communalism). The state is also expected to curtail individual self-interested action when it threatens public goods such as environmental quality, public safety, or public health. Communalism may be applied across generations, as when today's wage earners support Social Security payments to the elderly or when conservation policies are justified as necessary to preserve resources for future generations. In religion, communalism identifies the primary moral project as "building the Kingdom of God," establishing an alternative social order rather than reforming individuals.

So far, I have presented the dominant paradigms as a fairly strict typology with mutually exclusive categories. Empirically, however, these categories occur together in various configurations and interact dynamically. American mainstream and peripheral ideologies contain a wide spectrum of ideas and symbols. Some fall neatly into the given categories, while others are highly ambiguous. Ideas are never simply given and are rarely stable, but are constantly contested, refined, and adapted, leading to dynamic relationships within and between paradigms.

In thinking about plausible configurations of the paradigms discussed above, one might intuitively expect the individualistic paradigms of modernism and libertarianism to occur together and be opposed to an alliance between the collective paradigms of traditionalism and communalism. In fact, American political culture has been counterintuitive in this respect. Although they may have used different terms, various writers have noted the paradoxical combination of traditionalism and libertarianism in conservative or right-wing American ideology (e.g., Nash 1976; Lipset and Raab 1978; Himmelstein 1983; Platt and Williams 1988). Although many scholars view this paradox as primarily a characteristic of post-1945 American conservatism, de Tocqueville, as far back as the 1830s, noted in *Democracy in America* ([1850] 1969) that traditional religion in the United States had combined with unrestrained self-interest to promote the general welfare.

In contrast, the American Left has combined modernism with communalism, supporting both the moral autonomy of the individual and the regulation of economic and political activity in defense of the public good. These are, of course, ideal-typical characterizations. They represent two poles on the American ideological spectrum. Clearly, there is a large ambiguous middle position; but there is, nevertheless, a clear contrast between the Right and Left in its "pure" forms. Recognizing the contrasts between and paradoxes within mainstream American ideological positions is important for understanding specific cases of ideological conflict.[4]

Figure 1 is a graphic representation of what I call American mainstream ideological discourse. Here the dimensions defining the paradigms are represented as spectra rather than categories. The x-axis represents the locus of moral authority and the y-axis represents the moral project. Idea systems may theoretically be located at any position on the map. Although right-wing purists would tend to be located in the northeast corner and left-wing purists in the southwest corner, the boundaries of these categories are porous. The line connecting the two extremes is the realm of mainstream discourse. There are clear, sharp, often bitterly contested differences between positions along this line, but those located within the mainstream understand the differences. There are routinized vocabularies, procedures, categories, etc., for discussing and negotiating these differences. Most negotiation takes place in the "ambiguous middle." Here is where the majority of political institutions are located. This is the area where compromises are formed, where the observer finds the juxtaposition of seemingly incompat-

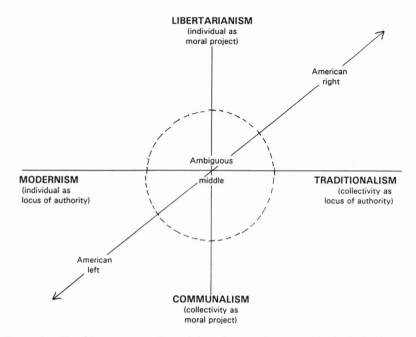

Figure 1. Graphic representation of American mainstream ideological discourse.

ible elements of opposing paradigms as "politics makes strange bedfellows."
The implementation of policies formulated at either "purist" location tends
to gravitate toward this middle.

IMPLICATIONS FOR CULTURAL CONFLICT

The heuristic model presented above has a number of substantive and
methodological implications that might be noted. In this section, I will discuss several that I have found helpful in my work on social change and
intrareligious conflict. An analysis of religious and cultural conflict will
provide an extended example.

The Significance of Peripheral Groups

I argued above that bipolar conceptions of cultural conflict ignored the
presence and role of peripheral groups—groups that did not fit either of the
two opposing categories. This is an important theoretical shortcoming, espe-

cially at a time when the importance of the periphery is being recognized in theories of social change. A promising logic for explaining cultural change and conflict is the dialectical relation between core and periphery, which has been used in world system theory and elsewhere. Wallerstein (1979) and Collins (1981) are the best known exemplars of this logic in the areas of economics and geopolitics, respectively. Wallerstein suggests that social change is driven by the rise and fall of world-economic systems. The rise and fall of these systems is, in turn, driven by inequalities between core and peripheral national or regional economies. Collins makes a logically similar argument about social change, except that he posits inequalities in power between "heartland" and "marchland" (i.e., geographic core and periphery) states as the engine of change. Wallerstein has been justly criticized for making the core's activities determinant in his explanations and ignoring the resources and alternatives that are available to the periphery. Both Wallerstein and Collins have been accused of proposing reductionistic causal models. But these criticisms are not really germane to my interest in borrowing their logical framework to explain cultural change and ideological conflict.

I am suggesting that cultural change and conflict operate within a dialectical system like that posited by Wallerstein or Collins. Rather than core/periphery or heartland/marchland, I refer to dialectical relationships between mainstream and fringe cultural groups. Elsewhere (Kniss 1988), I make this argument in some detail. To shorten the long story, I suggest that what Wallerstein has done for economics and Collins has done for politics might also be done for culture. Each of these domains can be studied within a similar dialectical structure of analysis and a similar logic can be applied to the question of change and conflict in each. If a similar logical structure can be applied to explain each social domain—economics, politics, and culture—then this structure of analysis does much to enrich grand theories such as Weber's that recognize their interpenetrating character.

The two-dimensional map proposed above helps to specify exactly how different fringe groups might be peripheral to the mainstream. Figure 2 suggests where some fringe groups might be located on the map. Recognizing the presence of groups that lie outside the mainstream and specifying the ways in which they are peripheral allows the analyst to include them in an explanatory model and to consider how they might affect or be affected by mainstream tensions and/or polarization. Note, however, that there is a significant difference between my conceptualization and some of the core/periphery theories. Consider, for example, Shils's (1975) theory of the cultural center and periphery. For Shils, the center is the "ultimate," "irreducible," "sacred" realm of society's most important symbols, values, and beliefs. I am suggesting that these values exist most purely at the periphery, while the center is the realm of ambiguity and competition over ideas.

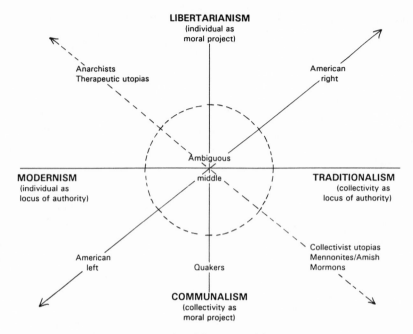

Figure 2. Peripheral location of fringe groups.

Understanding Intragroup Conflict

The moral order map also provides a useful heuristic for analyzing many of the specific cultural or religious conflicts that interest sociologists, especially those involving "sects" and "cults." These terms usually refer to groups that lie off the diagonal on the moral order map. The map helps us to be clearer about just how these groups differ from the mainstream. Mennonites are a good example of such a fringe group, because they combine the paradigms of traditionalism and communalism, a configuration that places them outside the mainstream of American ideological discourse. Throughout their history, they have combined an emphasis upon traditional moral and spiritual values, the importance of the family, biblical and communal authority, and denial of individual interests in favor of the collectivity (i.e., traditionalism), with a concern for egalitarianism, social justice, pacifism, environmental conservation, mutual aid, and the like (i.e., communalism).

This ideological peripherality has been a source of much intragroup conflict for Mennonites. Their combination of traditionalism and communalism has been especially uneasy within the context of twentieth-century America. Mennonite individuals and groups who are primarily concerned with traditionalism have often looked to the American Right for external supportive links. Those most concerned with communalism, on the other hand, have looked to the American Left. When these external links come to the fore, various social structural cleavages come into alignment. The internal cleavage between paradigms aligns with external cleavages between fundamentalists and modernists in American religion and between the Right and the Left in American politics. Increased conflict along external cleavages results in the emergence or intensification of internal conflict.[5]

The dashed-line diagonal in Figure 2 represents an imaginary line dividing the American Right from the Left. Note that the Right-Left division becomes an internal cleavage for Mennonite ideology. It would be expected that, during times of unusual ideological dynamism within the mainstream ["unsettled times" to use the concept suggested by Swidler (1986)], the internal cleavage between traditionalism and communalism would become more salient and thus conflict would be more likely to emerge around these paradigms. The hypothesis would be that if either or both of these paradigms are objects of contention in the mainstream, then the cleavage between them would become sharper within the Mennonite community and the number and intensity of such conflicts would increase.

A comparative historical analysis finds support for these hypotheses. The analysis (fully reported in Kniss 1997) is based on a set of archival data on 208 distinct conflict events occurring within the Mennonite church in Virginia, Pennsylvania, Ohio, and Indiana between 1870 and 1985. The 208 cases constitute the entire population of events that could be identified in secondary and primary archival sources. The sources include more than one hundred denominational and congregational histories; official records of bishop boards, regional conferences, executive committees, and district ministerial boards; and the correspondence and personal papers of key actors in the conflicts.

There were two periods during this century when, for Mennonites, internal polarization between the traditionalist and communalist paradigms generated numerous conflicts leading to schism or expulsion of individuals and congregations. One was during the 1920s to mid-1930s. The other was during the late 1960s through the mid-1980s. During the former, the primary instigators of conflict were progressive communalists who challenged the legitimacy of traditional authorities. During the latter, the modal conflict was instigated by traditionalists attempting to restore the authority of traditional sectarian standards. In each case, contenders on both sides of the conflict had ready access to ideological and material resources because of polarization in the mainstream religious and political culture. Here, I will focus on the earlier period to highlight how a multidimensional conception of cultural conflict provides insight into the experience of a particular fringe group.

For American Mennonites, the first two decades of the twentieth century were a period of relative calm and consensus under the authority of traditional religious hierarchs. However, during the twenties and thirties, following World War I, Mennonites experienced a dramatic surge of (often bitter) internal conflicts in which the instigators were, in various ways, challenging the legitimacy of traditional authorities. This surprising pattern, not true of other more mainstream German-speaking minorities,[6] can be best understood by focusing on the relationship between Mennonites' particular peripherality and events occurring within the mainstream religious and political domains.

By 1914, Mennonites (and especially their leaders) had been focused primarily on internal concerns for nearly two decades. The sudden external pressures applied by the onset of war caught them unprepared. During the late nineteenth century, Mennonites had instituted a number of religious and cultural innovations (such as Sunday schools, higher education, and English-language worship services) that had been made with an eye to external issues and interests. By contrast, changes during the first fifteen years of the 1900s were internally oriented, aimed at the reconsolidation of traditional authority and the production of ideological and cultural uniformity among ordinary Mennonites. These changes included the strengthening of central denominational authority, and the elaboration of theological and cultural disciplinary codes.

World War I once again confronted Mennonites with important external issues and strained the recently strengthened internal/external boundaries. The reassertion of traditional sectarianism in visible forms such as dress helped to highlight Mennonites as a people apart at a time when the policies of total war were asking for the united efforts of all American citizens. The fact that many of these sectarian people were German-speaking and that many of their cultural distinctions had Germanic roots heightened the tensions between them and their surrounding communities, making their American loyalties suspect. Added to this was the fact that Mennonites were pacifists. The official position of the Mennonite Church was that its young men should not participate in the war effort in any way, including noncombatant service. Neither should other Mennonites support the war effort through means such as the purchase of Liberty Bonds.

Unfortunately, denominational leaders during the war years were not prepared to deal with such external exigencies because their attentions and energies had been directed inward for most of their careers. They had neither the expertise nor the experience to deal adequately with the external institutions impinging on their community. This was painfully obvious in their dealings with the government over conscription issues, but it also was evident in negotiating relations with local community institutions.

At 1915 and 1917 general conference meetings, Mennonites adopted strong statements against participation in or support of the war and conscription. Members who bore arms would risk excommunication. Unfortunately, the denominational leaders were much less certain or forceful in dealing with the government about the draft than they had been in dealing with their own members. The Selective Service Act made provision for conscientious objectors, but required them to participate in noncombatant service within the military. This was a position that was unacceptable to Mennonites, but their delegations to Secretary of War Newton Baker were naively mollified by his assertions that "we'll take care of your boys" (Keim and Stoltzfus 1988). As a result, church leaders offered mistaken assurances to Mennonite parents and young men that the noncombatant service would be "not under the military arm of the government" (Juhnke 1989). This error was corrected after Quaker and Church of the Brethren delegations were able to extract more forthright positions from Baker and General Crowder, Baker's Judge Advocate General. In fact, Mennonites, even though they were hesitant to cooperate with Quakers and Brethren, often benefited from the latter groups' more sophisticated dealings with the government (Keim and Stoltzfus 1988).

Instead of presenting a unified front in dealing with the war department, numerous Mennonite groups, in addition to Quaker and Brethren groups, sent an unorganized series of delegations to Washington. Baker and Crowder seldom gave more than verbal responses to these groups. The responses themselves were sometimes conflicting, so that communication between the "historic peace churches" themselves was marked by confusion and uncertainty.

The ignorance and uncertainty of Mennonite leaders regarding government policy meant that young Mennonite conscientious objectors (COs) were poorly prepared to face government and military officials when they were drafted. This state of affairs was not unnoticed by the officials. In one meeting, where Secretary Baker met with twenty-six conscientious objectors, one of the young men, who probably was not fluent in English, repeated Jesus' admonishment to "render unto Caesar what is Caesar's" as "Give to the Kaiser what the Kaiser's is." Baker left the meeting describing the COs as "well-disposed," but "simple-minded," "imprisoned in a narrow environment," and having "no comprehension of the world outside of their own rural and peculiar community." He said that "only two . . . seemed quite normal mentally." In another setting, a general described COs as "of such a low grade mentality, they are actually too stupid to form any argument against military service except ready-made biblical phrases supplied them by their preachers, lawyers, and brighter associates" (all quotes from Juhnke 1989).

In the end, government policy was that COs were required to report to military camp, but could refuse to follow any orders to which they conscientiously objected. If they demonstrated the sincerity of their convictions, there was the possibility that they would receive an unpaid furlough for agricultural service. This of course placed Mennonites in the camps under considerable pressure, frequently subjecting them to mistreatment. Refusal to put on the uniform or perform noncombatant duties under military direction in the camps frequently resulted in beatings, various forms of torture, death threats, and imprisonment. Some of these were "normal" forms of military discipline, but in the case of COs, were violations of War Department policy.

In local communities, as well, leadership confusion and indecision had ill consequences for Mennonites. Most of the local trouble revolved around Mennonites' refusal to purchase Liberty Bonds. This was official denominational policy, but its practical application was varied and at times confused. Some leaders at first supported participation in Liberty Bond drives, but later opposed it. Others initially opposed their purchase, but later capitulated. In some communities, there were creative compromises worked out with bankers so that Mennonites technically would not purchase war bonds, but would deposit money in local banks, thus freeing other bank funds for investment in Liberty Bonds (Juhnke 1989).

In the face of confusing signals from denominational leadership, Mennonites needed to deal with harsh opposition from their neighbors. The government was promoting the war effort as a total war requiring extreme patriotism and sacrifice from citizens at home. Those who did not offer sacrificial support for the war were derided as "slackers." Patriotic fervor was high all across the country. Naturally, sectarian German-speaking minorities who refused to buy Liberty Bonds were not treated as model citizens. Especially in the West and Midwest where Mennonite communities were smaller and more scattered and where there was not a long tradition of toleration for Mennonite groups, local opposition ran high. There were vitriolic speeches, near-lynchings, and churches were burned or smeared with yellow paint. Individuals were burned or buried in effigy, whipped publicly, or tarred and feathered.

Given the difficult experiences of ordinary Mennonites during the war, it is not surprising that the years immediately following saw a sharp increase in conflict frequency. Although there were only five documented conflict events between 1907 and 1920, twenty-three events occurred during 1920–1924. Of these, sixteen concerned authority issues. The war had heightened the tension over the issue of authority and the traditionalist consensus Mennonite leaders had imposed. On the one hand, the war had heightened perception of the separation between Mennonites and others, justifying the need for consensus and strong authority to maintain it. On the other hand, it had brought Mennonites face-to-face with the world and they had survived. Mennonites had been required to take positions on complex national and international issues. Leaders had been dealing with government officials, even if ineffectively, and had developed relationships with leaders of other denominations. Many Mennonite young men had been exposed to other worldviews in the military camps. This exposure, thanks to the disoriented denominational leadership, had occurred outside the restrictions of religious authority or community. All these factors induced a turn toward external concerns rather than the internal focus characteristic of established authority in the previous decades. Those in denominational leadership positions were caught in the middle of this tension at the same time that their legitimacy had been weakened by wartime events.

Another internal threat to traditionalist authority was the resurgent communalist impulse that appeared after the war. Mennonite farmers had prospered during the war, thanks to increases in the prices of agricultural goods. They were probably carrying some philanthropic guilt over their inability to contribute to wartime public-spiritedness. Their surplus wealth and eagerness to reestablish themselves as legitimate citizens led to a boom in externally oriented benevolent activities. Mennonites gave hundreds of thousands of dollars to postwar relief efforts in Europe, not only through their own Board of Missions and Charities, but also through the Red Cross and other Protestant relief agencies (Juhnke 1989). Some of the giving was in the form of Liberty Bonds that had been reluctantly purchased under wartime pressure and now weighed heavily on their holders' consciences.

Many returning COs also decided to donate time in positive activity by assisting with relief efforts in Europe. Some, dissatisfied with the response of Mennonite agencies to the situation of COs in the war, signed on to work with Quaker relief programs (Meyer 1919). In 1920, the Mennonite Central Committee (MCC) was formed to coordinate the various Mennonite denominations' relief activities. MCC was an explicitly communalist institution that threatened the traditionalist hegemony in the Mennonite Church. The establishment of MCC was difficult precisely because of Mennonite Church fears that such inter-Mennonite cooperation would hamper efforts to maintain sectarian discipline among volunteers working far from home shoulder-to-shoulder with Mennonites from more lenient groups.

The broader postwar American culture also provided a sympathetic context for challenging traditional authority. All across American cultural fields, traditional positions were embattled. Modernist theology was defeating the traditional Protestant orthodoxies. In science, Einstein's theories were overthrowing the old Newtonian paradigm. Rationalist philosophy was being attacked by early existentialists. In general, there was a growing emphasis on individual experience and moral authority as opposed to the authority of tradition. Knowledge and perception were seen as relative rather than absolute, subjective rather than objective. Marsden (1980) shows how the raging controversy between fundamentalists and modernists during this period was related to these broader cultural changes. In politics, the scandals of the Harding administration shook the old progressive faith in rational policy and objective management as a legitimate tool for promoting social reform. Karl

(1983) describes the America of this era as an "uneasy state" and identifies the 1920s as a period of particular "uncertainty." He emphasizes the role of new communications technologies in tuning everyone in to the cultural transitions that were taking place.

As noted above, challenges to established denominational authority began immediately upon the close of the war. The young volunteers in the relief effort in Europe provided some of the earliest expressions of these challenges. In 1919, the Mennonite relief workers in France organized a conference to discuss the future of the church in America. They generated a list of sixteen "Expressions of interest and concern for the future of Mennonitism." Ten of these were direct criticisms of established denominational authority (its lack of proper qualifications for its tasks and its authoritarian character) or calls for a more active and powerful laity. For example, one of the points called for "a definite repudiation of the idea that laymen are simply to pray, pay, and obey," another for "greater emphasis on the part played by women in church organization," and another for "a relief commission whose members are competent to meet the officials of government and of other organizations" (Meyer 1919). Out of this meeting there emerged a series of Young People's Conferences held in the United States. These conferences, run by postwar activists, pursued a similar agenda to the meeting in France. They were not officially sanctioned by the church and were an ongoing thorn in the flesh of denominational leadership. Between 1924 and 1928, the younger activists even published a magazine, *Christian Exponent,* that offered a progressive alternative to the official denominational magazine, which had grown increasingly traditionalist and authoritarian under the editorship of a conservative Pennsylvania bishop.

Meanwhile, in the years following the war, the denominational establishment's response to the new challenges to their legitimacy was to reassert authoritarian discipline over doctrine and practice. The role of bishops and conference executive committees in enforcing religious orthodoxy and sectarian cultural practices was expanded. Each of the regional conferences adopted strengthened statements of doctrine and sectarian discipline. Most also adopted statements against the Young People's Conference. The denomination's general conference adopted a "Statement of Christian Fundamentals" in 1921 that included most of the standard fundamentalist dogma and added some peculiarly Mennonite points. In 1923, the temporary closure of Goshen College, the most progressive of the Mennonite colleges, provided a capstone to the reestablishment of authoritarian traditionalism.

Following 1923, however, there was a ten-year period that saw many challenges to conference and bishop authority by congregations (rather than simply disgruntled "young Turks") who were not willing to submit wholeheartedly to traditionalist authority. Clergy and lay leaders in many of the challenging congregations had been activists in the European relief effort and/or in the Young People's Conferences. Challengers were surprisingly successful. Out of fifteen progressive challenges to established authority during 1923–1933, only three ended in defeat. Four ended in schism and six ended in either compromise or victory. My point here is not really about who won or lost, but rather to show that understanding the patterns of conflict frequency and content requires focusing on the interaction between the internal characteristics of Mennonites that made them a fringe group and upheaval and polarization in the mainstream. Attention only to the mainstream, as in most bipolar conceptions of cultural conflict, would have excluded the experience of peripheral groups like the Mennonites. At best, it would have produced inaccurate hypotheses, likely predicting (with respect to cultural polarization) that Mennonites would be like other fundamentalists (and they were not), or (with respect to wartime upheavals) that their experience would parallel that of other German-speaking minorities (and it did not).

Impact of Fringe Groups on the Mainstream

In the previous section, I argued that bipolar conceptions of cultural conflict lead to ignoring or misunderstanding the experience of sectarian, utopian, or other peripheral groups and movements. But some may argue that this is no great loss—that fringe groups may be interesting curiosities, but are, after all, peripheral and thus relatively insignificant for understanding large-scale cultural conflicts occurring in the mainstream. However, another implication of the moral order map I propose is that the interaction between groups on and off the diagonal has an impact on both.

My examination of intra-Mennonite conflict, by focusing on internal events as the dependent variable, highlighted the causal effects of external factors on internal cultural dynamics. But it is a logical implication of the model I propose that fringe groups like the Mennonites should also have an impact on the larger environment. This kind of argument is much more difficult to make concisely or coherently because the dependent variable, impact on the sociocultural environment, is so diffuse. However, if we focus on specific characteristics of the environment, it is possible to make such an argument.

Probably the best example in the case of Mennonites would be American government policy toward conscientious objectors to war. The rapid succession of wars in this century and the disastrous experience of Mennonites during the first one led to their increasingly sophisticated dealings with the government (in cooperation with other "peace churches") in developing CO policies. The successful institution of such policies in U.S. law changed at least this one aspect of the political environment, making conscientious objection to war more respectable and more accessible to many people other than Mennonites. Institutionalizing and expanding the legitimate bases of conscientious objection was one important element of the widespread antiwar activism in the 1960s and 1970s.

Another more recent example, and one that is missed by simple bipolar conceptions of cultural conflict, is the public discourse around abortion and capital punishment. The irony of people's positions on the value of human life has been pointed out by partisans on both sides of the abortion and capital punishment debates. That is, pro-choice parties in the abortion debate accuse pro-lifers of being concerned about saving the life of the fetus, but being unconcerned about the life of the mother, or of prisoners on death row, or of victims of American military interventions. Pro-life parties, on the other hand, suggest that pro-choicers are inconsistent in being willing to "kill" innocent unborn children, yet being unwilling to kill convicted murderers and rapists.

The seeming paradox in this debate vanishes if we consider it in light of the moral order map I propose. That is, the accusations of each party ignore the location of the specific issues with respect to the larger moral questions, since the issue of abortion is primarily an issue of the locus of moral authority, while the issue of capital punishment regards the moral project. The point I want to highlight here regards the impact of fringe groups on the mainstream discourse. A relatively recent development in the public debate is the entrance of Mennonites, Catholics, the "New Evangelical Left," and other groups located off the diagonal in the southeast corner of the moral order map who oppose both abortion and capital punishment and claim to hold a "consistent ethic of life." They have built alliances with groups on both sides of the culture wars, thus opening space for accommodation and the lowering of tension. For example, there are emerging groups like Common Ground, a midwestern organization that brings together pro-choice and pro-life activists in cooperative efforts toward lowering rates of unwanted pregnancies and providing services such as improved prenatal care to women who find themselves in that position.

CONCLUSION

In this essay I have made the argument that cultural conflict should be seen as multidimensional rather than as unidimensional bipolar tensions. I argued that most unidimensional conceptions are overly simplistic. As an alternative, I proposed a slightly more complex two-dimensional map that accommodates most of the bipolar oppositions that various analysts have proposed. Adding a dimension enables a more sophisticated analysis of specific conflicts and allows interesting distinctions to be drawn between different issues—distinctions that are blurred or ignored in unidimensional conceptions. A multidimensional mapping of the cultural terrain has the further benefit of highlighting the role of peripheral groups and ideologies in the larger cultural system. This enables a more complete explanation of intragroup conflict for groups that have different locations in the moral order. It also provides new insights on some of the dynamics of intergroup conflicts over specific issues and permits consideration of the impact of fringe groups on mainstream discourse.

This more complex picture of cultural conflict raises some serious questions for the argument that there is a unique and significant culture war underway at the moment. Certainly there is evidence of increased polarization in public discourse and there have been attempts on both the Left and the Right to frame the polarization as a war. This is a useful rhetorical strategy because it simplifies the issues and makes recruitment and coalition-building easier. But simplification and political expediency should not be the goal or motivation of sociological analysis. The attention to empirical specificity and historical dynamics that is highlighted by a multidimensional map suggests that the polarization we see may be one part of a picture that is much more complex than partisans would have us believe. Some issues, for example, are crosscutting and may produce attenuation rather than intensification of conflict. Different issues have different histories, different ideological components, and different constituencies. It does not behoove us as sociologists to share in the simplistic apocalyptic vision of those who have a particular ideological battle to fight.

ACKNOWLEDGMENTS

Thanks to Mark Chaves, Anne Figert, Wendy Griswold, Dan Olson, Mark Shibley, and Rhys Williams for helpful comments.

NOTES

1. I apply the conceptual scheme proposed here to Marty's "two-party" argument about American religion in Kniss (forthcoming).

2. Will and Williams (1986) propose a similar typology. However, by making right vs. left one of the dimensions, they preclude the possibility of anomalous paradigm configurations of the sort I will be discussing here.

3. Nozick (1974) attempts a philosophical justification of this paradigm.

4. One can speculate about the reasons for these paradoxical configurations. Perhaps there is a "need" for a balance between individual and collective values. Himmelstein (1983) suggests that, on the right, neither traditionalism nor libertarianism carries much appeal on its own, but each provides a corrective to the unappealing aspects of the other.

5. Coleman (1956) argues for the importance of such potential lines of cleavage within a group. The extent to which various lines of cleavage coincide will determine the extent and intensity of a conflict. Coleman refers to the process of heightened intensity as the elevation of a conflict from the level of within individuals to between individuals. I prefer to think of this as the coming into alignment of two or more structural cleavages; but regardless of how this is conceptualized, the result is a heightening of conflict.

6. Marty (1986) shows that, for both German Catholics and Lutherans, World War I facilitated their assimilation as "true Americans" due to their intense efforts to demonstrate loyalty and support for the war. No doubt Mennonites' pacifism precluded such a process for them.

REFERENCES

Bellah, Robert N. 1975. *The Broken Covenant: American Civil Religion in Time of Trial*. New York: Seabury.

Bellah, Robert N., and Phillip E. Hammond. 1980. *Varieties of Civil Religion*. New York: Harper and Row.

Bellah, Robert N., Richard Madsen, William M. Sullivan, Ann Swidler, and Steven M. Tipton. 1985. *Habits of the Heart: Individualism and Commitment in American Life*. Berkeley: University of California Press.

Bloom, Harold. 1992. *The American Religion*. New York: Simon and Schuster.

Coleman, James S. 1956. "Social Cleavage and Religious Conflict." *Journal of Social Issues 12*(3):44–56.

Collins, Randall. 1981. *Sociology Since Midcentury: Essays in Theory Cumulation*. New York: Academic Press.

Davis, Nancy J., and Robert V. Robinson. 1996. "Are the Rumors of War Exaggerated? Religious Orthodoxy and Moral Progressivism in America." *American Journal of Sociology 102*(November):756–87.

de Tocqueville, Alexis. [1850] 1969. *Democracy in America,* transl. by George Lawrence, edited by J. P. Mayer. Garden City, NY: Anchor.

DiMaggio, Paul, John Evans, and Bethany Bryson. 1996. "Have Americans' Social Attitudes Become More Polarized?" *American Journal of Sociology 102* (November):690–755.

Himmelstein, Jerome L. 1983. "The New Right." Pp. 133–48 in *The New Christian Right,* edited by Robert C. Liebman and Robert Wuthnow. Hawthorne, NY: Aldine de Gruyter.

Hirschman, Albert O. 1991. *The Rhetoric of Reaction: Perversity, Futility, Jeopardy.* Cambridge, MA: Belknap Harvard.

Hoge, Dean R., and David A. Roozen. 1979. "Some Sociological Conclusions about Church Trends." Pp. 315–34 in *Understanding Church Growth and Decline: 1950–1978,* edited by Dean R. Hoge and David A. Roozen. New York: Pilgrim.

Hunter, James Davison. 1991. *Culture Wars: The Struggle to Define America.* New York: Basic Books.

———. 1994. *Before the Shooting Begins: Searching for Democracy in America's Culture War.* New York: Free Press.

Hutchison, William R. 1982. *The Modernist Impulse in American Protestantism.* Oxford: Oxford University Press.

Juhnke, James C. 1989. *Vision, Doctrine, War: Mennonite Identity and Organization in America, 1890–1930.* Scottdale, PA: Herald.

Karl, Barry D. 1983. *The Uneasy State: The United States from 1915 to 1945.* Chicago: University of Chicago Press.

Keim, Albert M., and Grant M. Stoltzfus. 1988. *The Politics of Conscience: The Historic Peace Churches and America at War, 1917–1955.* Christian Peace Shelf. Scottdale, PA: Herald.

Kniss, Fred. 1988. "Toward a Theory of Ideological Change: The Case of the Radical Reformation." *Sociological Analysis* 49(Spring):29–38.

———. 1997. *Disquiet in the Land: Cultural Conflict in American Mennonite Communities.* New Brunswick, NJ: Rutgers University Press.

———. Forthcoming. "Listening to the Disenfranchised: Toward a Multiparty Conception of American Religion." In *Re-Forming the Center,* edited by Doug Jacobsen and William Vance Trollinger, Jr. Grand Rapids, MI: Eerdmans.

Lipset, Seymour Martin, and Earl Raab. 1978. *The Politics of Unreason: Right-Wing Extremism in America, 1790–1977.* Chicago: University of Chicago Press.

Marsden, George M. 1980. *Fundamentalism and American Culture: The Shaping of Twentieth-Century Evangelicalism, 1870–1925.* Oxford: Oxford University Press.

Marty, Martin E. 1970. *Righteous Empire: The Protestant Experience in America.* New York: Harper and Row.

———. 1986. *Modern American Religion,* Vol. 1, *The Irony of It All, 1893–1919.* Chicago: University of Chicago Press.

McKinney, William, and Daniel V. A. Olson. 1991. "Restructuring among Protestant Denominational Leaders: The Great Divide and the Great Middle." Paper Presented at American Sociological Association Annual Meeting, Cincinnati, Ohio.

Meyer, J. C. 1919. Notes on the "Development of the Young People's Conference in France from Jan. to Sept. 1919." Document in archives of the Mennonite Church, Goshen, Indiana.

Nash, George H. 1976. *The Conservative Intellectual Movement in America, Since 1945.* New York: Basic.

Nozick, Robert. 1974. *Anarchy, State and Utopia.* New York: Basic Books.

Platt, Gerald M., and Rhys H. Williams. 1988. "Religion, Ideology and Electoral Politics." *Society* 25(July/August):38–45.

Roof, Wade Clark. 1978. *Community and Commitment: Religious Plausibility in a Liberal Protestant Church*. New York: Elsevier.

Roof, Wade Clark, and William McKinney. 1987. *American Mainline Religion*. New Brunswick, NJ: Rutgers University Press.

Shils, Edward. 1975. *Center and Periphery: Essays in Macro-sociology*. Chicago: University of Chicago Press.

Swidler, Ann. 1986. "Culture in Action: Symbols and Strategies." *American Sociological Review 51*:273–86.

Wallerstein, Immanuel. 1979. *The Capitalist World Economy: Essays*. Cambridge: Cambridge University Press.

Weber, Max. 1978. *Economy and Society: An Outline of Interpretive Sociology*, edited by Guenther Roth and Claus Wittich. Berkeley: University of California Press.

Will, Jeffry, and Rhys Williams. 1986. "Political Ideology and Political Action in the New Christian Right." *Sociological Analysis 47*(2):160–68.

Wuthnow, Robert. 1987. *Meaning and Moral Order: Explorations in Cultural Analysis*. Berkeley: University of California Press.

———. 1988. *The Restructuring of American Religion: Society and Faith Since World War II*. Princeton, NJ: Princeton University Press.

AFTERWORD

Culture Wars, Social Movements, and Institutional Politics

RHYS H. WILLIAMS

Due to the popularity and visibility of James Hunter's book *Culture Wars,* many of the contributors to this volume have targeted his version of the culture wars thesis. The preceding chapters strike a number of telling blows. In this afterword, I review briefly Hunter's argument and summarize the critiques in the previous substantive chapters. I then want to offer a perspective on politics in contemporary America that keeps some of the insights in the culture wars thesis—broadly construed—without buying into the narrow version of the argument.

HUNTER'S CULTURE WAR

Hunter made three basic points in building his argument. First, qualifications notwithstanding, Hunter portrayed basically all important political opinion and its supporting activism as lined up along an orthodox vs. progressive continuum. This continuum is thought to express *the* basic dimension of public political culture. The opinions of individuals and the political profiles of groups that are not easily captured by this continuum can be dismissed as irrelevant. Even if they do not align with the progressive-orthodox divide, the coercive nature of that division forces them into at least public agreement. A dimension of this claim, and an important one, is Hunter's attendant position that political discourse is a discourse of elites and activists, only imperfectly reflected in grass roots opinion.

Second, Hunter argued that positions on the conflictual issues in American politics not only run along a single axis, but also cluster around the two poles of that axis; that is, each worldview position leads to a cluster of inherently related opinions on issues as varied as abortion, gay rights, welfare reforms, school prayer, and economic policy. These issue clusters lead to polarization due to their inherently contradictory logic, and to conflict and perhaps even violence due to their origins in uncompromisable moral visions. Further, the current polarization represents a significant realignment of social divisions. The orthodox vs. progressive polarization cuts across many of the social structural cleavages that organized American politics in the past.

Third, Hunter's explanatory variable is the "worldview"—the mental, symbolic systems that "construct" the social world. This idea emerges out of a sociological version of phenomenological constructionism (see Berger 1967; Evans 1996). Worldviews are a melding of notions of "ought" and "is" such that the social world becomes taken-for-granted, and disagreements at the level of "ideology" can easily threaten core assumptions about personal identity and social reality. Thus, disagreements over cognitive ideas have the potential for expanding into uncompromising, identity-based confrontations. Hunter's account of these worldviews is relatively shorn of institutional, social network, or material groundings. While there is some consideration of the "knowledge class" base of many active political partisans, and the role that traditional religious communities play in the orthodox cultural camp, Hunter's explanation is fundamentally rooted in symbolic mentalities that cut across other social identities such as class, race, or religious affiliation; it is, in effect, a version of cultural idealism (cf. Evans 1996).

Along with this ideological realignment Hunter is also committed to what he calls a "Durkheimian" understanding of the autonomy of public culture from individuals' lives (cf. Hunter 1996). As he sees it, the adversarial rhetoric used by partisan elites is grounded in moral worldviews, promoted by activist groups that need conflict for justification, and then reinforced by media industries that thrive on sensationalized reporting. Over time the public adversarial political culture gains a momentum of its own, and forces more moderate positions to one of the extremes. The out-of-control and self-reinforcing qualities of the culture wars process paint a gloomy portrait indeed.

A SERIES OF CRITIQUES

The critiques in this volume follow these three major contentions. First, it is clearly not true that a single continuum can capture American political opinions, attitudes, or values, nor is it the case that opinions cluster at the poles of the axes that do divide American political culture. Several contributors to this volume have attempted to operationalize Hunter's continuum, and have analyzed survey data, particularly the General Social Survey conducted by the National Opinion Research Center, against its dimensions. The assertion of a single axis with polarized-attitude clusters does not stand up. The consistent finding, although articulated differently by different scholars, is that there are at least two axes along which issue-attitudes are arrayed: one for issues pertaining to the distribution of economic and political resources; another one for issues of personal and cultural morality. And as the data reveal, in many cases these dimensions are orthogonal to each other. This offers the possibility for a fourfold distinction, rather than a two-sided war. That is, if the economic and morality dimensions are arrayed against the principles of individual liberty versus collective regulation, one finds a fourfold table representing four ideal-typical ideological positions: those who are libertarian on both moral and economic issues; those who are communalist on both types of issues; those who are moral libertarians and economic collectivists (sounding much like Great Society Democrats); and those who are moral collectivists and economic libertarians (sounding very much like the current Republican coalition).

Several authors represented here, along with other political analysts (e.g., Dionne 1991) draw upon these findings to claim that this opinion diffusion may be *why* political conflict does not get upgraded to "war" status: simply not enough people feel represented by the current configurations of the Republican and Democratic parties to be organized into reliable armies. "Crosscutting cleavages" intersect the body politic in a variety of ways, making the mobilization of a mass collective action more difficult. In sum, the conceptual logic of a *biaxial* grid produces differences in "issue domains" that the narrow version of the culture war thesis conflates. Unidimensional conceptions of political opinion leave out at least as many people, and issues, as they include.

While recognizing that survey data of mass opinion does not reveal the culture war, there remains the important caveat that political discourse is a matter of elites. This functions as something of a "side bet" for Hunter's argument; since there is evidence that activists' opinions cluster more than nonactivists, mass opinion can be downplayed [Davis and Robinson (1996:250) do note that Hunter often relies on public opinion survey data to support his argument]. Certainly the bipolar rhetoric of partisan mobilizers and activists, the political elites that concern Hunter most (and not to be confused with the elites that actually sit atop America's political and economic institutions), lends itself easily to images of war.

Also, limiting the culture war to elites resonates, at least in part, with a long tradition in political science that finds apathy and a lack of interest to be the dominant features of general public opinion. Philip Converse's (1964) classic article described the phenomenon in terms of the relative ideological "consistency" between elite and mass opinion—elite opinion having greater logical and issue coherence. But it is not necessary to treat logical consistency as a normative value in order to recognize that many people do not think about politics in the same ways as pundits, activists, and scholars do. Russell Neuman (1986) has also demonstrated that there simply aren't very many reliable "soldiers" in the general American public. Neuman's convincing estimate is that only 5 percent of the general public can be considered politically engaged beyond the level of voting, and thus termed "activist"; concomitantly, a solid 20 percent are resolutely apolitical. The remaining 75 percent can be mobilized and activated, but their interest is situational, contextual, and intermittent.

Shanto Iyengar's (1991) work on media and opinions produces a related finding: the generative principles that undergird many specific political opinions (what he calls "attributions of responsibility") are unstable. People switch between individualist and communalist arguments for attributing responsibility for social problems depending upon issue domain, the category of person being discussed (in racial, age, or gendered terms), and the framing of the story by the media. For example, Iyengar's respondents made different decisions about whether the individual was responsible for her/his own problems or whether government should take problem-solving responsibility, depending on the circumstances under which the issues were presented to them. They were not always "consistent," if that term means a regular application of an absolute moral principle. Situational context shapes political attitudes, and hence issue positions, as much as personal characteristics, whether cognitive or psychological.

Together, these studies of political attitudes make an important point: the connections between worldview, opinion, and action are tenuous indeed. But there is an irony here. At first glance the existence of "opinion instability" among many people in the general population seems to support Hunter's claim that elites are the relevant actors in the culture war. However, if we think of the phenomenon less as "inconsistency" and more as context-based decision-making, then we discover a potential flaw in the use of the worldview as the main explanatory factor. That is, a reliance on a transcendent source of moral authority (the defining characteristic of the orthodox worldview) does *not* automatically produce a general ideological principle from which specific attitudes are deduced. These connections are constructed by people in particular social contexts regarding particular social issues (cf. Evans 1996). Opinions, beliefs, and attitudes are generated and made meaningful embedded in contexts. Abstracting too far from these contexts invariably loses some of the meaning.

Further, particular attitudes, even if firmly held, do not necessarily generate political action (cf. Williams and Blackburn 1996). There is a fairly consistent finding that on many dimensions of social location, structural position, and cultural engagement, "activists" on either (or any) side of an issue have more in common with each other than either set of activists has with nonactivists. Studies of social movement recruitment have shown consistently that social *networks,* rather than previously existing *attitudes,* are the mechanism through which people become involved politically (e.g., Friedman and McAdam 1992; Klandermans and Oegema 1987). Once involved, it is true that attitudes and beliefs among activists on different sides often become more distinct and less compromising. For example, both Luker's (1984) analysis of the differences between pro-life and pro-choice abortion activists, and Ginsberg's (1989) analysis of a community conflict over abortion, suggest that the process of activism itself is a polarizing one. But it is less a matter of moral worldviews than it is a matter of social networks and "socio-logical" perspectives. If there is a culture war going on, it may well be between those who are trying to rally armies and those who simply refuse to be rallied.

Thus, in my view Hunter's (1996) use of Durkheim in defending his thesis relies on the wrong founder. Hunter claims that public political culture is a set of Durkheimian symbolic structures that have become detached from social groupings and have an external, coercive force of their own (whether that is a truly Durkheimian position is a different matter). I would counter that it would be better to consider political culture more in terms of Max Weber's (1946) "switchman" metaphor, where ideas help direct social interests along particular tracks, while still recognizing that the connections between ideas and action require active interpretations by human agents (see, for example, the case studies of religiously based activism in Demerath and Williams 1992).

Nonetheless, while Hunter's scheme cannot capture the diversity of general public opinion, if we take studies of political apathy and opinion instability seriously we find some support for a bipolar notion of cultural conflict, rooted in activist elites. The survey data that indicate widely dispersed attitudes generally do not tell us anything about *salience*—how much respondents *care* about the issues they are professing to have opinions on. Many "pseudo-opinions" are expressed because of an interviewer's promptings— these are things not tightly held or invested with much meaning. Political mobilization, on the other hand, requires salience. Getting people to act means getting people to invest meaning, interests, or identity in an issue.

This reveals an important implication of the culture wars thesis developed in several of the chapters included here. One reason the "Left" and the "Right" are organized as they are in the current versions of the Democratic and Republican parties (that is, economic communitarians with moral libertarians, and economic libertarians with moral communitarians, respectively) is that those positions largely reflect the salient positions of the major active interest groups within the two parties. Democrats don't win without blue-collar workers, African Americans, and "knowledge class" liberals voting for them. Republicans don't win without white-collar managers, small business owners, and White Evangelicals voting for them. Data show a general dispersion of attitudes, but they also show clearly that the major parties have put together logically inconsistent platforms in order to accommodate the specific, impassioned, but often limited visions of their major constituencies.

Thus, there is something to the claim that cultural war is built on "elite" discourse. But that discourse should not be understood as representing homogeneously clustered attitude groupings among either grass roots voters or political elites generally; rather, the discourse should be analyzed as a language used by coalitions of activists, many of whom are themselves only in partial agreement with each other. Voting is usually a binomial choice, an either/or. Voters must often choose the candidate who approximates their commitments; they must put issues into priorities. Because it is an either/or choice, voting is relatively easy for social scientists to predict, and elections are structured so that they lend themselves to Manichean rhetoric.

Political activism, however, is not so reducible—there are many ways of getting involved, many issues around which to become active, and a variety of rationales for such participation. Political conflict, particularly that lying on the edges of party politics, reflects the coalitional nature of the contending sides. Conflict may be couched in expansive rhetoric about "the American people," or in the clarifying military metaphor of a two-sided war; but political rhetoric is a series of symbolic gestures meant to appeal simultaneously to only partially overlapping social groups—public political discourse is a system of symbolic gestures that typically allow enough flexibility in interpretation to keep a coalition together.

Hunter and other culture war proponents, despite disclaimers about the autonomy of extremist political language, err by seeming to take the rhetoric of conflict at face value—believing it to be an accurate collective representation of a polarized social and cultural divide in society. But the often alarming rhetoric is not a reliable guide to public opinion, activist opinion, or the coalitions that constitute the major political parties; it is instead strategically instrumental language used by activists to mobilize adherents.

But here again, Hunter displays a curious inconsistency in his analysis of mobilizing rhetoric. He is critical of the "discourse of adversaries" used by partisans that so easily escalates into absolutist, moralized rhetoric. It is, in his terms, a "grammar of hostilities" that reveals a "symmetry of antipathies" (1991:135, 143, 156), in which opponents become enemies. There is, of course, a bit of irony in blaming the media and partisans for exacerbating conflict by sensationalizing it—in two books titled *Culture Wars* and *Before the Shooting Begins* (1994). Nonetheless, Hunter's first example of over-the-top rhetoric is the tendency of partisans to label their opponents as extremists in order to discredit them. But extremism is only an effective epithet if moderation, reasonableness, and positions near the center are considered a virtue. Presumably, in a deeply divided culture partisans might attract like-minded persons to their cause if they are indeed relatively extremist. And there are, after all, people in American society who are extremists in their attitudes; thus some of the discourse of adversaries is undoubtedly effective in motivating activists. But activist rhetoric is also meant to persuade by-stander publics—and calling your opponents extremists in order to discredit them seems to indicate that activists recognize that most of the game is played in the center of the field. It may even indicate that activists prefer to think of themselves as moderate and reasonable compared to their adver-saries. In any case, it is a de facto recognition of the normative importance of consensus in American politics. This does not seem like strong support for the contention that our culture has a deep political divide, pulling the com-peting sides into extremism.

MOVEMENT MOBILIZATION AND INSTITUTIONAL POLITICS

As noted above, the survey results that show a dispersion of political attitudes reveal that the combinations of individualism and communitaria-nism currently used by Democrats and Republicans do not align well with many people's attitudes. Many observers claim that as people recognize that they are not being represented by the major parties they drop out of active participation in politics. It is significant to note that this argument is the reverse of the traditional argument in *favor* of mass political parties. In the traditional view, parties are *supposed* to aggregate interests and opinions, forcing groups into compromises and voters into choosing the "better" of two choices. Historically, this has been an institutional mechanism for dif-fusing conflict by forcing moderation on the contending parties; the necessi-ty of compromise balances the tendency to polarize (cf. Brint 1992). I am not arguing for the continuing vitality of a "strong center" in American life (see Hunter 1996:247). Rather this is an argument that recognizes that American political institutions cannot, and are not intended to, represent all the opin-ions of all Americans. They are designed to marginalize uncompromising minorities. The institutions of American politics aggregate and prioritize interests, preferences, and values. That aggregation effect is one reason why parties and institutions serve the body politic differently from social movements—they diffuse and defuse the passion necessary for war.

What would be the outcome, for example, if each social group in the United States that holds a particular set of issue-positions had its own politi-cal party? Would politics be more or less chaotic than it is currently? Would political conflict be heightened or attenuated? Pat Buchanan may run a moral crusade with war rhetoric, but he cannot get nominated by a political party that also represents large numbers of socially tolerant, college-educated, but economically mobile yuppies.

The defining function of an institution is the routinization of social life. Institutions remove some of the overt conflict from social processes by making it part of the taken-for-granted order. Struggle becomes submerged by standardized procedures. This process has an inherent injustice to it; some will have more access to institutions than will others, and those who have will be able to use the institutions themselves to reinforce their privilege. The American government's separation of powers and the polity's two-party system have functioned to swallow many political challenges in the swamp of necessities that constitute institutional routines. On the other hand, the success of movement mobilization—again by definition—requires calling into question those very routines. That is why social movements are most usefully thought of as extrainstitutional; they operate outside, and often challenge directly, the taken-for-granted distributions of institutionalized power.

Thus the processes that the culture war thesis identifies as *the* defining characteristic of contemporary politics—the polarization of ideologies leading to escalating, uncompromising conflict—is more accurately understood as a fundamental dynamic of *social movement mobilization*. The institutionalized polity has a two-party system; movement discourse produces bipolar rhetoric that also constructs a two-antagonist world. But beneath that similarity, the sociopolitical processes are different. Scholars and pundits too often use the terms liberal and conservative, or orthodox and progressive, to describe the divisions in contemporary opinion; in that function the terms are imprecise, inconsistent, and largely inaccurate. The current divisions in American politics are quite distant from any coherent ideological system. What is more important is to recognize that *activists* use terms such as liberal, progressive, and conservative as *identity markers* for symbolically constructing their movements. The terms can help evoke the sense of injustice and identity necessary for movement mobilization.

A focus on ideology and symbols as the identity markers necessary to generate the symbolic frames for collective action marks another critique of any narrow version of the culture wars scheme. Whether one distinguishes the relevant political groupings as the Left and the Right, or the orthodox and the progressive, is less significant for what it says about the content of the beliefs involved than it is significant for what it says about the construction of the principal political groupings. That is, the divisions between the groupings are more important than the operative principles of the ideologies. Political conflict *is* often between the orthodox and the progressive, but these are not as much descriptions of attitude clusters as they are symbolic markers of identity and difference (cf. Lamont and Fournier 1992).

Hunter maintains that ideological principles, drawn from moral world-views, are the independent variables that then organize the resulting political formations. Those critics who complicate Hunter's scheme by offering a second dimension claim that the ideological divisions are not so clear-cut, and the connections between ideology and identification support the truth of the old saying that "politics makes strange bedfellows." But many of these critics still see the principles as the major divide. I am arguing instead something of a reverse position, that "bedfellows make strange politics."[1] There is an autonomy to the dynamic of identity and opposition that shapes ideological adaptation and cultural understandings, but also constrains such adaptation. This is where conflict is happening: not between abstract world-views, but between an "us" and a "them" constructed through a host of cues such as race, life-style, education, and other identity markers. The dynamic of conflict is located between "us" and "them," because we are "us" and they are "them."

Many public opinion scholars find that partisan identification remains stubbornly important as a political predictor variable. Often partisanship is interpreted as a proxy for adherence to a belief system; but it may be instead a proxy for an important identity marker. We are who we are because we identify with some and oppose ourselves to others. Even if there is not complete ideological agreement, and clearly the open character of American political culture makes clearly articulated ideologies and widespread consensus relatively rare, there is still a sense of participation and commitment generated through the dynamics of identification. We are who we are because we are who we are; and we are who we are because we are not them.

In this light, the use of the label "extremist" to discredit opponents is easier to understand. The labeling itself helps to produce a boundary of identity and distinction: they are extremists and we are not. At the same time, the content of the label "extremism" itself recognizes the normative importance placed on consensus (i.e., extremism is bad because moderation is good) while it simultaneously creates an inclusive definition of who "we" are. In other words, the label does "create" an adversary through us/them rhetoric, but it leaves the boundaries of who can be with us very open and easily expanded—all one need do is side with the sensible, moderate middle and not be "extremist." The extremist label, used as a weapon, does create an enemy, but it does not lock those who wield it into a position that would limit their ability to gather allies.

A focus on the processes that escalate conflict through identification and distinction keeps questions of power at the center of the study of politics; that is, abstract principles of regulation take a back seat to the practical realities of who regulates whom, about what. Further, identification and distinction help account for the persistence of warlike imagery among activists, the tendency of partisans to overlook ideological paradoxes, and the concomitant frustrations of those who do not share the partisan loyalty. Such "noncombatants" can easily see partisan politics as unreasonable, unchari-table, and perhaps ultimately fruitless.

It has often been noted that American politics readily takes on the person-ality of a religious revival. Just as revivals need both the "saved" and the "damned" to generate a sense of moral urgency, politics seems to require an "us" and a "them" to generate political passion and mobilization. Gamson's (1992) analysis of the language necessary for collective political action con-cludes that mobilization requires constructing a sense of *injustice* (existing social arrangements are morally flawed), a sense of *identity* (a boundary between us and them), and a sense of *agency* (our involvement will make a difference). One can easily see how the rhetoric of a cultural war would serve activists and partisans trying to rally interest and action. The process of generating distinctions, particularly the boundaries between us and them, produces an autonomous dynamic of struggle. It is not reducible to issue-attitudes alone, but neither is it an irresistible force unconnected to social groupings and collective identities.

As Kertzer (1988) notes, symbols are particularly crucial to the enactment of politics because they are multivocal and ambiguous. Their flexibility allows for interpretations along similar, although not identical, lines. A polit-ical or social movement can use its symbolic repertoire to produce soli-darity, even without consensus on particular issues or interpretations. The collective action frames that Gamson considers necessary for mobilization do require notions of injustice, agency, and identity among adherents. But those need not come from the same symbolic sources, nor be manifested in the same manner. Thus dimensions of cultural "style" can be important clues for creating social distinctions because they are often vaguely articulated. They are identity markers, but can be fluidly interpreted (cf. Platt 1980).

This is not to say that the content of movement ideology has no conse-quences, that it is completely open to the whims of individuals. While I disagree with Gitlin's (1995) assessment of American politics as a culture war, he does make an insightful point about the clash between more partic-ularistic "identity politics," based on ascriptive characteristics such as race and gender, and the universalizing tendencies of class-based, Marxian ideol-ogies. Gitlin argues that this has fragmented the American Left to the point where it is ineffective in national politics. Whether that is the case is a subject for a different book. The insight, however, that less flexible identity markers create potential problems for movement mobilization is a useful corrective to perspectives that focus too much on abstract and cognitive factors, disconnected from social and institutional processes. The hetero-doxy in the composition of social movements does indeed call attention to the important role of symbolic and cultural factors (the broad reading of "culture wars"), but it undermines the claim that coherent worldviews are the true independent variable animating political differences (part of the narrow thesis).

In sum, there is truth in both a broad reading of the culture wars thesis and in the criticisms of narrower versions. That paradox is built upon the *institutional* tendency of American politics to produce centrist political solutions and the *cultural* tendency of movement-style politics to inflate identity and ideological differences into cultural war. Institutional pressures force political parties, interest group organizations, and even many social movement organizations into behaving more and more similarly—a process often referred to as "institutional isomorphism" (DiMaggio and Powell 1983). But these organizations are still struggling within a competitive market, and to attract adherents often feel pressured to distinguish themselves from other similarly situated groups. The use of extreme, adversarial rhetoric is one such response. Thus, organizational pressures are centripetal even as ideological tendencies are centrifugal. This disjunction between the dynamics of political culture and the dynamics of institutional routine may be at the heart of the current disaffection with American politics. The two-party organization of American politics and political institutions seems to resonate with the bipolar dynamics of mobilizing movement discourse. But in fact the two processes operate differently. One operates to aggregate differences, force compromise, and facilitate cross-cutting cooperation. The other operates to polarize the constructions of "us" and the "other," and leads to a tendency for uncompromising, moral absolutist, mobilization-style politics. This difference in the logic of the political dynamic distinguishes movement politics from institutional politics. And it leads to the clear implication that one version of the culture wars thesis—and many of the criticisms leveled against that thesis—are simultaneously true. It is another paradox of current American politics that eschews an "either/or" understanding for a "both/and" reality.

NOTE

1. A phrase suggested by R. Stephen Warner.

REFERENCES

Berger, Peter L. 1967. *The Sacred Canopy.* New York: Anchor/Doubleday.

Brint, Steven. 1992. "What if They Gave a War . . . " *Contemporary Sociology* 21(4):438–40.

Converse, Philip E. 1964. "The Nature of Belief Systems in Mass Publics." Pp. 206–61 in *Ideology and Discontent*, edited by David Apter. New York: Free Press.

Davis, Nancy J., and Robert V. Robinson. 1996. "Rejoinder to Hunter: Religious Orthodoxy—An Army without Foot Soldiers?" *Journal for the Scientific Study of Religion* 35(3):249–51.

Demerath, N. J. III, and Rhys H. Williams. 1992. *A Bridging of Faiths: Religion and Politics in a New England City.* Princeton, NJ: Princeton University Press.

DiMaggio, Paul J., and Walter W. Powell. 1983. "The Iron Cage Revisited: Institutional Isomorphism and Collective Rationality in Organizational Fields." *American Sociological Review* 48(April):147–60.

Dionne, E. J., Jr. 1991. *Why Americans Hate Politics.* New York: Simon & Schuster.

Evans, John H. 1996. " 'Culture Wars' or Status Group Ideology as the Basis of U.S. Moral Politics." *International Journal of Sociology and Social Policy* 16(1/2):15–34

Friedman, Debra, and Doug McAdam. 1992. "Collective Identity and Activism: Networks, Choices, and the Life of a Social Movement." Pp. 156–72 in *Frontiers of Social Movement Theory,* edited by A. Morris and C. M. Mueller. New Haven, CT: Yale University Press.

Gamson, William A. 1992. *Talking Politics.* New York: Cambridge University Press.

Ginsberg, Faye D. 1989. *Contested Lives.* Berkeley: University of California Press.

Gitlin, Todd. 1995. *The Twilight of Common Dreams: Why America Is Wracked by Culture Wars.* New York: Metropolitan.

Hunter, James Davison. 1991. *Culture Wars: The Struggle to Define America.* New York: Basic Books.

———. 1994. *Before the Shooting Begins: Searching for Democracy in America's Culture War.* New York: Free Press.

———. 1996. "Response to Davis and Robinson: Remembering Durkheim." *Journal for the Scientific Study of Religion* 35(3):246–48.

Iyengar, Shanto. 1991. *Is Anyone Responsible? How Television News Frames the Issues.* Chicago: University of Chicago Press.

Kertzer, David I. 1988. *Ritual, Politics, and Power.* New Haven, CT: Yale University Press.

Klandermans, Bert, and Dirk Oegema. 1987. "Potentials, Networks, Motivations, and Barriers: Steps toward Participation in Social Movements." *American Sociological Review* 52:519–31.

Lamont, Michelle, and Marcel Fournier, eds. 1992. *Cultivating Differences: Symbolic Boundaries and the Making of Inequality.* Chicago: University of Chicago Press.

Luker, Kristin. 1984. *Abortion and the Politics of Motherhood.* Berkeley: University of California Press.

Neuman, W. Russell. 1986. *The Paradox of Mass Politics: Knowledge and Opinion in the American Electorate.* Cambridge, MA: Harvard University Press.

Platt, Gerald M. 1980. "Thoughts on a Theory of Collective Action: Language, Affect, and Ideology in Revolution." In *New Directions in Psychohistory,* edited by Mel Albin. Lexington, MA: Lexington.

Weber, Max. 1946. "The Social Psychology of the World Religions." In *From Max Weber: Essays in Sociology,* edited by H. H. Gerth and C. Wright Mills. New York: Oxford University Press.

Williams, Rhys H., and Jeffrey Neal Blackburn. 1996. "Many Are Called but Few Obey: Ideology and Activism in Operation Rescue." Pp. 167–85 in *Disruptive Religion: The Force of Faith in Social Movements,* edited by Christian Smith. New York: Routledge.

Index

A

Abortion, 41, 71–3, 86, 90, 95n.12, 105, 111, 151, 182–3, 232–3, 239, 242, 276
African Americans, 30, 48, 54–6, 83, 103, 130–2, 134, 142, 161, 178–80, 193nn.1,6, 231, 247, 250

B

Bennett, William, 2, 20, 79
Buchanan, Patrick, 1, 39, 160, 289–90

C

Catholics/Catholicism, 84–5, 103, 105, 108, 113–5, 146, 148–50, 152–4, 226–7, 250, 276
Christian Right, 2, 39, 43–5, 57, 59n.10, 84, 146, 153, 160–2, 164, 168–70, 176, 178, 181–2, 192, 211, 233, 248, 255
Civil religion, 206–7, 221, 225–6, 234
Converse, Philip, 65, 244, 254, 285–6
Culture
definitions of, 6–7, 214–6

D

Defense and security issues, 104, 107–8, 111–3, 233, 252, 275
Democrats/Democratic party, 30, 87–9, 146, 149, 153–4, 160, 169–70, 172n.2, 230–2, 249, 255, 285, 287, 289

E

Economic class, 3, 4, 42–3, 48, 248
Economic justice issues; 30, 40, 42–3, 50–2, 72, 103, 105, 107, 178, 224, 230, 240, 242, 248–9, 252, 257n.7, 264
Education, 2, 4, 76, 79, 159, 166–7, 183–9, 245–7, 253
in seminaries, 122–43
European Americans, 54–6, 142, 147, 193n.1

F

"Family" issues, 40–1, 48–50, 145, 150, 183–9, 263–4

G

Gay rights/homosexuality, 1, 41, 105, 111, 148, 239, 242